ALSO BY ANDREW COCKBURN

Out of the Ashes: The Resurrection of Saddam Hussein
(with Patrick Cockburn)

RUMSFELD

An American Disaster

ANDREW COCKBURN

VERSO

London • New York

First published in the USA by Scribner 2007
This edition published by Verso 2007
Copyright © Andrew Cockburn 2007
All rights reserved

The moral rights of the author have been asserted

1 3 5 7 9 10 8 6 4 2

Verso
UK: 6 Meard Street, London W1F 0EG
USA: 180 Varick Street, New York, NY 10014-4606
www.versobooks.com

Verso is the imprint of New Left Books

ISBN-13: 978-1-84467-128-1

British Library Cataloguing in Publication Data
A catalogue record for this book is available from the British Library

Typeset in Sabon
Printed and bound in the UK by CPI Bath

For Leslie, Chloe, Olivia,
Charlie, and Tao

CONTENTS

CHAPTER ONE

Making History

Just after 9:37 a.m. on the morning of September 11, 2001, Officer Aubrey Davis of the Pentagon police was standing outside Donald Rumsfeld's office on the third floor of the Pentagon's E Ring. Inside, Rumsfeld, though aware that the World Trade Center towers in New York had already been hit, was proceeding with his regularly scheduled CIA briefing. Davis, on the other hand, had concluded from watching the TV news that the country was under attack and the Pentagon might be a target. Assigned to the defense secretary's personal bodyguard, he had come on his own initiative, ready to move Rumsfeld to a better-protected location.

"There was an incredibly loud 'boom,'" says Davis, raising his voice slightly on the last word. Fifteen or twenty seconds later, just as his radio crackled with a message, the door opened and Rumsfeld walked out, looking composed and wearing the jacket he normally discarded while in his office. "Sir," said Davis, quoting what he had heard on his radio, "we're getting a report that an airplane has hit the Mall."

"The Mall?" replied Rumsfeld calmly. Without further word, the secretary of defense turned on his heel and set off at a sharp pace toward the so-called Mall section of the Pentagon. Down the hall, someone ran out of a VIP dining room screaming, "They're bombing the building, they're bombing the building." Davis frantically waved for colleagues to catch up as the stocky, 5' 8'' defense secretary marched ahead of his lanky escort.

The group, which grew to include several more police officers as well as Rumsfeld's personal communications aide, turned into the wide passageway running along the Mall face of the building. Thick crowds of Pentagon staff, in and out of uniform, were hurrying past in the opposite direction. They could smell smoke, but there was no sign of any damage here. "I thought you said the Mall," said Rumsfeld.

"Sir," responded Davis, holding his radio, "now we're hearing it's by the heliport." This meant the next side of the building farther along from the Mall. Rumsfeld set off again without a word, ignoring Davis's protestations that they should turn back. "At the end of the Mall corridor, we dropped down a stairway to the second floor, and then a little farther we dropped down to the first. It was dark and there was a lot of smoke. Then we saw daylight through a door that was hanging open." Groping through the darkness to the door, the group emerged outside. In front of them, just thirty yards away, roared a "wall of flame."

"There were the flames, and bits of metal all around," Davis remembers, as well as injured people. He noticed the white legs of a woman lying on the ground, then realized with a shock that she was African-American, horribly burned. "The secretary picked up one of the pieces of metal. I was telling him he shouldn't be interfering with a crime scene when he looked at some inscription on it and said, 'American Airlines.' Then someone shouted, 'Help, over here,' and we ran over and helped push an injured person on a gurney over to the road."

While the secretary of defense was pushing a gurney, Davis's radio was crackling with frantic pleas from his control room regarding Rumsfeld's whereabouts. "It was 'Dr. Cambone [Rumsfeld's closest aide] is asking, Dr. Cambone wants to find the secretary.' I kept saying, 'We've got him,' but the system was overloaded, everyone on the frequency was talking, everything jumbled, so I couldn't get through and they went on asking."

An emergency worker approached, saying that equipment and medical supplies were needed. "Tell this man what you need," said

Rumsfeld, gesturing to the communications aide, apparently oblivious of the fact that there were no communications.

Once they had pushed the wounded man on the gurney over to the road, the bodyguard was finally able to lead his charge back inside the building. "I'd say we were gone fifteen minutes, max," he told me in his account of what happened that morning. Given the time it took to make their way down those Pentagon corridors—each side of the enormous building is the length of three football fields—Rumsfeld was actually at the crash site for only a fraction of that period.

Yet those few minutes made Rumsfeld famous, changed him from a half-forgotten twentieth-century political figure to America's twenty-first-century warlord. On a day when the president was intermittently visible, only Rumsfeld, along with New York mayor Rudy Giuliani, gave the country an image of decisive, courageous leadership. According to his spokesman, the sixty-nine-year-old defense secretary's "first instinct was to go out through the building to the crash site and help." Over time, the legend grew. One of the staffers in the office later assured me that Rumsfeld had "torn his shirt into strips" to make bandages for the wounded.

As we shall see, Rumsfeld was first and foremost a politician, though not always a successful one. The weeks before the attacks had been one of the unsuccessful phases, with rumors spreading in Washington that he would shortly be removed from his post. Only the day before he had lashed out at the Pentagon workforce, denouncing the assembled soldiers and civilians as "a threat, a serious threat, to the security of the United States of America." Now, his instinctive dash to the crash site could inspire loyalty and support among those he had derided. An official in the Office of Plans, Analysis and Evaluation, whose office was close to Rumsfeld's, saw him walking swiftly down the hall in the first minutes after the crash. Later, when he heard where Rumsfeld had been, he thought, "very astute, politically."

Hatred and resentment among those in his wake had been a regular feature of Rumsfeld's career, and 9/11 proved no exception. I first realized this while discussing that day with a senior White House official who had been in the Situation Room, desperately trying to coordinate a response to the bewildering disaster of the attacks. As he reminisced, I mentioned that despite the legend, it didn't seem as if Rumsfeld could have had much time for rescue work that morning.

"What was Rumsfeld doing on 9/11?" said the former official with sudden anger. "He deserted his post. He disappeared. The country was under attack. Where was the guy who controls America's defense? Out of touch!"

"He wasn't gone for very long," I observed mildly.

My friend waved his coffee mug in emphatic rebuttal. "How long does it take for something bad to happen? No one knew what was happening. What if this had been the opening shot of a coordinated attack by a hostile power? Outrageous, to abandon your responsibilities and go off and do what you don't need to be doing, grandstanding."

This conversation took place in March 2006, just before it became commonplace in Washington to speak disrespectfully of Rumsfeld, at least in anything louder than a whisper, so I was taken aback by the vehemence of his response. A minute later, this sober bureaucrat burst forth with renewed passion. "He's a megalomaniac who has to be in control at all times," he fumed. "He is the worst secretary of defense there has ever been, worse than [Robert] McNamara. He is playing a major part in destroying this presidency."

Clearly, Rumsfeld was reviled in certain parts of the Bush administration. Yet such antagonisms occur in every presidency. But what did it mean, I wondered, that Rumsfeld had "deserted his post"? Though most people assume that the chain of command runs from the president to the vice president, the cold war bequeathed a significant constitutional readjustment. In an age when an enemy attack might allow only a few minutes for detection and reaction, control of American military power became vested in the National Command Authority, which consists of the president and the secretary of defense. Collectively, the NCA is the ultimate source of military orders, uniquely empowered, among other things, to order the use of nuclear weapons. In time of war, therefore, Rumsfeld was effectively the president's partner, the direct link to the fighting forces, and all orders had to go through him.

Such orders were supposed to be transmitted from a two-story complex at the end of a narrow passageway across the corridor from Rumsfeld's office. This was the National Military Command Center, staffed twenty-four hours a day with as many as two hundred military officers and civilian staff and equipped with arrays of communications systems, including multiple screens for video conferences. "All very Star Trek," recalls an official who formerly served there.

This was the operational center for any and every crisis, from nuclear war to hijacked airliners. The command center organized conference calls enabling key officials around the government to communicate and coordinate. At 9:39 a.m. that morning, just over a minute after the Pentagon was hit, the navy captain in charge of the command center announced on the "air threat conference call" that had just begun that "an air attack on North America may be in progress," and asked that the secretary of defense come to the center. A few minutes later, the secretary's office reported back that he was nowhere to be found. The chain of command was broken.[1]

In fact, Rumsfeld was at the crash site, though eventually it occurred to him that he might perhaps be in the wrong place: ". . . at some moment I decided I should be in here," he told *Parade* magazine in his office a month later, "figuring out what to do, because your brain begins to connect things."

Rumsfeld was back in the building by ten o'clock, but despite the anxious pleas from the military, he did not go to the command center. Instead, he headed for his office, where he spoke to President Bush, though afterward neither man could recall what they discussed. Next, in his words, he moved to "a room about 30 yards away here in this building . . . that's sealable." That would have been the Executive Support Center, conference rooms "secure" against electronic eavesdropping right next door to the military command center.

Waiting here was a small group, distinguished above all else by their personal loyalty to Rumsfeld. One was Stephen Cambone, the aide who had been inquiring so anxiously for his whereabouts minutes before. Of all in Rumsfeld's court, Cambone cast the longest shadow, energetically accumulating power thanks to the protective embrace of his mentor and his acknowledged intelligence.

Also there was Rumsfeld's personal chief of staff, Larry Di Rita, a former naval officer who had moved into Rumsfeld's orbit from the right-wing staff of Senator Kay Bailey Hutchison. Di Rita's defining characteristic was his devotion to the boss. (An Olympic-standard squash player, he would still dutifully lose to Rumsfeld.) The third person in the room was his spokesperson, Victoria (Torie) Clarke, a consummate public relations professional, artful enough to promote Rumsfeld—who was so secretive that he would refuse to tell his own deputy what had happened in White House meetings—as a paragon of openness and transparency.[2]

After a brief discussion with this select group, Rumsfeld finally made his way to the military command center. It was almost 10:30. Only then, as he later explained to the 9/11 Commission, did he begin to gain "situational awareness" of what was going on. After a brief interval he spoke with Vice President Dick Cheney, who was in a bunker under the White House and for the previous forty minutes had been issuing orders to shoot down suspicious airliners.

"There's been at least three instances here where we've had reports of aircraft approaching Washington—a couple were confirmed hijack," Cheney told Rumsfeld in his favored clipped, macho style. "And pursuant to the President's instructions I gave authorization for them to be taken out."

Actually, the presidential authorization cited by Cheney consisted, at best, of the words "You bet" from Bush as *Air Force One* streaked out of Orlando, Florida. In any event, it was Rumsfeld, not Cheney, who was legally in the chain of command and authorized to give such an order.

"So we've got a couple of [military] aircraft up there that have those instructions at this present time?" asked Rumsfeld, still catching up.

"That is correct," replied Cheney. "And it's my understanding they've already taken a couple of aircraft out."[3]

Together, these two men dominated the U.S. government for six years. They must have had thousands of conversations, but this snatch of dialogue, as released by the 9/11 Commission, is the only known publicly available sample of a private conversation between them. Though brief, it is instructive. Not for the last time, they were reacting to information that was wholly inaccurate—there were no more hijacked airliners in the sky. One of the planes Cheney had ordered "taken out" was United Flight 93, which crashed in Pennsylvania ten minutes before he issued the command. The other was a low-flying medevac helicopter on its way to the Pentagon. Neither man seemed concerned that the president was not involved. Cheney was usurping his authority, since he was not in the chain of command. Lacking any experience in the military, the vice president may not have realized that military commanders like precise orders, and will not proceed without them, which was why the fighter commanders chose not to pass on his aggressive instructions to the pilots.

Rumsfeld, once he had finally settled into his place at the command center, got to work on the "rules of engagement" for the fighter pilots. This was an irrelevant exercise for he did not complete and issue them until 1:00 p.m., hours after the last hijacker had died.

Later, when asked why he had taken no part in military operations that morning, Rumsfeld blithely insisted that it was not his job. "The Department of Defense," he told the 9/11 Commission in 2004, "did not have responsibility for the borders. It did not have responsibility for the airports . . . a civilian aircraft was a law enforcement matter to be handled by law enforcement authorities and aviation authorities." Expanding on this theme, he explained that the Defense Department's only responsibility when a civilian plane was hijacked was to "send up an aircraft and monitor the flight, but certainly in a hijack situation [the military] did not have authority to shoot down a plane that was being hijacked."[4] This statement was flat out untrue, but none of the commissioners dared call him to account.

Having absented himself from military involvement while the al Qaeda attacks were actually in progress on the morning of 9/11, Rumsfeld began the afternoon with the first fateful steps toward the war that would secure his historical reputation. At 12:05 p.m., CIA director George Tenet called to report that just fifteen minutes after the Pentagon had been hit, the National Security Agency (NSA) had intercepted a phone call between a known associate of Osama bin Laden in Afghanistan and someone in the former Soviet Republic of Georgia. The bin Laden associate announced that he had heard "good news," and that another target was still to be hit (presumably the intended target of Flight 93). Tenet also reported that one of the hijackers on the Pentagon plane had been linked to someone involved in the suicide attack on the USS *Cole* in 2000. Here was clear confirmation that the millionaire Saudi leader of al Qaeda was behind that day's attacks.

Rumsfeld was having none of it. According to Cambone's cryptic notes, the secretary felt this intelligence was "'vague,' that it might not mean something, and that there was 'no good basis for hanging hat.' " So whatever the terrorists might be saying on the phone, the secretary of defense was reserving judgment. The moment was a textbook example of Rumsfeld's standard reaction to information that did not suit his preconceptions. It would recur in the years to come.[5]

In a brief televised press conference at 6:40 that evening, in which Rumsfeld's calm demeanor much impressed viewers, veteran Reuters Pentagon correspondent Charlie Aldinger asked, "Mr. Secretary, did you have any inkling at all, in any way, that something of this nature and something of this scope might be planned?"

"Charlie," responded Rumsfeld quickly, "we don't discuss intelligence matters." The response appeared to reflect his tough-minded prudence in times of crisis. Yet in retrospect, it is easy to understand his reluctance to pursue the subject. Two months before, an intelligence report prepared for the National Security Council (NSC) had concluded "we believe that UBL [Usama bin Laden (sic)] will launch a significant terrorist attack against U.S. and/or Israeli interests in the coming weeks. The attack will be spectacular and designed to inflict mass casualties against U.S. facilities or interests. Attack preparations have been made. Attack will occur with little or no warning."[6]

It is an inescapable and now well-documented fact that the Bush administration had serial warnings prior to 9/11 that bin Laden was preparing a major attack, and routinely dismissed these warnings. On July 10, 2001, one such alarm was delivered to National Security Adviser Condoleezza Rice in the form of a briefing from Tenet and his counterterrorism chief, Cofer Black. According to some accounts Rice did take this presentation seriously. (When news of the warning first surfaced in Bob Woodward's book *State of Denial,* Rice denied that it happened at all, then recalled that it had.) On her recommendation, Rumsfeld received the same briefing on July 17, along with Attorney General John Ashcroft.[7] Ashcroft immediately stopped flying on commercial airliners.[8]

Rumsfeld's reaction has never been previously revealed, but according to several intelligence sources his response was one of vehement dismissal, complete with cutting observations about the CIA falling victim to "vast doses of Al Qaeda disinformation" and "mortal doses of gullibility." It had been a classic example of how Rumsfeld reacted to anything he thought might become a problem. He took this position, so the CIA believed, because agitation about terrorist threats might pose a distraction from his cherished goals of shrinking the army, investing in a new generation of high-technology weapons, and deploying a ballistic missile defense system.

Now Osama bin Laden and his teams of hijackers had proved Rumsfeld spectacularly wrong. So, on the afternoon of September 11, with part of his building still burning and smoke eddying through the corridors, Rumsfeld was already pondering how to shift attention in a new direction. At 2:40 p.m., still in the command center, he told General Richard Myers to find the "[b]est info fast . . . judge whether good enough [to] hit S.H. @ same time—not only U.B.L." S.H. was of course Saddam Hussein, while U.B.L, in Cambone's preferred spelling, was Usama bin Laden. "Hard to get a good case," mused Rumsfeld, pondering what he needed from his intelligence agencies. "Need to move swiftly—Near term target needs—Go massive—sweep it all up, need to do so to get anything useful. Things related and not."[9]

It was the first step on the road to Baghdad. The notion of attacking Iraq had been rumored in the Pentagon since George W. Bush and the Republicans had taken power. But this had been wishful thinking rather than any firm decision. Now, thanks to the events of the morning, war became inevitable.

Most of the things we need to know about Donald Rumsfeld were on display that day. The country was under attack, but he went off to micromanage operations at the crash site. He had clearly defined responsibilities, but later claimed he did not. As was often the case, his actions enraged colleagues. As usual, he turned first for advice to a small group on whose loyalty he could count. He worked closely with Vice President Cheney. He disregarded intelligence he did not want to hear. Warnings he had dismissed were now horribly vindicated, so he opted to change the subject. At the end of the day he gave a powerful performance on TV, impressing the country with his leadership qualities.

For Rumsfeld, in other words, it was a day much like any other. On 9/11, his future was assured. But to understand why his future took the path it did, we must visit his past.

CHAPTER TWO

A Ruthless Little Bastard

Nearly everybody liked the Rumsfelds, the former high school sweethearts from Chicago who lived in a tiny house in Georgetown with three young children and a dog named Otto and threw spaghetti parties in their backyard.[1] "They were so much fun," remembers one longtime friend and former neighbor. "They never had any money, but they were great to have around." Columnist Joe Kraft affectionately nicknamed the young Republican congressman "Boy-Boy." "It was because he was just so boyishly exuberant," recalls Polly Kraft.

Kraft was a liberal, a former Kennedy speechwriter who ultimately landed on Richard Nixon's enemies list. But Rumsfeld, at least in those days, never had trouble making friends across party lines. This was partly due to the effect of his good-natured wife, Joyce, who commanded widespread affection and loyalty.[2] Ever since his arrival in 1962 as a thirty-year-old congressman from an affluent Chicago district, he had cultivated friendships across party lines and with journalists such as Kraft, *Washington Post* editor Ben Bradlee, and the up-and-coming CBS White House correspondent Dan Rather. A keen wrestler in his college days, one of Rumsfeld's closest friendships was with a fellow wrestler, antiwar activist and Democratic congressman Allard Lowenstein, later tragically murdered by his gay lover. His fellow Illinois Republican boy-wonder politician, Charles Percy, who later served in the U.S. Senate from

1968 to 1984, long remembered that Rumsfeld had dropped every-thing in the middle of a campaign to rush and offer assistance to the Percy family on the awful day when Percy's daughter Valerie was found murdered in the family home. For a personal problem, Rums-feld could be counted on as a friend in need.

At the carefree Georgetown gatherings, when the popular young host was not demonstrating his ability to perform backflips with his pipe in his mouth, he liked to quote a profile published during his first congressional campaign that described Rumsfeld as "distinguished by his total lack of social, financial and political standing in the district." He loved that line so much he would still be quoting it in 2003,[3] but it was far from the truth. In his first congressional campaign, no less than fourteen chief executives of major national corporations, as well as powerful lawyers and academics, endorsed him.[4]

This potent support derived from the fact that Rumsfeld grew up in Winnetka, one of the wealthier suburbs on Chicago's North Shore, "where all the CEOs lived," according to one former resident. George Rumsfeld, his father, a real estate salesman, managed the local office of a realtor firm. His mother, Jeanette, worked as a sub-stitute teacher. The Rumsfelds "were not exactly in the same club" as their well-heeled neighbors, recalls William Cohea, former pastor of the Winnetka Presbyterian Church, "but they were well known. His uncle was a professor at Northwestern University." New Trier high school, which Rumsfeld attended, was famous for its excellence and therefore attracted the sons and daughters of the local elite. By the time he began running for Congress as a twenty-nine-year-old, the young man who had attended Princeton on an ROTC scholar-ship, which he followed with three years in the navy, had forged relationships that would still be serving him half a century later.

"When I met him for the first time, he was eighteen," says Cohea, "and all he talked about was going into politics." Following his mil-itary service, Rumsfeld started on the bottom of the political ladder, working as a congressional staffer. But after managing a losing campaign for one of his bosses, he moved back to Chicago to work in an investment bank, buying a house in Glenview—within calling distance of the grand Winnetka mansions. It was not long before opportunity knocked.

Early in 1962, Marguerite Stitt Church, his local congresswoman, announced her retirement. The thirteenth Illinois district, which included much of the North Shore, was one of the most solidly Republican in the nation, so the crucial race was the Republican primary. Rumsfeld filed for the primary—one of several eager aspirants. He was sponsored, according to a well-connected former Winnetka resident, by Art Nielsen, son of the founder of the TV ratings company and a local power broker who rounded up support among neighborhood corporate heavyweights such as Dan Searle, heir to the G.D. Searle drug company.

Before commencing his campaign, the ambitious young politico had one very important personal decision to make. What, actually, were his political views? According to local Republican sources, Rumsfeld sought outside help in settling the issue. Approaching the chairman of the Chicago Republican Party, Francis X. Connell, he asked whether he should run as a conservative or as a moderate. For the young Rumsfeld, ideology was a matter of tactics. In any event, Connell seems to have advocated a conservative approach, advice that would have momentous effects far into the future.

State representative Marion Burks was the initial favorite, and was expected to receive the popular Mrs. Church's endorsement. But Rumsfeld's chances suddenly improved when the *Chicago Sun-Times,* which had already endorsed Rumsfeld, headlined a story that money in an insurance company of which Burks was chairman had gone missing. The ambitious twenty-nine-year-old (he turned thirty in July 1962) had recruited an equally youthful team of helpers, including an MBA student from the University of Chicago named Jeb Stuart Magruder, later jailed in the Watergate scandal for his role in the Nixon administration's criminal dirty tricks operation. "I already had experience from the 1960 Nixon campaign in Kansas City, so it was natural for me to get involved," Magruder, now a minister of the Presbyterian Church, told me in 2006.

Rumsfeld himself affected a statesmanlike attitude during the campaign, never mentioning the allegations against Burks, while Magruder and other Rumsfeld operatives reportedly arranged for someone to raise the issue at every one of Burks's meetings, disregarding his repeated protests of innocence.[5] "I did what I did best," the seventy-two-year-old Magruder replied when I asked him about his role. "I don't remember much about Burks." In his 1974 memoir, *An American Life,* a younger Magruder recalled, "We did everything we could to keep the [Burks] issue alive. Don never mentioned it in public, but whenever Burks spoke we would send our people to pepper him with questions about the scandal." The allegations were a total smear; Burks retired as a respected circuit court judge.[6] But meanwhile Rumsfeld had won the primary.

His margin was huge, more than two to one, a spectacular victory for a political neophyte, but in one sense it proved a poisoned chalice. "That was the one and only election contest Rumsfeld ever had to face," a veteran of Illinois politics pointed out to me. "In that district, once he was in, he could keep on getting reelected till the end of time, barring the proverbial discovery of a dead girl or live boy in his bed. But he thought he knew everything about politics after that one race, and had nothing more to learn."

Congressional Republicans had yet to evolve into the grim partisans of the Newt Gingrich era and beyond, so Rumsfeld managed to serve six years in the House, predictably reelected by his affluent constituents without acquiring any ideological label more striking than that of a conventional conservative, loyal to his business sponsors and the routine prejudices of their class. Militant anticommunism came with the territory—this, after all, was the party of Joe McCarthy, whose witch-hunting days had ended only seven years before young Rumsfeld's election to Congress.

Soon after taking his seat in Congress, Rumsfeld issued a fierce denunciation of a Kennedy administration nominee for a Pentagon post as "soft" on the communist foe. The individual had attended a National Council of Churches meeting at which pacifist ideas had been debated. The statement proved only to demonstrate Rumsfeld's ignorance of the wider world, for the man he attacked was none other than Paul Nitze, whose entire government career had been devoted to highlighting the Soviet threat.[7]

Rumsfeld later apologized to Nitze for his ill-founded abuse, but other positions carved out by the ambitious young legislator were to remain as enduring themes for years to come. In response to John F. Kennedy's ringing call for an expedition to the moon—"We choose to go to the moon in this decade and do the other things, not because they are easy, but because they are hard"—Rumsfeld, unmoved, joined five fellow right-wing house Republicans in a public complaint that the administration was ignoring "the main thrust of the Soviet space aim, which is to dominate inner space thru the ability to exercise control over the surface of the earth."[8] It was a theme he never let go. Forty years later, he was pouring out $9 billion a year to defend inner space with the missile defense program, even though by then the Soviets were long gone from the surface of the earth.

Aside from such public announcements, Rumsfeld was exercising a craft in which he was already displaying great ability: backroom intrigue. In 1965 he played a leading role in a maneuver that displaced the House Republican floor leader, a venerable party stalwart named Charles Halleck, known as "Two Cadillac Charlie," in favor of a younger though equally conservative congressman from Michigan named Gerald R. Ford.[9] "Getting rid of Halleck and putting in Jerry Ford was the best thing he ever did in Washington," said Charles Bartlett, a veteran political reporter who came to know the Rumsfelds when they first arrived in Washington. "Everyone knew Halleck had to go, but most of those Republican congressmen were just sitting on their hands." Nevertheless, this power play exposed another feature of Rumsfeld the politician, one that served him ill in the career of which he dreamed: his tendency to leave a trail of embittered enemies behind him. Glorious though the Halleck victory may have been, especially for the future of Jerry Ford, it left Halleck's good friend Congressman Leslie Arends of Illinois deeply displeased. Arends was not only the Republican whip but also the dean of the Illinois Republican delegation. Even worse, an attempt in January 1969 to unseat Arends from his post as whip failed, which meant that Rumsfeld had now directly provoked a powerful enemy in his own backyard. Bob Michel, a colleague from the Illinois Republican delegation, told him that he would never get a leadership post so long as Arends was around. "Well," Rumsfeld reportedly replied, "I better see if I can get a job with the administration."

The newly elected Richard Nixon had retrieved the White House from the Democrats in the 1968 election largely as a result of the unpopularity of the Vietnam War launched and pursued by his

Democratic predecessors. While his mandate may have been to end the war, his agenda was to reverse some of the socially progressive initiatives of John F. Kennedy and Lyndon Johnson.

Johnson had promised to create a "Great Society" in which poverty would be abolished thanks to a host of programs that catered in various ways to the needs of the poor, including Head Start, aimed at needy preschoolers, and the Federal Legal Services Program, which enabled poor people to litigate their rights. These programs were under the central supervision of the Office of Economic Opportunity. It was politically impossible for Nixon to do away with the poverty programs, though he disliked them intensely, and he was looking for a politically reliable operative who would at least rein them in. Offered the job, the thirty-five-year-old Rumsfeld used the fact that several other candidates had already rejected the job to bargain successfully for cabinet rank and the title of assistant to the president.

In Congress, Rumsfeld had proudly proclaimed himself a foe of the War on Poverty. "I voted to revise the poverty and the Model Cities programs," he boasted to his well-heeled constituents during the 1968 campaign. "I oppose the rent supplement program . . . I opposed increasing the Federal Debt limit . . . I joined a group of Republicans to cut Federal spending $6.6 billion."[10] Thus, when his appointment was announced, liberals quaked at the prospect of this rabid ideologue taking over the chicken coop. But of course, now that he had his own little empire, Rumsfeld was not about to dismantle it.

Rumsfeld's stewardship of the antipoverty effort was to do much for his subsequent reputation. The fact that he kept the agency going while mouthing supportive statements about its mission was taken to indicate that he was no hard-line right-wing ideologue, but an open-minded individual ready to fight for a liberal cause when it was justified. In fact, Rumsfeld's record at the antipoverty agency fits neatly into the same pattern as those of his subsequent jobs. That is to say, he devoted most of his energies to imposing his unchallenged political control on the organization while cultivating an ill-merited reputation for administrative competence. Hence, among his first acts was the creation of an internal security unit in OEO headquarters charged with sniffing out "revolutionaries" who might be funneling government funds to "subversives."[11]

The management team assembled by Rumsfeld at the dawn of his administrative career was to show remarkable longevity. A third of a century later many of them were still by his side, either directly in his employ or close at hand to proffer advice and counsel. Kenneth Adelman, for example, was an accomplished amateur Shakespeare scholar and ardent supporter of Israel who later carved out a niche as an authority on defense matters. Adelman was joined by his wife, Carol, who, decades later, would find herself recommending personnel choices for Rumsfeld's Pentagon when he took over in 2001. Frank Carlucci was a diminutive lawyer who later reaped a multimillion-dollar fortune as a defense contractor as well as serving in a variety of high-level national security posts.

Most fateful of all was the addition of a young and so far undistinguished man from Casper, Wyoming, Richard Cheney. Arriving in Washington in 1968, Cheney had found service as the political equivalent of a field hand in the office of a Republican congressman before landing in the office of the newly appointed head of the poverty program. Rumsfeld had actually rejected Cheney when the self-effacing youngster had earlier applied for a job in Rumsfeld's congressional office, but there now began a relationship that would endure for decades to come, with fateful consequences for the country and the world.

Observers of this relationship in its early years were in no doubt as to its internal dynamic: Rumsfeld ruled; Cheney served. As Jerry Ford's sharp-tongued amanuensis, Robert Hartmann, observed a few years later, Cheney's "adult life had been devoted to the study of political science and the service of Donald Rumsfeld." A serious student of political power, he "derived both his employment and his enjoyment from it. Whenever his private ideology was exposed, he appeared somewhat to the right of Ford, Rumsfeld, or, for that matter, Genghis Khan." Hartmann, a former newspaperman, summed up Cheney as a "presentable young man who could easily be lost in a gaggle of Jaycee executives. His most distinguishing features were snake-cold eyes, like a Cheyenne gambler's."[12]

To the extent that the Rumsfelds' social circle took note of the dour young assistant and his buxom spouse, a former drum majorette with literary pretensions named Lynne, it was to remark on Cheney's subservient attitude to his ebullient boss. "Flunky" is the word that most often comes up in reminiscences of the period. "Cheney was so much Don's faithful assistant, with Don so clearly the mentor, I can't believe that relationship ever changed," insists one friend who remained close enough to be invited to all of Rumsfeld's formal swearing-in ceremonies.

But the relationship did change. Eventually, the student of political science calculated, like the gambler to which he was compared, that he had learned enough to play his own hand. It was a turning point that, as we shall see, came as a shock to the man who had always considered himself the senior partner, but the relationship eventually reestablished itself on a different course. Even so, asked about Cheney in a 2006 interview, Rumsfeld struck a slightly patronizing note: "I used to think of him as a promising young man, when I hired him. . . . It was so many years ago, 1969. I hired him as my—one of my special assistants. . . . He's a very talented fellow."[13]

Hartmann, in a penetrating character sketch, describes Rumsfeld as "expansive and, when it suited him, all smiles." The smiles were no doubt a contributing factor in Rumsfeld's popularity on the Washington scene, but for Rumsfeld, career came ahead of friendships. His relationship with Al Lowenstein ended when Rumsfeld, unwilling to court Nixon's disfavor, endorsed his old friend's opponent in a congressional race in 1970. Lowenstein lost and never forgave his former wrestling companion.[14] Rumsfeld made a similar call in the case of Terry Lenzner—today one of Washington's most successful private investigators, but then a trenchantly progressive young lawyer. Lenzner was director of an OEO subsidiary, the Federal Legal Services Program, an effort designed to give poor people the means to pursue litigation.

The right-wingers hated Legal Services with an especially vitriolic passion, their attacks spearheaded by Governor Ronald Reagan of California, and the even more conservative Governor Claude Kirk of Florida. In November 1970, Rumsfeld announced he had fired Lenzner and his assistant because the pair were either "unwilling or unable" to carry out his policies. This justification was swiftly rebutted by Lenzner, who described it as "mere cover up." He charged that the real reason for his dismissal lay in the baleful opposition of Reagan, Kirk, and others who were "determined to keep us from suing special interests close to them on behalf of the poor."[15]

In subsequent accounts, Rumsfeld and his supporters sought to portray Lenzner as a wild-eyed radical who plastered his office walls with posters of Che Guevara and whom no responsible administration could continue to employ. But, at the time, Rumsfeld's action was greeted with stormy opposition not just from activists but also from the legal community at large.

The day before he fired Lenzner, Rumsfeld met with the president of the American Bar Association, an Arkansas attorney of impeccable establishment credentials named Edward L. Wright. Twenty-four hours later, he simultaneously issued two press releases, one announcing Lenzner's dismissal, the other reporting on his meeting with Wright. The obvious inference was that the ABA endorsed the firings, a point Rumsfeld sought to emphasize by mentioning his meeting with Wright. Wright was having none of it: "Since the releases were issued concurrently," he shot back, "an impression was created that I had knowledge of the dismissals. This is untrue." He added that the bar association did not support or endorse the firings.[16]

This awkward maneuver was to prove more typical of Rumsfeld's style than that of the deftly competent Machiavelli later touted by friends and enemies alike, a telling clue to what would be his failure ever to achieve elective office again. In the backroom politics of the Nixon court, however, where Rumsfeld's style found many admirers, it was a different story. In his diary for May 21, 1970, Nixon's chief of staff, H. R. Haldeman, recorded how he and Rumsfeld had been summoned by Nixon to discuss how to handle the problem of disloyalty in the cabinet and among the staff. The president was in favor of "cracking down hard," but Rumsfeld "made point you have to establish record of trying to work things out before you fire someone." Nixon liked this kind of thinking, and, as Haldeman noted, "Wants Don Rumsfeld brought more into the inner councils."[17]

It seems Rumsfeld fit right in. "At least Rummy is tough

enough," President Nixon remarked in March 1971. "He's a ruthless little bastard. You can be sure of that."[18]

Rumsfeld appealed to Nixon because, as one seasoned Republican operative explained to me, "Don understood that Nixon liked
protégés with an Ivy League background from silk-stocking districts,
and he knew how to appeal to that. George Bush Sr. was another
protégé; he got Nixon to make him U.N. ambassador because he
promised to fight his own class at the U.N. on behalf of Nixon."
Thanks to the silently turning tape recorders in the White House
basement, we can eavesdrop on counseling sessions between the
mentor and the protégé from Winnetka. On July 22, 1971, for
example, Nixon held forth to Rumsfeld on the topic of Spiro Agnew,
his vice president, who had publicly expressed some crass comparisons between American blacks and Africans while on a trip to
Africa, claiming that African blacks were "smarter."

Nixon: "It doesn't help. It hurts with the blacks. And it doesn't
help with the rednecks because the rednecks don't think any
Negroes are any good."

Rumsfeld: "Yes."

Nixon: "Coming back and saying that black Americans aren't as
good as black Africans—most of them, basically are just out of the
trees. Now, let's face it, they are. My point is, if we say that, they
[opponents] say [here Nixon drops into a Southern drawl], 'Well, by
God.' Well, ah, even the Southerners say, 'Well, our niggers is just
better than their niggers.'"

Rumsfeld laughs.

Nixon: "Hell, that's the way they talk!"

Rumsfeld: "That's right."

Nixon: "I can hear 'em."

Rumsfeld: "I know."

Nixon: "It's like when our black athletes, I mean in the
Olympics, are running against the other black athletes; the South-
erner may not like the black, but he's for that black athlete."

Rumsfeld: "That's right."

Nixon: "Right?"

Rumsfeld: "That's for sure."

Nixon: "Well, enough of that."[19]

In August 1971, Nixon found new employment for his "ruthless little bastard." The colossal expenses of the Vietnam War had sapped America's global economic supremacy to the point where the United States was forced to abandon the gold standard, allowing the dollar to float and potentially opening the door to runaway inflation. Scenting opportunity in this debacle, Nixon decided to impose wage and price controls on the American economy while simultaneously expanding the money supply. Thus the American people, their pockets bulging with cash to spend on price-controlled goods, would coast toward Nixon's 1972 reelection in a suitable mood of financial gratitude. Rumsfeld, while protesting to the president how philosophically opposed he was to the whole idea, took on the job.

While Rumsfeld did much to gain approval in the eyes of his mentor, Nixon, he also managed to provoke some dangerous antagonisms, which, paradoxically, were to serve him well in the years to come. The point of contention was Vietnam. Having gained the White House on a pledge to end the war via a "secret plan," Nixon's policy, as crafted with the help of Henry Kissinger, was to try to win the war by expanding it into neighboring Southeast Asian countries. At the same time, Nixon and Kissinger hoped to negotiate an overall geostrategic arrangement with Russia and China as part of a Vietnam settlement. This was not necessarily a popular option on the right, which bridled at the notion of regulating global affairs hand in hand with the communist enemy. "The conservative position was we should get out," recalls Rumsfeld's old friend Richard Allen, who later served as Ronald Reagan's first national security adviser.

By 1971, Rumsfeld was letting it be known that he was one of those opposed to the policy of holding the line in Vietnam, an attitude that, by extension, constituted a critique of the Kissinger line. Why not move toward a quick end to the war? he began suggesting at staff meetings. Concurrently, he began angling for a high-level post in charge of postwar reconstruction in Southeast Asia, a part of the world Henry Kissinger very much regarded as his own.

Thus was born the notion that Rumsfeld had in his younger days been something of a dove on Vietnam. At the time, no one in the Nixon inner circle seems to have thought that Rumsfeld was acting out of anything approaching principle.

"He's ready to jump the ship, Rummy," Nixon remarked to Haldeman and Kissinger following an April 7, 1971, staff meeting at which Rumsfeld had once again proved obstreperous.

"No, I don't think he's ready to jump," responded Haldeman. "And I doubt if he ever would, just because [staying on in the administration] serves his interests more than not."

"He's just positioning himself to be close to the *Washington Post* and the *New York Times*," added Kissinger.[20]

"You have to remember," notes Richard Allen, "that these people didn't trust anybody. They didn't even trust their wives. They used people. Nixon knew that Kissinger was betraying him at every dinner party he went to, but he figured he would be able to let Kissinger take the fall if things went down the tubes."

Nixon and his closest advisers took Rumsfeld's consuming ambition as a given, and perceived his maneuverings in that light. At one point Haldeman grumbled in his diary that Rumsfeld had agreed in a meeting with John Ehrlichman, another senior Nixon aide, that he would return to Illinois to run for the Senate, but had then promptly reneged, telling Nixon that he insisted on a senior administration post for a year. "Typical Rumsfeld," noted Haldeman, "rather slimy maneuver." John Ehrlichman, Haldeman's equally formidable colleague, stated in his memoirs that "the senior staff grew to realize that the ambitious Rumsfeld would decline every assignment that did not enhance his personal goals."

Finally, they got him to accept an overseas post as the U.S. ambassador to NATO in Brussels. As things turned out, it was a golden parachute, fortuitously proffered at a time when the Nixon machine was headed for a very hard landing. After fixing up a job for his faithful flunky Cheney with Bruce Bradley, an investment banker and squash-playing friend from his congressional days, Rumsfeld packed up the family and headed for Europe.

Among Rumsfeld's more famous utterances has been his derisive reference to "Old Europe," inspired by French and German reluctance to support the invasion of Iraq. For statesmen with long memories, such displays came as something of a shock. "He's an enigma to me," sighs a former very senior official. "I've known Don Rumsfeld for thirty-five years and I still have no idea what he really thinks. I first knew him when he was ambassador to NATO. Do you know, in those days he was rabidly pro-European. His closest colleague was the French ambassador!"

Rabidly pro-European sentiments were not especially popular in Washington at that time, especially not in the offices of Henry Kissinger, who dominated U.S. foreign policy, serving simultaneously as both secretary of state and national security adviser. Kissinger, irked at European reaction to issues such as American support of Israel, let it be known that he was "disgusted" by the allies' behavior.[21] Rumsfeld, clearly, felt no need to join in the official chorus of disapproval. Had Kissinger's team been watching more closely, they might have noted a budding Rumsfeld friendship with a frequent visitor to Brussels, Paul Nitze, the preeminent cold warrior, whom Rumsfeld as a callow young congressman had once denounced as "soft."

The most important feature of Rumsfeld's time in Brussels, however, was where he wasn't. "Fortune," noted Robert Hartmann in reviewing Rumsfeld's role in the turbulent events to come, "often favors those who have the rare gift of being in the right place at the right time. Even rarer, however, is the knack of being somewhere else. Donald Rumsfeld possessed both."[22]

An old friend and former colleague of Rumsfeld, who spent so much time discoursing on the subject at a Washington restaurant that lunch gradually morphed into an early dinner, explained this "uncanny knack" in these terms: "Don looks at everything from the point of view of his own position. So no issue is so important that he will not be able to avoid it if there's a downside. He has a very, very high-level radar system that gives him a sense of incoming lethality so he can stay away. He is very good at keeping his fingerprints off things."

In Brussels, Rumsfeld was safely distanced from the stench of Watergate and its associated crimes that was beginning to swirl around the Nixon White House. Over the course of the next year and a half it would waft many of Rumsfeld's erstwhile colleagues off to the jailhouse, and eventually force Richard Nixon to resign in disgrace. During all this time the ambassador to NATO was happily consorting with his new French friends, or engaging in such carefree pursuits as running with the bulls in Pamplona in the mode of Ernest Hemingway. He even sought out some distant German cousins, who, at the time, thought him a "genuinely nice man."[23]

Despite such carefree diversions, Rumsfeld's eye never shifted very far from Washington and the ongoing decline of his mentor. Afterward, he described how he learned that Richard Nixon had resigned the presidency from the *International Herald-Tribune* while on holiday on the French Riviera, whereupon he flew back to Washington to see what he could do to help Jerry Ford.

Others contest this impression of disinterested detachment. "Don't believe it," laughs one former political associate. "When Don was at NATO, he was always flying back to Washington and spending a lot of time with Mel Laird [the former Wisconsin congressman who served as secretary of defense and then as a senior White House official under Nixon]. Laird had been very close to Ford when they were both in the congress. As Nixon got in worse trouble Don came back more and more often, positioning himself for an appointment after Nixon fell. I think Laird promoted him to Ford."

Thus Rumsfeld was well prepared for Nixon's departure, and was immediately on hand to proffer Ford advice on the transition. Ford's initial honeymoon came to a jarring end when he pardoned Nixon, but Rumsfeld, displaying his useful knack for being somewhere else, missed that political earthquake, having nimbly skipped back to what he said were urgent duties in Brussels.

At last, untainted by any of the scandals that had brought down Nixon and were already weakening Ford, Rumsfeld rode back into town as the rescuer, sliding into the White House as chief of staff to the president, retrieving Cheney from his private employment, where he had been parked, to serve once again as his assistant. (Interestingly, Cheney had reservations about returning to service, consulting his employer Bruce Bradley as to whether becoming deputy chief of staff at the White House was a good career move. Bradley gently assured him that it probably was.) Now at last Rumsfeld had real power, yet his ambition was evidently not even briefly satisfied. Within weeks of his moving into the West Wing, newspaper columnist Jack Anderson was already reporting that "Donald Rumsfeld won't be around the White House more than six months" because Ford intended to send "the able Rumsfeld" to run the Pentagon.

Those who remembered the new chief of staff winning favor with Richard Nixon for his ruthlessness and general political skills were either in jail, spending their waking hours with their lawyers, or at least hoping to hang on to their White House jobs.[24] He himself had no public comment on the criminal activities recently rampant in the building. In fact, few people had much idea of what Rumsfeld thought about anything. He had been compiling a little book of aphorisms—"Rumsfeld's Rules"—which he began circulating in 1974. Such nostrums as "In the execution of Presidential decisions, work to be true to his views, in fact and tone," may have excited little comment (apart from quiet derision among colleagues), but they certainly gave no insights on what Rumsfeld thought about the constitutional earthquake through which the Republic had recently passed.

"How did Rumsfeld react, for example, over the discovery of the White House taping system?" remarked the old friend toward the end of our very long lunch. "He made no comment, on that or any other significant event, but I happen to know he was utterly disgusted with Alexander Butterfield [the patriotic White House official who told congressional investigators about the taping system] for having spilled the beans."

Butterfield was fired in March 1975. This move could only win the applause of the many Nixon holdovers still infesting nooks and crannies of the White House bureaucracy and who were reassured to find that their jobs were secure under the new regime, for whom Rumsfeld was, as one Ford loyalist sardonically observed, "the prodigal returned."[25] Jerry H. Jones, for example, had been a staff member in the field division of the notorious CREEP—Committee to Re-Elect the President. Jones had gone on to serve as deputy to Alexander Haig during the latter's reign as chief of staff. Following Haig's replacement by Rumsfeld, Jones bobbed up again like a cork on the bloodstained political waters as staff secretary to the president. Twenty-five years later, when Rumsfeld moved into his spacious E Ring suite at the Pentagon for the second time as secretary of defense, Jones was simultaneously taking up quarters in the Pentagon personnel office down the hall. Rumsfeld always liked to have familiar faces around him.

As with any job he occupied, Rumsfeld moved swiftly to get control of the levers of power. Ford's old friend and adviser Robert Hartmann was deftly edged out of his office immediately next door to the Oval Office by means of a Rumsfeld-inspired redecoration scheme. While announcing that the title of "White House Chief of Staff," rendered infamous under the iron-fisted regime of H. R. Haldeman, was being discarded, Rumsfeld swiftly arranged matters so that he exercised the powers, even without the title (he modestly styled himself assistant to the president) of that office.

Survivors of the Ford White House tend to concur with the assessment of William Seidman, chief of Ford's Economic Policy Board, who insisted to me that Rumsfeld had been "an incredibly talented and efficient chief of staff." However, as Seidman, the man later called in to clean up the catastrophic disaster of the savings-and-loan crisis in the Reagan era, explained in a 2006 interview, Rumsfeld had his mind on a lot more than running the White House efficiently: "Like a lot of people in Washington, Donald Rumsfeld wanted to be president. He figured the way to get there was to get to be Jerry Ford's vice president, and move on from there." Recalling the power struggle of thirty years ago with crystalline clarity, Seidman described how "the Rumsfeld plot" faced two obstacles. First of all there already was a vice president. Nelson Rockefeller, the fabulously wealthy former governor of New York, had been named to the post by Ford not long after Nixon's resignation. Second, the chief of staff position was not considered a suitable stepping-stone to the vice presidency. He needed something more impressive on his résumé. To achieve his goal, Rumsfeld would not only have to get him himself appointed to run a major department, but also get Ford to drop the existing vice president from the ticket. "Not an easy thing to do," observed Seidman, "especially as Ford was the most loyal person in politics."

In pursuit of his first objective, securing a major cabinet slot, Rumsfeld, according to Seidman, scanned the list of possibilities and concluded that the Department of Treasury would suit him fine. Of course there already was a secretary of the treasury, William E. Simon, but soon there began to appear a spate of news stories, sourced to unnamed White House officials (including a detailed column by Rumsfeld's friend Joseph Kraft), announcing confidently that Ford had lost confidence in Simon and was about to fire him. "Simon was going nuts," remembered Seidman, and was on the point of resigning. The campaign only came unstuck when the journalist Charles Bartlett discovered that Jerry Ford had no desire to fire Simon, and began making inquiries to find out who was spreading the malicious leaks. Washington journalists are, of course, ready to protect their sources unto death, but their peers can as often as not find out who is behind a leak anyway. It did not take Bartlett long to discover that the anti-Simon leaker was none other than Dick Cheney, clearly acting on behalf of Rumsfeld. "I sat down and wrote a piece detailing the whole story," Bartlett told me, "then I called Rumsfeld and read it to him and said, 'This is going out in ten minutes.' There was a silence at the other end and then he said, 'This will stop, right now.' I said, 'That's not good enough. First, I want to see a picture of Ford and Bill Simon on the front page of the *New York Times,* and second, I want you to call Simon immediately and tell him he has the president's full confidence.' And he did both those things." Rumsfeld's first effort to create a cabinet vacancy for himself had been run aground.

The Ford White House was a maelstrom of intrigue and backbiting, with various factions openly sabotaging both one another's and the president's initiatives. Rumsfeld featured openly in a multitude of leaks as a contender for power with other major figures such as Henry Kissinger or Vice President Rockefeller. Whereas disputes between Rumsfeld and Kissinger appear to have been a function of rivalry for power, Rumsfeld and Rockefeller "simply loathed each other," recalled a former White House aide who dealt with both men, "far beyond what the professional competition would have predicted. [Rumsfeld] had wealth issues." Relations were not helped by Rockefeller's habit of poking his head around Rumsfeld's office door and saying, "Don, you *know* you will never be president."

"Rumsfeld always reminded me of the Wizard of Oz," chuckled

Seidman, an astonishingly energetic eighty-four years old, as he recalled the distant days of the Ford White House. "He thought he was invisible behind the curtain as he worked the levers, but in reality everyone could see what he was doing." Another former Ford White House official recalled Rumsfeld as "very hard to do business with." Musing further, the official strove to define his old colleague's effect on people he worked with. "I'd say intimidating—he has a way of making people uneasy and off-balance."

One crisis that flared up in May 1975, however, stood out as a significant milestone in Rumsfeld's career, for it marked the first time that he played a role, albeit a minor one, in sending men to their deaths. It happened just a few short weeks after the fall of Saigon and the final defeat of the United States in the Southeast Asian wars. Cambodia, of course, had also fallen to the cruel and intransigent Khmer Rouge, who seized an American merchant ship, the SS *Mayaguez,* which had strayed into Cambodian territorial waters and imprisoned the crew.

For Ford and his close advisers, including Rumsfeld, this brazen affront to American power so soon after the humiliating retreat from Saigon was an opportunity to show some muscle. A rescue force was hurriedly dispatched, but they suffered heavy casualties while assaulting an island in the mistaken belief that the captured crewmen were being held there. The intelligence was false. While the battle raged, the crew was picked up from a Thai fishing boat. They had been released unharmed shortly after their capture. Altogether, forty-one American servicemen and an unknown number of Cambodians died in the incident, all for nothing.

The political calculations driving the White House response proved correct. *Time* magazine expressed the general media mood in its cover story: "Ford Draws the Line"—over a dramatic picture of marines storming out of a helicopter.[26] It has become conventional wisdom that the United States, at the time of the defeat in Southeast Asia, was already swinging back to the right after the progressive euphoria of the Watergate era. But in 1975 the American people were still in a fairly radical mood. Opinion polls registered strong distrust of presidents and skepticism of military commitments abroad.[27] An April 1975 Gallup survey found only 37 percent willing to send troops if England were attacked, while similar help to Israel drew the support of only 11 percent. A February poll that year opposed increasing the defense budget, as requested by Ford, 46 to 43 percent. As we shall discover, however, there were potent forces ready and willing to reverse these sentiments, forces that offered Rumsfeld a natural home.

In the meantime, the differences between Kissinger and Rumsfeld were about a lot more than differing perceptions of the public mood. Rumsfeld, for example, had discovered that Kissinger routinely recorded all his phone calls. At an opportune moment, he revealed the secret to President Ford. Hence, in the midst of a foreign policy discussion with his national security adviser, Ford playfully interjected, "Henry, Don tells me that you're taping all of this." Kissinger simply continued speaking, ignoring the accusation faithfully preserved in Kissinger's transcripts. In another conversation, Ford quoted an observation made by Rumsfeld. "Don't listen to that man, Mr. President," retorted Kissinger angrily. "He's running for president in 1980."[28]

Many in the White House understood that Rumsfeld, whatever his 1980 plans, was maneuvering to be nominated as Ford's vice presidential running mate in 1976. By September 1975, columnists Rowland Evans and Robert Novak were reporting that "a 34-year-old Presidential aide named Dick Cheney" was "increasingly taking charge of the day-to-day White House business" while his "boss and mentor" Donald Rumsfeld was deepening his involvement in the Ford reelection campaign. "And that," reported the columnists, "is widely viewed in upper reaches of the administration as a means to one end: putting Rumsfeld on the 1976 ticket as Vice President."[29]

Of course, there already was a sitting vice president, Nelson Rockefeller, with every expectation of being on the ticket, assuming, of course, that Ford himself would be the Republican nominee. But Ford's campaign for the nomination was showing signs of trouble. Local organization in key states was in disarray, important state party chairmen were not being contacted, and so on. Meanwhile, on the right, there was the menacing specter of California governor Ronald Reagan, well financed and organized and remorselessly assailing the centrist policies of Ford and his "liberal" vice president, Rockefeller.

How could the efficient Donald Rumsfeld, supposedly the overseer of the campaign, be permitting his president's political fortunes to fall into such dire straits? Seidman, a high-ranking official with a nose for intrigue, concluded that the chief of staff was engaged in a supremely Machiavellian maneuver: the more Ford's nomination chances sank in relation to Reagan's right-wing challenge, the more the "liberal" Rockefeller would be seen as the millstone that must be jettisoned. By the late summer of 1975, a year away from the election, Rumsfeld was getting close to overcoming the obstacles in his path. One evening in September, Seidman happened to overhear two of Ford's closest political allies and advisers, Senator Bob Griffin and Federal Reserve Board chairman Arthur Burns, discussing the president's perilous situation. "It was getting dark, and I don't think they realized I was in an armchair at the end of the room," Seidman told me cheerfully. "They were saying, 'the way Reagan's going, Ford will not be nominated unless we dump Rockefeller from the ticket.' Ding! Rummy had gained the first of his objectives."

At the end of October, everything fell into place. It was known as the "Halloween massacre," the political coup de grace that earned Rumsfeld his reputation as a supreme bureaucratic warrior, even if few then or since have understood the full scope of his maneuvers. In short order the White House announced that Rockefeller had "voluntarily" withdrawn from the 1976 ticket, Henry Kissinger had lost his post as national security adviser, CIA chief William Colby had been fired, as had defense secretary James Schlesinger. Colby was replaced by George Bush, then serving as ambassador to China. Replacing Schlesinger at the Pentagon was Rumsfeld, at forty-three, the youngest man ever to hold the job.

"Ford had two principal goals," recalled a former senior official from the Ford White House. "One was to get rid of Jim Schlesinger," the arrogant defense secretary who made no secret of his disdain for the president. "It had been clear for months that he had to go. The other was to get rid of Colby," the CIA chief enmeshed in widening congressional probes of the agency's misdoings. "Bill was a broken man by that point, almost dysfunctional. He had turned into a total creature of Congress. On the other hand, the whole thing certainly did seem to promote Rumsfeld. Remember, he and Ford were *close* friends," continued the former official.

Two people never forgave Rumsfeld for his role in this massive intrigue. One of them was Vice President Rockefeller, who detected the chief of staff's manipulative hand behind his displacement. As he correctly divined, Rumsfeld played a major role in persuading Ford to jettison his allegedly liberal vice president as a means of warding off the looming far-right threat of Ronald Reagan in the upcoming Republican primaries.

The other lifelong enemy acquired by Rumsfeld was George Herbert Walker Bush. When Ford was originally pondering whom to nominate as vice president in 1974 (with his accession to the presidency, the post was vacant), he polled Republican senators and congressmen. The senators' majority for Barry Goldwater could be discounted as sentimental, but the congressional Republicans opted for their former colleague George Bush, then serving as ambassador to China. As it happened, Ford chose Rockefeller, but Bush was obviously a front-runner if the slot again became vacant.

"Bush had thought he would get Commerce" in a reshuffle, one old friend and political adviser of the former president told me. "That way he could come back from Beijing and burnish his economic credentials for any future White House run." But instead, Bush found himself shunted off to the woods of northern Virginia as director of the CIA. This was considered a "nonpolitical" position, precluding the occupant from any future political career. To put the seal on this political emasculation, Bush was asked at his confirmation hearings to pledge that he would not politicize the CIA by running for office in 1976. Cornered, Bush did as he was asked.

"Bush thought Rumsfeld planted that question," the friend revealed. "George Bush is the most polite of men, never speaks ill of anyone. In all the time I've spent with him, I've only ever heard him speak with bitterness about two people. One was Dick Snelling, the governor of Vermont who broke his word without warning on supporting him for the nomination in 1980. The other was Donald Rumsfeld. Real bitterness there. Makes you wonder what was going through Bush 43's mind when he made him secretary of defense."

As it was, Bush swallowed his bile and retreated to CIA headquarters with good grace while Rumsfeld, at his swearing in as secretary of defense on November 20, 1975, heard himself warmly described by President Ford as "the most able public servant I have ever known." In a mere two and a half years, he had emerged from the diplomatic exile to which he had been consigned by Haldeman and Nixon, banished his enemies, achieved the extraordinary feat of displacing a sitting vice president, and installed himself as the chief of the most powerful department in the U.S. government.

Not long after Rumsfeld had departed for the Pentagon, the Library of Congress sought the papers he had generated as chief of staff, but the archivists could find few pieces of paper bearing his actual signature. "He wanted to leave no tracks in the snow," said Bill Seidman at the end of a long afternoon's conversation. "That way there was nothing anyone could use against him. Remember, the name of the game in this town is to get to be president."

CHAPTER THREE

Secretary Rumsfeld:
The Prequel

Donald Rumsfeld will forever be associated with the catastrophe of the Iraq War. Once it became clear that the intelligence used to justify the operation was wholly flawed, and the ensuing occupation had been grievously mismanaged, the defense secretary's reputation, so recently held in high esteem by press and public, went into an accelerating decline.

Yet much of the Iraqi experience, at least from the point of view of Rumsfeld, was a rerun. Years before, he had brandished intelligence reports on a growing military threat. Doubters within the intelligence community were overridden. He had acted in alliance with a powerful neoconservative lobby. Subsequent investigation revealed that the intelligence on which he relied was almost entirely baseless. His actions were a major factor in the political ruin of the president he served.

There was, however, one significant difference between the two episodes. The Iraq adventure led to what has been called "the greatest strategic disaster in the history of the United States." The prequel took place during the cold war, which America ultimately won, though the world very nearly blew up on various occasions along the way. Nevertheless, a proper understanding of Rumsfeld's role in the Iraq War, as well as his overall performance as defense secretary, requires knowledge of his performance as secretary of defense over a quarter century earlier, during the Ford administration.

Today's generation knows little of the bitter arguments and fears aroused in those days by the nuclear standoff between the superpowers. When Rumsfeld arrived at the Pentagon in November 1975, the relaxation of tension, or détente, initiated by Richard Nixon with the Soviet Union was still theoretically in effect. Henry Kissinger was negotiating a follow-on agreement to the Strategic Arms Limitation Treaty signed two years earlier. More important, the Vietnam War was finally over, America was at peace, and the average American, as indicated by polls, seemed to believe that it was time to devote resources to domestic needs rather than military spending.

Not everyone agreed, especially not the U.S. military and its allies in industry and Congress. After the colossal buildup of the late 1960s caused by the Vietnam War, defense budgets had steadily declined in the early 1970s. To counter this trend, interested parties were raising progressively louder complaints that America was letting its guard down at a time when the Soviet enemy was rearming with malign intent.

The single most effective proponent of this viewpoint was a man Rumsfeld later eulogized as his "dear friend," Paul Nitze. The friendship that blossomed during Rumsfeld's Brussels sojourn deepened after his return to Washington. When Ford offered him the job of secretary of defense, Rumsfeld revealed at a Pentagon ceremony in 2002, he had called to consult with Nitze before accepting the job.[1]

Wealthy, generally feared rather than loved, extraordinarily crafty in high-level bureaucratic intrigue, Nitze had played a pivotal role in U.S. national security policy since the dawn of the cold war. In fact, he had almost single-handedly heralded that dawn in April 1950 when, as a senior State Department official, he had written a top-secret planning document arguing that the communist Soviets were bent on world domination and that America must rearm to confront them anywhere and everywhere. Since the document's acceptance as policy by President Harry Truman, the U.S. defense budget has never looked back.

The story of the Gaither Report—a top-secret inquiry into the strategic nuclear balance crafted by Nitze in 1958—serves as a perfect illustration of his goals and methods. Drawing on military intelligence assessments that were hotly contested by the CIA, the report asserted that the Soviets were not only growing ever more powerful economically, politically, and militarily, but would before long have as many as five hundred long-range nuclear missiles ready to launch at an unprepared United States. Swiftly leaked, almost certainly at Nitze's instigation, the report generated widespread and uncritical coverage on the "almost immediate threat" facing the United States from the "missile-bristling Soviet Union," which would require an "enormous arms outlay" if the nation was to survive. Picking up the theme, presidential candidate John F. Kennedy soon began invoking the "missile gap" in his campaign speeches, attacking the Eisenhower administration for lowering America's guard. The issue was an important factor in swinging the close-fought 1960 election in Kennedy's favor. In reality, as confirmed by CIA spy satellites at the time, the Soviets had just four missiles deployed, while the United States had ten times that many. Kennedy's defense secretary, Robert McNamara, later admitted, "Yes, there was a gap. But the gap was in our favor."[2] It did not matter. The United States had already embarked on a huge missile buildup to compensate.

A decade and a half later, this pattern was recurring. Pressure was mounting to reverse recent declines in U.S. defense spending on the grounds that there was a "spending gap" of as much as fifty percent in the Soviets' favor. President Ford's first defense secretary, former economics professor James Schlesinger, was a leading exponent of this view. Schlesinger was heedless of the discomfort he thereby caused Ford, who was still pursuing Richard Nixon's policy of détente and arms control negotiations. In 1974, Nitze, who had been an adviser to the Strategic Arms Limitations Talks (SALT) negotiating team, resigned from the government and went before Congress to announce that the Soviet Union was well on its way to achieving usable strategic superiority over the United States, and the administration was doing nothing to stop it.[3]

In replacing Schlesinger with Rumsfeld the following year, Ford hoped that his old friend from the House of Representatives would be more supportive. Rumsfeld's ambiguous answers to aggressive questions from hawkish senators at his confirmation hearing may have lent comfort to this view.[4]

During his second spell in the Pentagon, as we shall see, Rumsfeld tended to treat Congress with a disdain bordering on contemptuous. At his confirmation hearings on November 12, 1975, however, he was all charm, impressing his audience with a fluent discourse on NATO. This cooperative attitude continued when he took up his new responsibilities. Not long after he settled into his Pentagon office, a powerful senator, John McClellan (D-Ark.), called to demand that Rumsfeld dismiss a senior Pentagon official, Len Sullivan, who headed the Office of Plans, Analysis and Evaluation. Sullivan had irked the senator's friends and allies in the navy high command by critiquing one of their cherished programs, so Rumsfeld dutifully summoned Sullivan and fired him on the spot.

Many former Pentagon staffers recall the early defense secretary Rumsfeld as "generally affable, though he could be vicious when crossed." Nevertheless, even then there were glimpses of the character reviled in 2006 by senior retired officers as "abrasive, dismissive, contemptuous." One such example occurred on Rumsfeld's very first day at the office. The office staff had prepared a little welcoming ceremony for the new boss, and one of the secretaries had gone down to the Pentagon flower shop and purchased an expensive bouquet of flowers, which were then arranged in a vase just inside the door. According to one of those present, Rumsfeld walked in, saw the flowers, plucked them out of the vase using both hands, and "without breaking stride, thrust them into the trash." The consensus explanation was that he was making a point about wasting money.

It did not take long for Ford and Kissinger to find their arms control policy also headed for the trash, though there was no question of saving taxpayer dollars—quite the opposite. The warning signs came early. "One of the things Rumsfeld started doing once he became secretary was staging regular briefings for congressmen on the growing Soviet threat," recalls a veteran of Ford's National Security Council staff. "Somehow he managed to hold these at the White House, and he brought over a very hawkish analyst from DIA [Defense Intelligence Agency] to give the briefings. There must have been about half a dozen of these meetings in the winter of 1975–1976."

The briefings were carefully stage-managed, as a former official involved in the arrangements recalls with some pride. "We picked a perfect Joe Palooka type [Palooka was a heavyweight boxing champ featured in a 1930s comic strip] from DIA, so that after his scary introductory remarks the congressmen would consider him crazy. If one of them didn't then rise up and ask, 'How do *you* know all this?' we'd plant someone to do it, all so he could answer in an ominous whisper, 'Because we can count.' And then there'd be a huge picture on the screen of a Soviet airfield with the camera focusing ever downward to the letters on one plane's weapons. It was powerful stuff."

Coincidentally or not, by early January, *Aviation Week*, the bible of the defense aerospace business, was purring, "There has been a marked change in congressional attitude toward the U.S. defense posture and the Soviet strategic surge during this winter."[5]

At the White House, meanwhile, seasoned Rumsfeld-watchers simply assumed he was maneuvering for political advantage as he positioned himself for a presidential run in, so Kissinger believed, 1980. "He was making a tactical shift to the right," Brent Scowcroft, Kissinger's former assistant who succeeded him as national security adviser, told me. "Insofar as I was concerned, it was merely a matter of political convenience."

There was certainly considerable political logic behind this move. As we have seen, this was an election year, and Ronald Reagan was making ever-deeper inroads from the right into Ford's political base in the Republican Party. To counter this, Ford was himself already swinging to the right, most obviously by dumping the supposedly liberal Nelson Rockefeller from the ticket. Even so, the contest for Republican delegates, organized on Ford's side by the Houston lawyer James Baker, was bound to be tight. According to two high-ranking Republican operatives from that period, Rumsfeld was promoting the concept that Ford's chances with the delegates would be vastly improved if he named a running mate of solid right-wing credentials. Who better for this role than his hawkish defense secretary? A former Pentagon official recalled for me a long plane trip out of Washington on which Rumsfeld talked about his chances of selection for the ticket. "He said that his best shot at VP was doing a good job at DoD, by which he meant, of course, being politically relevant. If the country leaned right, and the propelling mechanism was the red threat, whose remedy was on his turf, things would move his way. It was always at the root of his thinking."

Rumsfeld could see the political advantage to himself of an aggressive defense policy, but he had no idea how to do this. Fortunately for him, he had Paul Nitze ready at hand to instruct him. Nitze soon had reason to feel gratified at his pupil's performance. In late January 1976, Kissinger flew to Moscow for a long-planned negotiating session with the Soviets that he and Ford hoped would produce a second SALT treaty. Rumsfeld had managed to have the trip delayed while he queried every detail of the secretary of state's negotiating position. "He had a penchant for complicating the decision process," recalls a former senior White House official of his performance at the time. "In policy making, he took delight in throwing monkey wrenches into the works, not to alter course, but simply to impede."

Specifically, Rumsfeld took aim at a central plank of Kissinger's negotiating strategy. The major sticking point in the negotiations concerned the U.S. cruise missile and the Soviet Backfire nuclear bomber, deemed by the United States, on the basis of somewhat shaky intelligence, to have intercontinental range. Each side wished to limit the other's weapon under the proposed treaty, while excluding its own. On his Moscow trip, Kissinger agreed on a compromise deal and briefed the press to make it a fait accompli. But Rumsfeld and the Joint Chiefs of Staff refused to accept the agreement, humiliating the secretary of state by forcing him to back down. "I never saw the president confront Rumsfeld directly on these issues," recalls one former high-level White House staffer, "except once." One of Rumsfeld's objections to a cruise missile limit was because, as he claimed at an NSC meeting, "we've already got a whole program for putting cruise missiles on ships," which were far too valuable to be traded away. At a later NSC meeting, Ford mentioned this program to the chairman of the Joint Chiefs, who revealed that in fact it did not exist. "Ford really blew up at Rumsfeld over that."

Not only did Kissinger return from Moscow empty-handed, he was greeted by Rumsfeld sounding the alarm from the battlements. Delivering the defense secretary's traditional annual report to Congress, he called for a $9 billion increase in defense spending, gravely announcing that "confidence in the future adequacy of our force structure is gradually declining" because of the increasing Soviet military momentum. There had been a "gradual shift in the power balance," which would "continue to shift unless United States defense outlays are increased in real terms."[6]

Rumsfeld not only echoed Schlesinger's bellicose themes, he raised the ante. The former secretary had denied the navy a new nuclear aircraft carrier? Rumsfeld gave the go-ahead. Was there a mere $144 million for cruise missiles in the previous budget? This year he would almost double that amount.[7] There seemed to be no military request so excessive, no scenario of malign Soviet intentions so outlandish, that Rumsfeld would not endorse it. Nitze had recently published an article in *Foreign Affairs* positing a doomsday scenario in which newly detected and supposedly superaccurate Soviet missiles would be targeted on America's land-based missiles, the only ones capable of hitting Russian missiles in their silos. The Soviets, meanwhile, would have evacuated their entire urban population into what the author claimed was a vastly expanded and more efficient civil defense program. The United States would be left with submarine-based missiles, accurate enough to hit only Russian cities—which would now be empty, thanks to civil defense. If the United States did fire at the empty cities, this would invite Russian retaliation against the unsheltered inhabitants of American cities. So the U.S. president would have no option but to surrender.

Even for Schlesinger, this had been too much to swallow. He argued, sensibly enough, that the Soviets could never have a "high confidence" that they could wipe out the Minuteman weapons in a surprise attack. (He was aware of a very highly classified study that revealed U.S. missiles as less accurate than advertised and could assume that Soviet ICBMs were no better.) Rumsfeld had no such problem, and dove right in. Even under a new SALT treaty, he told Congress, ongoing Soviet strategic programs "might give them the ability to knock out the highly accurate Minuteman force, depriving the American President of being able to use them for surgical strikes before resorting to all-out nuclear war."[8] Meanwhile, he added, "an asymmetry has developed over the years [in civil defense] that bears directly on our strategic relationship with the Soviets and on the credibility of our deterrent posture. . . ."[9]

Fortunately, the secretary assured his audience, this looming danger could yet be averted by his $30 billion program to develop a brand-new missile, the MX. Three times larger and more accurate than the Minuteman, this weapon would not only be able to hit Soviet missile silos, but would also be mobile, moving between launch sites, thus frustrating Soviet efforts to target the force.[10]

Rumsfeld was certainly doing his best, but it was proving difficult to work the American people into a satisfactory state of fear. Asked in a June 1976 Gallup poll whether current defense spending should be increased, kept at the same level, or reduced, 42 percent of Americans thought that the then-current level was fine, while only 27 percent thought it should be increased. A considerable number, 21 percent, thought it should be reduced. Only a small minority thought the United States either was becoming or would become weaker than the Soviet Union anytime soon.[11]

Clearly, there was much work still to be done. One of the problems was the CIA, which persisted in reporting that the Soviets were by no means as formidable as claimed by the Pentagon. To correct this state of affairs, the alarmists lobbied vigorously for a reconsideration of the CIA conclusions by an "independent" group. In May 1976, newly installed CIA director George H. W. Bush agreed, and "Team B," codirected by Nitze, was in business. Among its senior staff members was an affable young defense intellectual out of the University of Chicago named Paul Wolfowitz, who had gotten his start in the national security world when hired by Nitze to lobby for missile defense in 1969. Now he joined his fellow team members in rummaging through the agency's classified files, sniffing out neglected evidence of Soviet perfidy.

Predictably, given its staff and sponsors, the team's final report duly endorsed the wildest speculations of the right-wing defense lobby. The "Backfire bomber will probably be produced in substantial numbers, with perhaps 500 aircraft off the line in 1984." The Sovi-

40

ets were on the verge of fielding "a significant ABM [antiballistic missile] capability" including lasers and charged particle beams with potentialities "of a magnitude that it is hard to overestimate." Ever more bizarrely, Team B looked for confirmation of speculation that the ingenious Russians had developed a unique method of detecting submarines that did not rely on sound. Their failure to find any evidence of this was taken as evidence that the Soviets had succeeded.[12]

"The B Team," Wolfowitz later complacently reminisced, "demonstrated that it was possible to construct a sharply different view of Soviet motivation from the consensus view of the analysts, and one that provided a much closer fit to the Soviets' observed behavior."

It was all utter nonsense, a farrago of speculation and fantasy, as was the entire array of "evidence" concocted by Nitze and his allies to support the defense buildup. Information that emerged when the USSR fell and the files were opened revealed that there weren't five hundred of the dreaded Backfire bombers in 1984, or even half that number, nor was it capable of reaching the United States. The Soviets had no "significant ABM capability," then or ever. A nuclear death-ray test facility identified by excited members of Team B was in fact a site for testing rocket engines. Even the most basic and widely accepted calculations were later proven false. At a time when Team B, as well as defense secretary Rumsfeld, was preaching about the Soviets' "intense military buildup," Soviet defense spending was slowing down, with weapons production staying flat from 1976 until well into the next decade.

A review of the exaggerations, misapprehensions, and straightforward lies regarding the Soviet military current in those years reveals in stark detail that the marketing of Saddam Hussein's weapons of mass destruction a quarter century later was merely history repeating itself as tragedy. All that was required in both cases was a suspension of disbelief and a lack of intellectual scruple. There was, however, an important difference. The prize sought by players in the 1970s exercise was success in the struggle for power in Washington, as well as unhindered access to the taxpayers' dollar. No one died. When the same techniques were deployed against the gimcrack Iraqi regime early in the twenty-first century, the cost was counted not just in billions of dollars, but in hundreds of thousands of Iraqi and American lives.

Team B was not the only initiative Nitze was working behind the scenes in 1976. He was also building what would become one of the most successful lobbies in Washington history. The instrument was a broad-based coalition of powerful individuals, drawn from across the political spectrum but united in a common goal. Later, as Ford prepared to leave office, this coalition would be officially unveiled to the world as the Committee on the Present Danger. The board was studded with former defense officials, such as former deputy defense secretary David Packard, founder of the computer company Hewlett-Packard; powerful Washington players such as lawyer Max Kampelman; retired military commanders such as former chief of naval operations Admiral Elmo Zumwalt; well-connected defense intellectuals like the future national security adviser Richard Allen; labor leaders like AFL-CIO chief Lane Kirkland; along with high-powered business types, including future CIA director William Casey. "We didn't announce the committee until after the [1976] election," Richard Allen told me, "but we started work well before that."

Beyond the general objective of lobbying for rearmament, Nitze had a specific objective in mind for the organization, which can be discerned from the interests represented by two of its leading members, Eugene Rostow and Charls Walker. Walker was the leading corporate lobbyist of the day, with many major defense contractors among his clients. "Walker got us the money; that was his job," says W. Scott Thompson, Nitze's son-in-law and himself a founding board member of the committee. Rostow, on the other hand, along with other committee members of the board, such as Max Kampelman, and New York intellectuals Norman Podhoretz and his wife, Midge Decter (later author of a 2003 Rumsfeld hagiography), had been members of a group called Coalition for a Democratic Majority, which catered to Democrats who were also strong supporters of Israel. Nitze's strategy, according to his relative and close associate Thompson, was to fuse this group with the established military-industrial lobby.

Traditionally, while militant on any issue relating to Israel, pro-Israeli groups were dovish on other security matters. "A bunch of rabbis came to see me in 1967 to tell me I ought not to send a single screwdriver to Vietnam," Lyndon Johnson once complained, "but, on the other hand, [told me I] should push all our aircraft carriers through the Straits of Tirana to help Israel."

Within a few short years this anomaly had largely been eliminated. "The Israeli lobby in Congress is no longer in favor of cutting the defense budget," the politically astute congressman Les Aspin (D-Wis.) told an audience of defense contractors in Philadelphia in 1977. By 1982, pro-Israeli sentiment had shifted so far that the national director of the Anti-Defamation League, Nathan Perlmutter, could claim in his book *The Real Anti-Semitism* that contemporary anti-Semitism lay in the actions of "peacemakers of Vietnam vintage," and that "nowadays war is getting a bad name and peace too favorable a press" from a left that is "sniping at American defense budgets."

It was the birth of a movement. "We were the real neoconservatives," Richard Allen remarked proudly, thirty years later, rattling off the names of Rostow, Kampelman, Kirkland, and Nitze as examples. It was also the start of a potent alliance between Rumsfeld and some of these neoconservatives that was not to reach its full fruition until the dawn of the next century. Discussing two influential advisers to Rumsfeld in the years after 2001, a former State Department arms-control official remarked, "Most of these relationships go back in history, to the battles over arms control. One of the foremost enemies of Kissinger and the whole détente process was Richard Perle, the chief aide to Senator [Henry "Scoop"] Jackson [D-Wash.]. Rumsfeld was a major Kissinger adversary, so they made common cause, and it was an alliance that endured." Among other skills, Perle was highly adept in using the currency of strategic leaks in securing useful press coverage, as well as spotting weaknesses in the arcane arms agreements negotiated by Kissinger with the Soviets. In 1974 he permanently hobbled future negotiations with the USSR by crafting legislation that punished the Russians for restricting Jewish emigration. The Russians promptly cut the number of Jews permitted to emigrate, but Perle's stock as a neoconservative champion soared in Washington. Perle was to play a major role in fomenting the invasion of Iraq, as of course was his friend Paul Wolfowitz. The pair had first worked together on a Nitze-sponsored project lobbying for missile defense in 1969. "You can't overestimate Perle's influence," a former senior official in the Ford administration told me. "On a personal level, too. After he stopped working for Jackson, Scoop became a different person, reasonable, open-minded."

Pentagon staff soon noted Rumsfeld's taste for secrecy in his approach to management. "He would never make a decision in public," remembers a former senior analyst who frequently briefed the secretary. "We would brief him on an issue in a meeting, but he wouldn't react, wouldn't say what he thought. Then he would disappear into a back room with a trusted aide, who would come out later and tell us what he had decided."

In later years, Rumsfeld became known for impatiently demanding reports from operatives in such places as Abu Ghraib and Guantánamo. But he had always been keenly aware of the power of intelligence and equally determined to control it. Hence, soon after his arrival in 1975, he slotted another old friend and Nixon administration alumnus, former congressman Robert Ellsworth (R-Kans.), into the newly created post of deputy secretary of defense for intelligence. Ellsworth was a strong opponent of Kissinger and had long chafed at the latter's ability to control the flow of information to the president.[13] Now he would have the chance to correct matters.

Of course, the most important intelligence was that concerning Rumsfeld's own subordinates. Here, he could rely on "Doc" Cook, a fabled bureaucrat who served as director of administration at the Pentagon from the 1950s into the twenty-first century. Among other potent responsibilities, such as control of all office space, Cook ran an in-house intelligence service on behalf of whoever happened to be secretary of defense. "He worked directly for the secretary," one former official explained. "If you were lying, cheating, stealing, fucking, he'd find out." (Dick Cheney, one of the secretaries loyally served by Cook, later described him as "the kind of career professional who really makes the government work.")[14]

It did not take long for Rumsfeld's appreciation of intelligence to pay off where it really counted: in the vicious battle for power and influence ongoing inside the Ford administration. At that time all but the most sensitive State Department communications were routinely transmitted over Department of Defense links. In Rumsfeld's day at least, the Pentagon took full advantage of this to read the diplomats' mail, and the aide specifically assigned to this task was none other than Scott Thompson, Nitze's son-in-law. As Thompson revealed to me in 2006, he issued strict instructions to the technicians downloading the traffic to bring him any message from or concerning Kissinger or his principal aide, State Department counselor Helmut Sonnenfeldt. In mid-March, Thompson was handed a cable giving the text of a talk delivered the previous December by Sonnenfeldt to a London meeting of U.S. ambassadors in Europe. Kissinger himself had been present. In his remarks, Sonnenfeldt had suggested that it was in America's interest to encourage an "organic union" between the Soviet Union and the countries it dominated in Eastern Europe in place of the existing relationship, which was based on military power.

Thompson was "awestruck" by the implications of what he was reading. Spun the right way, these remarks could be used to depict both Sonnenfeldt and Kissinger as enablers for the Soviet empire. As was often the case, Nitze was in the building, and Thompson showed him the document first. They agreed it was a "moment of history." Then he took it to Rumsfeld, whom he found walking down the E Ring corridor. "He brought me back to his office, kicking out a couple of congressmen who were waiting there. We read it over and over and I explained what I thought were the implications. I then asked Don what he wanted me to do with it, give it to those with the need to know? He nodded. I said to how many, about five hundred? He said 'two hundred should suffice.' Of course I gave it to Perle, and he passed it to Evans and Novak." Though asked to comment on his role in this maneuver, Perle declined to answer any of my questions on this or any other topic.

The columnists' dramatic report on "the Sonnenfeldt doctrine" appeared in their widely syndicated column on March 22, the eve of the North Carolina Republican primary, a campaign that had hinged on the administration's foreign policy record.[15] Ford lost, only the third time in U.S. history that a sitting president had been defeated in a party primary. Nor did the issue go away. In the presidential debates that fall, Carter was able to belabor Ford over "the so-called Sonnenfeldt document."[16] Ford never knew whom to thank.

To an alumnus of the Nixon and Ford White Houses, such back-stabbing maneuvers must have seemed like second nature, and it was his skill in this mode of bureaucratic politics that made Rumsfeld feared in Washington. But the responsibilities of the secretary of defense extend beyond political vendettas, and here a recurrent paradox that has defined Rumsfeld's career was on full display. The bully who dumped the flowers seemed strangely uninterested in confronting more powerful forces, such as the military bureaucracies that ruled the Pentagon.

The man with the reputation as an able manager when he took office in 1975 was soon known to insiders for his laissez-faire attitude to the demands of the services and their partners in the business community. The sole weapons program he actually terminated was a navy fighter jet called the A-7, so antiquated that even the admirals raised only pro forma protests. After dealing with Rumsfeld, a senior general in the armed forces of a close U.S. ally described him as "political, forceful, shallow, immature, inexperienced in defense matters." Richard Helms, who had directed the CIA for many years before becoming ambassador to Iran, remarked in August 1976, "he had never seen . . . so many people out of control in the Pentagon."[17]

The saga of Malcolm Currie and the Condor missile helps illustrate Helms's observation. Currie, a former executive with Hughes Aircraft, was under-secretary of defense for research and engineering, a position of enormous power. His decisions on weapons development programs could mean billions of dollars for the relevant contractors, not to mention tens of thousands of jobs in weapons plants across the country. One of the issues occupying Currie's attention when Rumsfeld arrived at the Pentagon was an air-to-surface missile called Condor under development for the U.S. Navy by the Rockwell International Corporation. The navy planned to spend half a billion dollars buying eight hundred Condors, with another $200 million required to modify the planes that would carry it.

Unfortunately, the weapon was overbudget and didn't work anyway. The General Accounting Office (GAO) concluded that there were serious questions about Condor's "affordability, operational utility, effectiveness, vulnerability to enemy countermeasures, as well as the Navy's and contractor's ability to maintain adequate quality control." Inside the Pentagon, there were moves to cancel it outright. It seemed that the project was doomed.

Such was the situation when Currie opted to spend the 1975 Labor Day weekend at Rockwell's fishing resort on North Bimini Island in the Bahamas, one of several retreats maintained by the company for the entertainment of valued friends including congressmen, high-ranking military officers, and senior Pentagon officials.[18] Traveling on a Rockwell plane and lodged in a Rockwell guesthouse, Currie was accompanied by a female friend, as well as his thirteen-year-old daughter.

Host and guest later insisted that no business was discussed over the weekend. On his return, however, Pentagon colleagues noted that Currie had become an ardent Condor partisan, vigorously opposing those who suggested killing the program. Ultimately, whistle-blowers from inside Rockwell exposed the coincidence of Currie's trip—some months after circulation of an explicit Defense Department prohibition on accepting such favors—and his deep interest in the missile's fate.

Under pressure from Congress, Rumsfeld commissioned an investigation. "We all expected Mal to be fired," remembered one former official. Instead, Rumsfeld treated Currie to a "severe reprimand" and docked him a month's pay. In a press conference, he asserted that "the facts" did not justify any further punishment for Currie, who had meanwhile been promoted to "acquisition executive" in charge of all military weapons purchases. When outraged congressional critics cried "whitewash," Rumsfeld defended his subordinate as "the architect" of a plan adopted some months before to delay Condor production pending further reliability tests. Thus, he claimed in his subordinate's defense, Dr. Currie "acted contrary to the business interests of Rockwell International."

As the *New York Times* noted, "The Defense Secretary's conclusion runs contrary to the recollection of several Pentagon staff officials who participated in the discussions of the Condor program. According to these officials, the issue before the review panel was whether to cancel the program, as had been proposed by two members of the committee.

"Dr. Currie, these officials reported, argued that the company would overcome the reliability problems besetting the missile and urged as a compromise that a commitment be given to production after further testing. This was the position ultimately adopted by the Defense Department."[19]

Rumsfeld saved Currie, who ultimately returned to his former haunts in the defense industry. But Congress took its revenge on the Condor, voting to kill it the same day Rumsfeld delivered his merciful sentence. Though this was a blow to Rockwell, the company had bigger and more lucrative contracts to defend, most especially the $21 billion B-1 bomber program.

Commissioned by Nixon in 1970, the B-1 was supposed to be capable of flying to the Soviet Union and back, even, when necessary, skimming the treetops faster than the speed of sound. With the Los Angeles–based Rockwell as prime contractor, its primary mission had been to boost the Southern California aerospace economy in time for Nixon's 1972 reelection campaign. By 1976 the project was rife with technical problems, delays, and vast cost overruns, rendering it the most expensive airplane ever built up to that time, while at the same time incapable of performing its mission as specified. Critics were clamoring for cancellation. Instead, Rumsfeld affirmed his faith in the project by flying it himself, or at least handling the controls of a prototype during an hour-long flight over southern California. Afterward he posed for pictures in his dashing orange flight suit while commenting knowledgeably on the aircraft's flying characteristics. *Newsweek* noted churlishly that the plane had "little need for such public relations efforts as Rumsfeld's wild-blue-yonder showmanship last week—and most insiders thought the defense secretary was doing some high-level politicking on his own behalf. Rumsfeld has ambitions for the Vice Presidency and beyond, and some flight-suited visibility might help."[20] In any event, the pictures reportedly soon joined many similarly flattering portraits of himself with important people on his crowded office wall.

Though Rumsfeld could probably not have defied the coalition of political and economic interests behind the B-1 even had he dared, his willingness to bend before corporate requirements was already evident and would soon be further demonstrated in the case of the M-1 tank.

In later years, Rumsfeld took to recalling fondly his role in the birth of the army's main battle tank as a bold exercise in visionary management. Discussing new defense technologies in a 2001 interview, for example, he recalled how the army "came to me to make a decision. We had always had diesel tanks and I made the decision to go to a turbine tank for the first time in the history of the world."[21] Five years later, in April 2006, when under assault by retired army generals who had taken their disgust at his performance to the press, he brought up the episode again.

"The Army was in favor of the 105 [millimeter tank gun] and in favor of a diesel engine," he said at a contentious press conference. "And the other approach would have been for the— To standardize with our NATO allies at 120 millimeters and also to move away from the diesel engine to a turbine engine. I decided I wanted to take some time to think about it, and ultimately announced that I thought that the turbine engine and the 120-millimeter cannon was preferable to the 105 and the diesel engine."[22]

It is possible that Rumsfeld does remember the episode that way, but it is certainly not what happened. By 1976 the army had been trying for years to develop a new tank, leaving a string of costly failures along the way. However, following a competition between two prototypes developed by the General Motors and Chrysler corporations respectively, the generals finally thought they had a clear winner. Chrysler, which was in severe financial difficulties and needed the contract, had opted for a turbine engine in its model, using a technology that was largely new and unproven, burning fuel at a very high rate and requiring delicate filters to keep out all dust. The rival diesel engine was based on a well-established technology, though it also had innovative features. Overall, the army experts concluded that the entry from General Motors, which was far less dependent on the tank business, was a better design all around, as well as cheaper, and agreed unanimously to give the corporation the contract. By lunchtime July 20, 1976, the documents on the contract award were ready for Rumsfeld's pro forma approval.

The first sign of trouble came when army secretary Martin Hoffman brought the tank team in to inform Malcolm Currie and deputy defense secretary William Clements, a politically well-connected Texas oilman, on the decision. This, too, was expected to be a rubber stamp. But the two officials tore into the generals' conclusions, insisting that the turbine would be a better choice. When the contending parties argued the case before Rumsfeld, he refused to ratify the army's decision, ignoring desperate pleas from the generals and his old friend Hoffman. He then ordered a four-month delay and finally made it clear that only the turbine-engine tank would be acceptable. "It was a political decision that was reached," the army's head of research and development said later, "and for all intents and purposes the decision gave the award to Chrysler since they were the only contractor with a gas turbine." Chrysler, searching for financial lifelines, had been lobbying the administration for a bailout.

There was more to come. The army wanted to use an existing and well-proven 105-mm gun, rather than a new and bigger 120-mm weapon, because the 105 would be almost as lethally effective while enabling the tank to carry more ammunition and in greater safety. The Germans, meanwhile, had developed their own 120-mm gun, and wanted to sell it to the Americans. If there was no U.S. sale, they made clear, the U.S. Air Force would have no chance of achieving its dream of selling the AWACS radar plane to the Luftwaffe. Pressured by the Germans and, more important, the air force, Rumsfeld once again overrode the army and signed off on the larger and more expensive gun.[23]

Years late and overbudget, the M-1 finally entered service in the 1980s. Thanks to intensive care, many of its technical problems had been fixed. But no one could find a way to get that turbine to use less gas. The inevitable consequence has been on display in both Iraq wars: hapless tank units waiting by the side of the road for the fuel truck to arrive.

Rumsfeld's recovered memory of having boldly gone where no tank general had gone before, as opposed to playing his assigned role in a political bailout, is significant. By 2001, when he made this claim, he had come to believe that he understood the future of defense technology, the need for a bold new transformation. Thus he was easy game for salesmen with futuristic, if expensive, high-tech projects to sell, fixing a legacy that will burden U.S. defense years after George W. Bush has left office.

Back in 1976, of course, Rumsfeld's mind was on higher things, such as the Oval Office, or at least the vice presidential residence at the Naval Observatory. The ambitions he had since returning from Europe were undiminished. No Republican politician would dream of offending the military-industrial interest groups whose support was so vital in any electoral race. The B-1 program, for example, was directly and indirectly responsible for 140,000 jobs nationwide. Rumsfeld thought he might soon be garnering those votes. His strategy of helping to push Ford to the right, first put into play the year before, had borne fruit, albeit at severe political cost to the president. Now the end was near. As they headed to Kansas City for the Republican National Convention in August 1976, Ford and Reagan were neck and neck. Each side was desperately trolling for individual delegates. This was the moment when Ford might perhaps have put in a call to the hotel room of his fire-breathing defense secretary and invited him to join the ticket before the delegates voted. But Rumsfeld was not in Kansas City, and friends recall him being "glum" while it was going on. The cause of both his absence and mood was Nelson Rockefeller.

Rockefeller had identified Rumsfeld as a source of his political grief early on. "Mr. President," he told Ford angrily soon after his removal from the '76 ticket, "Rumsfeld wants to be President of the United States. He has given George Bush the deep six by putting him in the CIA, he has gotten me out. . . . He was third on your list and now he has gotten rid of two of us."[24] But the former governor was still the undisputed master of the New York Republican Party, thereby controlling the votes of the 154 delegates the party would send to Kansas City, votes that Ford desperately needed to defeat his opponent. Not long before the convention was due to open, Rockefeller struck. According to a close friend and political associate, Rockefeller made the following demand: "Mr. President, if Donald Rumsfeld so much as appears at the convention, I will release my delegates." Ford, who ultimately won by only 117 votes out of

2,258 cast, had no hesitation in ordering his defense secretary to be elsewhere. The reason for his absence remained a closely held secret. Even thirty years later, a very senior official in the Ford administration, no friend of Rumsfeld's, still proffered as a point of indictment to me the fact that Rumsfeld "didn't even bother to show up" at the convention.

So Rumsfeld's strategy for boosting himself onto the ticket came to naught, but like some abandoned minefield, the effects of his schemes—the dumping of Rockefeller, the sabotage of arms control—lived after him. Having swung so far to the right in the primaries, it was far harder for Ford to gain centrist votes. An arms control agreement could have helped, especially with Rockefeller on the ticket. Some of Ford's White House officials believe to this day that such a foreign policy success might have saved their president. In the view of the Ford adviser quoted above, Rumsfeld had "actively undermined arms control talks with the USSR. This as much as anything stopped Ford's election, [because] he had nothing to show in foreign policy. A SALT II agreement might have tipped the balance."

In the November general election, Ford narrowly lost to Jimmy Carter, the Georgia governor who had campaigned on a promise to cut the defense budget and cancel the B-1 bomber. Shortly after the election, several Ford officials gathered in the White House for a gloomy postmortem. There were many factors, they agreed, that had contributed to the defeat, ranging from Ford's original pardon for the crimes of the disgraced Richard Nixon to the feeble condition of the economy. But if there was one single person who had contributed above all others to Jerry Ford's defeat, they agreed, it was Ford's old and close friend Donald Rumsfeld.

Meanwhile, his work almost done, Rumsfeld had time to prepare his legacy: a $123 billion defense budget to be bequeathed to the incoming Carter administration. Rumsfeld called this proposal, which increased spending on new weapons by 25 percent in a single year, "sound and austere." He added that "no attempt was made to please those individuals who have it as their task every morning when they get up to find a way to hack the defense budget."[25] Among the items on the shopping list were cruise missiles, nuclear missile submarines, the MX missile, and the B-1. Paul Nitze had been on the committee that recommended the bomber be approved for production.[26] Carter, pledging to trim the overall defense budget by $7 billion, had called the bomber "wasteful of taxpayers' dollars" during his victorious campaign. But despite such pledges, as *Aviation Week* smugly noted in its report on Rumsfeld's good-bye budget, the new president's "first real chance to shape his own budget will come in Fiscal 1979."[27] In 1977, opinion polls finally recorded a shift in public attitudes; a majority was now in favor of increased defense spending.

Rumsfeld and his guides had committed the nation to a vast military expansion that, despite the noisy claims of the Committee on the Present Danger and similar entities, was not reversed in the Carter years. To do this they had evoked a fearful specter of an impending military confrontation with the Soviet Union that would almost certainly involve massive use of nuclear weapons. Yet close examination suggests that few of the leading lights in this campaign really took these terrifying predictions seriously. Why else did they struggle so energetically to buy weapons that manifestly did not work, like the Condor? If there really was a predictable moment when America would be vulnerable to a surprise nuclear strike, why didn't Rumsfeld and those who echoed his statements send their families out of town when that moment came? The suspicion arises that for him and the others it was all a game, a game they could win.

Unfortunately, one day, he would get to play the game with live ammunition and angry people shooting back. But before then, there was money to be made.

CHAPTER FOUR

How $weet It Is

In early February 2006, following a lunchtime speech at the National Press Club, defense secretary Donald Rumsfeld was chatting informally with his hosts. When the discussion wound around to his earlier career, someone at the table mentioned his years running the pharmaceutical company G.D. Searle, which he had joined after leaving the Defense Department on the day that Jimmy Carter was inaugurated in 1977. Rumsfeld reached across to the sugar bowl on the table and picked out a little sky blue packet of Equal, the ubiquitous white powder sweetener. "This was one of our products," he remarked offhandedly, as if Equal had just happened to have been one among the multitude of items churned out in Searle's facilities. The statement was true, but his casual tone was about as misleading as his history of the M-1 tank.

Equal had not been just "one of" Searle's products. Bringing it and its sister brand NutraSweet to market had been the supreme achievement of Rumsfeld's business career. His success saved the company and made him rich—though some medical scientists believed it contributed to several thousand Americans developing a particularly malignant form of brain cancer.

Rumsfeld's eight-year career at Searle, from 1977 to 1985, is commonly described as a classic tale of the tough manager who takes charge of a troubled company and, by making the hard decisions and chopping out the dead wood, turns things around. The reputation as a decisive and effective CEO that he thereby acquired did much to burnish his aura when he returned to public life as secretary of defense under George W. Bush.

The true story of what happened in the Searle years is a little different, and a lot more interesting.

Rumsfeld had grown up with G.D. Searle, whose Skokie, Illinois, headquarters was close to his boyhood home. The Searles were North Shore aristocracy, one of the half dozen richest clans in all of Chicago. Dan Searle, great-grandson of the company founder, one of Rumsfeld's wealthier contemporaries in Winnetka, was a close enough friend to serve as finance chairman in that first hard-fought 1962 congressional primary campaign, with personal contributions to match. At that time the Searle heir was already vice president of the company and about to be promoted to executive vice president, riding high on the profits from Searle's introduction of Enovid, the first birth control pill. This spectacular innovation had been the result of good fortune rather than visionary management, since the company had initially refused to carry out research on oral contraception and marketed the pill only after one of their researchers discovered it by accident while experimenting with another product. Dan, joined in the upper tiers of the Searle hierarchy by his brother William and brother-in-law Wesley Dixon, spent the sixties on a shopping spree, pouring pill profits into a diverse assortment of unrelated businesses.

Fifteen years later, the glory days were over. G.D. Searle, in the brutal words of one Wall Street analyst, was "snuffing itself."[1] The stock, which had once soared to $110, was down to $12. The company's early monopoly on the pill had been lost, partly because of reports of some unpleasant side effects associated with Enovid. Unfortunately, the investments financed by the pill bonanza had proved disappointing. In addition, the Food and Drug Administration (FDA) was refusing to allow the company to release the one new product that might turn Searle's fortunes around. Worst of all, the company was faced with a looming grand jury investigation for what amounted to faking its drug testing reports. In short, the company was in serious trouble. So the Searles reached out to Rumsfeld and, in the words of one of his Chicago friends, "asked him to clean it up and sell it."

In May 1977, G.D. Searle formally announced that Rumsfeld had been appointed president and CEO. Dan Searle took himself off to the dignified pasture of the chairmanship, while assorted Searle relatives were similarly moved aside.

In accepting the Searles' offer to take over the troubled company, Rumsfeld did not abandon politics to enter business. He brought politics with him, and used his peculiar skills and connections in that field to rescue the corporation. It was a less common approach to business at the time, but as government generally developed a more supportive attitude to corporations in the eighties and nineties, similar examples of politician/bureaucrats deploying their special skills in business grew more common. Former Interior Department under-secretary Kenneth Lay built Enron from an obscure pipeline company into an infamous colossus largely by manipulating regional energy deregulation to his own advantage. Former defense secretary Dick Cheney's major contribution to Halliburton as CEO was to use his government experience and connections to shift the corporation's focus from the oil service business to the more easily managed environment of government contracts.

Of course, the defense business had been functioning this way for decades, with officials like Malcolm Currie shuffling back and forth between the Pentagon and the contractors without generating any particular public concern over conflicts of interest. A year after he became president of Searle, Rumsfeld told an interviewer that "the problems of running a company aren't much different from running a federal agency, such as the Defense Department."[2] To assist him in managing the company, Rumsfeld therefore reached out for men who knew the world of government, and how to use it.

John Robson was his first and most important recruit. Hired as executive vice president for planning and regulatory affairs, Robson knew nothing about the pharmaceutical business, but a lot about the business of bureaucratic regulation in Washington, where he had until recently been the chairman of the Civil Aeronautics Board (CAB). Equally significant, he had, as one mutual friend recalled, "played sandlot baseball with Rumsfeld" at New Trier high school.

He was one of the inner circle of men in whom Rumsfeld reposed his total trust, so long as they accepted his preeminent status in the group.

Joining the team as general counsel was Robson's former special assistant in the Transportation Department, Robert Shapiro, a sharp-tongued lawyer whose experience also lay in government, not pills. Bill Greener, Rumsfeld's loyal spokesman at the Ford White House and Pentagon, signed on as vice president for public affairs. Bill Timmons, a friend since the Nixon White House, was chosen to head up the Searle lobbying team in Washington. The new Searle management team "figured the business they were in was getting FDA approval" for their products, according to James Turner, a public interest lawyer who was to have ample opportunity to observe this group in action.

Later on, Rumsfeld liked to give the impression that he had opted for a business career only after thoughtful reflection in the groves of academe. (He delivered some lectures at Princeton and Northwestern.) However, in the very small print of the biographical summary he was obliged (with many grumbles) to submit to the Senate prior to confirmation as defense secretary in 2000, he records that he began work as a consultant for Searle—the only company so honored—in January 1977, within days of leaving the Pentagon.[3]

The detail is interesting, for it suggests that although he did not formally assume command, at a salary of $200,000 a year plus generous stock options, until the summer of 1977, he was well informed of the crises buffeting the firm—and furthermore was suggesting solutions—for many months beforehand.

One crisis urgently requiring a solution was the looming threat of a criminal indictment. In evaluating new drugs, then and now, the FDA in large part relied on honest reporting of the results of drug trials in company laboratories. Such trials generally involve dosing a select number of test animals, usually rodents such as rats, mice, or hamsters, with the relevant drug while a control group of exactly similar animals are left untreated. An accurate record of the condition of the animals during the tests, as well as the autopsies performed after they were killed at the end of the experiment, is of course essential.

Hence, senior FDA officials had reacted with outrage to the results of an investigation into the Searle research laboratory by a special task force. The eighty-four-page report submitted by the investigators reads at times like a treatment for an NC-17-rated horror film. Searle researchers had recorded malignant tumors as benign, and dead rats as still alive. Test animals that had developed tumors after being given experimental drugs would have the tumors cut out while they were still alive and would then be recorded as having suffered no ill effects as a result of the experiment. "They lied," one member of the task force said later. "They didn't submit the real nature of their observations . . . they did other terrible things." Other respected scientists involved in the scrutiny of the firm delivered similarly shocked verdicts, using words and phrases such as "sloppy" or "never seen anything as bad," and "scientifically irresponsible."

On January 10, 1977, the agency's chief counsel, Richard Merrill, dispatched a thirty-three-page letter detailing Searle's infractions to Sam Skinner, the U.S. attorney in Chicago. "We request that your office convene a Grand Jury investigation," he wrote, "into apparent violations of the Federal Food, Drug, and Cosmetic Act . . . and the False Reports to the Government Act . . . by G.D. Searle and Company and three of its responsible officers for their willful and knowing failure to make reports . . . and making false statements in reports of animal studies."

Sixteen days after FDA counsel Merrill sent his letter, a team from Sidley & Austin, the Chicago law firm that represented Searle, requested a meeting with Skinner in order to discuss the issue of the grand jury. Among the lawyers at the meeting was a partner named Newton Minow, a Democrat and a hero to the liberal intelligentsia for his stirring denunciation of network television as a "vast wasteland" while serving as Kennedy's Federal Communications Commission (FCC) chairman. At the same time, Minow was also an old friend of Rumsfeld from the days when he had studied under Rumsfeld's uncle at Northwestern University. In the world inhabited by such men, personal bonds and shared interests far outweighed politics.

As it so happened, Skinner was looking for a job. Following the arrival of the Carter administration, all Republican-appointed U.S.

attorneys were gradually being replaced by Democrats. So when Sam Skinner got the FDA counsel's fierce letter demanding the prosecution, or at least investigation, of Searle, he, too, was getting ready to pack up his office and explore new possibilities in the private sector. Whatever transpired at that January meeting, a spark was obviously set. Six weeks later, on March 8, Skinner circulated a confidential memo to his senior staff stating that he was withdrawing from any involvement with the Searle investigation because of "discussions about a possible job with the law firm representing the drug company." Skinner wanted the news kept confidential "to avoid any undue embarrassment" to Sidley & Austin.

In April, the Justice Department, apparently ignorant of Skinner's discreet withdrawal from the case, sent him a memo urging action on the case, and followed up with another memo some months later. The lawyers in Washington were concerned that the statute of limitations on the possible charges against Searle for withholding or falsifying evidence would run out by the end of the year. But the U.S. Attorney's Office, the Chicago arm of the Justice Department, seemed strangely paralyzed, even after Skinner left at the beginning of July. Following his withdrawal, the Searle file passed into the hands of senior prosecutor William Conlon, who announced three months later that he had decided to "reduce or end" his involvement in the case due to the pressure of other duties. He did manage to empanel a grand jury on Searle, just as time ran out for consideration of the most serious charges. Fourteen months later, Conlon, too, opted for private law practice, accepting an offer from Sidley & Austin. Not long afterward yet another prosecutor who had been working on the Searle file trod the by now well-worn path from prosecution to defense team. Finally, early in 1979, the U.S. Attorney's Office simply told the FDA that it was dropping the case on the grounds that the pertinent FDA regulations were "ambiguous." Neither Rumsfeld nor anyone else from Searle had had to spend a single day in court. Senator Howard Metzenbaum (D-Ohio) afterward noted that the steady migration of prosecutors to the Searle legal team raised "serious questions."

Sam Skinner, who went on to become George Bush Sr.'s chief of staff and then secretary of transportation, told me that he had no involvement in the case after he sent his letter to his staff in March 1977 and that an allegation concerning him had been fully investigated by the FBI and the U.S. Senate, which cleared him of any wrongdoing. William Conlon did not reply to my email requesting a comment on the case.

By the time the grand jury problem had completely melted away, Rumsfeld had been in the driver's seat at Searle for almost two years. He had sold off twenty divisions, gotten various members of the Searle family to take a backseat, fired half of the headquarters staff, and tyrannized the remainder. "Don was not really a manager," one former colleague told me. "He liked to fly along at thirty thousand feet, far removed from the day-to-day concerns of his subordinates, except when he impulsively felt like diving down into the weeds and seizing on some microissue. This gave the illusion that he was all-knowing. So people were terrified, they thought he knew everything, but of course he didn't, far from it."

His style of putting people off-balance with a barrage of interjections had already irked colleagues in the Ford White House, but Rumsfeld's manner was becoming steadily more intimidating as his direct power over the lives of underlings increased. (A presidential chief of staff cannot fire several hundred people overnight; a corporate CEO can.) One former Searle executive described his first encounter with Rumsfeld as "very unpleasant." Called back on short notice from a vacation in California, he had worked hard with his staff to put together a presentation demanded by the boss. "We must have been going five minutes when he began a rapid-fire series of questions. He was intolerant of sitting through the presentation. It was supposed to last twenty minutes. It lasted ninety, and I came out frustrated that I hadn't been able to tell my story."[4] This technique of inflicting hours of rapid and often disconnected questions on the people under him was to become a Rumsfeld hallmark. He referred to it as "wirebrushing," and while very effective as a tool to intimidate and keep people on their toes, its utility as a means of eliciting useful information is less clear. He also occasionally indulged himself with more straightforward harassment. Irked by one executive's weight, which he deemed to be excessive, Rumsfeld withheld the man's annual bonus until he shed some pounds.[5] Such behavior earned him a slot on *Fortune* magazine's 1980 list of the Ten Toughest Bosses in America.[6]

In the short term, his aggressive downsizing generated a salutary effect on the balance sheet. The company lost $28.4 million in his first year. The following year it earned $72.2 million. But this, as Wall Street well understood, had been the easy part. Most of the profit came from selling company assets (including the agriculture subsidiary's prize bull), a one-time benefit that could not be repeated. Analysts were quick to note that after-tax margins still lagged behind those of the rest of the pharmaceutical industry. Many of the company's drugs had been on the market for years with patents that would soon expire, and there were few promising replacements in the pipeline.

This dire situation was all the more galling because Searle did have a new product, already manufactured and sitting in the warehouse ever since 1974, that was almost guaranteed to sweep the market. Unfortunately, the FDA was refusing to allow the company to sell it, simply because of suspicions on the part of some scientists and consumer groups that this miracle product, aspartame, might give people tumors, or otherwise attack their brains.

Aspartame was not a new lifesaving drug, but a sweetener, intended for use as a calorie-free sugar substitute in foods and drinks. The potential market among the weight-conscious population was enormous, especially as the two leading artificial sweeteners on sale either had a slightly nasty taste, like saccharin, or were suspected health risks. Cyclamate, discovered in 1937, had actually been banned as a carcinogen in 1974, and saccharin, barely escaping a similar fate, bore the indignity of a federally mandated health warning on its packaging.

Like Searle's earlier discovery of the pill, the sweetener had emerged by accident. A researcher working on a possible treatment for ulcers spilled an experimental compound on his fingers, licked it off, and noticed that it was astonishingly sweet. Tests showed the compound was two hundred times sweeter than sugar, so the tiny dose required was essentially calorie free, and with no unpleasant aftertaste. In 1974, after reviewing the results of tests performed under Searle's auspices—all of which concluded that aspartame was utterly safe—the FDA approved the product for release as a food additive.

Then just as Searle, which had already spent $40 million on the product and had begun to manufacture it in quantity, could cash in, nemesis arrived in the form of Dr. John W. Olney, professor of neuropathology and psychiatry at Washington University School of Medicine in St. Louis, Missouri. Olney was a specialist in the toxic properties of consumer products as they affected the human brain. A few years before aspartame crossed his path, he had demonstrated that monosodium glutamate causes brain lesions in rats, and managed to end the use of MSG in baby food. Now he reasoned that aspartame had molecular similarities to glutamate and might therefore be equally dangerous. Testing a sample on rats he found that the animals suffered "acute death of nerve cells in the immature hypothalamus," a region of the brain that produces and secretes hormones into the bloodstream.

As if Olney weren't bad enough news for Searle, he found an ally in public interest lawyer James Turner. Turner was working with Ralph Nader in campaigns on behalf of the health and safety of consumers, who were all too often ignored both by corporations and the federal agencies charged with monitoring them. He had authored *The Chemical Feast,* a best seller in 1970, which laid out in chilling detail how the FDA was shirking its obligations to the public in the interests of the industry it was supposed to oversee. *Time* magazine had described it as "the most devastating critique of a U.S. Government Agency ever issued." Turner was thus keenly aware of the degree to which barely scrutinized food additives were being slipped into the American diet. Thirty years later, sitting in his Washington law office, his thirst for combat on behalf of the public still unslaked, he recalled how a fight that would last decades first began. "I had the FDA account from Nader, and someone suggested that I take a look at this new product aspartame."

The FDA commissioner, a medical academic named Alexander Schmidt, who had approved aspartame for release in July 1974, had relied solely on Searle's own interpretation of its experimental testing as evidence that the product was safe. He had allowed a mere thirty days for public comment before his order became final.

Noting the fluent ease with which the product had sped toward release, leaving barely any time for outsiders like them to comment,

Olney and Turner joined forces to petition the FDA to hold up the release pending further investigation. To their surprise, Schmidt agreed and promptly slapped a stay on the sweetener, pending a public inquiry at which all relevant information, including the company's own tests, would be disclosed.

The horror stories from the Searle labs began to emerge shortly afterward. In this atmosphere, especially with a grand jury in the offing, the chances of aspartame going on the market anytime soon began to recede. A special task force sent to Skokie, Illinois, in the spring of 1977 to examine the raw data used in the company's uniformly positive test reports on the product uncovered what the team said were falsifications and omissions. Among fifty-two significant shortcomings in just one of fifteen studies, the investigators noted, "Observation records indicated that animal A23LM was alive at week 88, dead from week 92 through week 104, alive at week 108, and dead from week 112."[7]

According to an investigation by UPI reporter Greg Gordon in 1987, Searle sent a key executive involved in aspartame tests out of town when the grand jury threat materialized, handing him $15,000 and immediately sending him on a three-year sabbatical.[8] But such desperate measures were not enough to hide the bad news about Searle's testing practices that were now being uncovered by a variety of investigative task forces. Meanwhile, the grand jury was still sitting, an unpleasant background threat, however weakened it may have been by the prosecutors' procrastination.

In the fall of 1978, therefore, Rumsfeld opted for a bold move, a face-to-face meeting with Turner to see if they could come to some agreement. "He called me, and said, 'Let's meet,'" recalled Turner in a 2006 interview. "So we met at the Madison Hotel," an expensive establishment in the heart of Washington. Sitting across the table from the Searle boss, who was flanked by two aides and his newly appointed head of research, Turner suggested that since this was a scientific argument, they should try to find the answers by scientific means. "I said, 'I've got scientists that say this stuff is unsafe. You've got scientists that say it's safe. Let's agree on a team that can evaluate the arguments from both sides so that we can reach some sort of consensus.'" The proposal met with a muted response.

"Rumsfeld wanted me to walk him through all the scientific material" that made up the case against aspartame, recalled the lawyer. "He had obviously been told that this material was not solid, and they could beat us with science, so I took him through all the stuff we had. We were there for two or three hours."

Reflecting on the encounter, Turner expounded an analysis of the Searle boss's attitude that could cover other aspects of his career. Rumsfeld, he concluded, was "not interested in facts, not interested in truth, not interested in finding out what the fundamental realities are, but is much, much more interested in setting a goal and then, by will and force, pulling all the resources that he could possibly pull together to achieve that goal: i.e., to get [aspartame] on the market and sold."

In January 1980, the long-awaited public inquiry finally opened in Washington. Three distinguished scientists led by Dr. Walle Nauta, a neuroscientist of towering eminence from MIT, were ready to consider at least some of the concerns about aspartame (many complaints were excluded in a procedural maneuver that favored Searle). Turner was convinced at the time that Rumsfeld assumed the inquiry would produce a favorable result, and the way for aspartame's release would finally be clear. Years before, however, Schmidt, the FDA commissioner who originally ordered the inquiry, had stipulated that all the data used by either side in support of their positions should be made publicly available. "There was a whole roomful of Searle's stuff," remembers Turner, "piled high on tables in the clerk's office. Ninety percent of it was crap. There were 103 studies in all, of which 11 were pivotal studies."

Dr. Olney, the scientist who had first raised the alarm, flew in from St. Louis, eager to see the raw studies underpinning the assertion that aspartame was safe. Somehow, amid the towering piles of paper, Olney unearthed a report detailing an experiment carried out on rats in the early seventies. "What startled me most," he told me, "was that it showed that aspartame had been causing brain tumors in rats, and the FDA [in originally reviewing the study] had just sloughed it off." Olney was not about to let that happen again. "I took it to the FDA commissioner and asked him to make sure that this was considered by the panel." As it turned out, this evidence of a possible link between aspartame and brain tumors had a decisive effect. In September 1980, the panel issued their verdict, a 3–0 vote to block the aspartame release pending resolution of the concerns about cancer. All three members of the panel have since died, but one scientist of their acquaintance reports all three were "totally convinced" that they had settled the matter once and for all. "They thought aspartame was dead," he says.

They were wrong. Two months later, Ronald Reagan was elected president. Wall Street was quick to appreciate the opportunities for Searle of a Republican administration. "The numbers are incredible," an excited analyst told *Forbes* magazine in reference to prospective aspartame-driven profits for the company.

Rumsfeld felt the same way. One week before the inauguration, he addressed a meeting of the Searle sales force. According to one of those present, he declared that he would "call in his markers" and "no matter what," he would see to it that aspartame "would be approved" by the end of 1981.

Those markers were all over the incoming administration. Rumsfeld himself had campaigned for Reagan in the general election. He was on Reagan's foreign and defense policy advisory committee. His old friend Richard Allen was the new president's national security adviser. Most important of all, John Robson, his right-hand man at Searle, was on Reagan's transition team.

The effects of the change in administrations were soon felt at the FDA. Jere Goyan, FDA commissioner at the time, informed me how he was "fired . . . in early November by a phone call to my California home at two a.m. California time by a very low-level member of the transition team who said that my services were no longer needed. It was the first time that a commissioner had been fired because of a change in administration. I was told to write a letter of resignation and to vacate my office on the day of the inauguration."[9]

On January 21, 1981, one day after Reagan had taken the oath of office, Searle petitioned to have the inquiry panel's verdict overruled. Goyan's place was temporarily occupied by his deputy, who reportedly was anxious not to make waves with his new masters. Finally, in April, the administration unveiled its very own FDA commissioner, Arthur Hull Hayes. Subsequent inquiries by investigators for the Senate Committee for Labor and Human Resources failed to uncover any account of how he had been selected for this important position, save that it had been the result of outside intervention in the regular selection process. A professor of pharmacology from Pennsylvania State College of Medicine, Hayes's only previous experience in public service had been as a doctor in the Army Medical Corps in the 1960s. Stationed at Edgewood Arsenal, the army's chemical warfare research center, Hayes had experimented on human guinea pigs with a class of mind-disorienting drugs called glycolates that could induce hallucinations or delirium and hence were of interest to the military for use as riot-control agents. The subjects in these experiments were army recruits who had volunteered for the role. However, the army's inspector general had reported in 1976 that these young volunteers might not have been fully briefed on the health effects posed by these experimental weapons. Hayes himself was quoted in a press report as admitting, "I did not tell them every specific," because "then very often they will tell you that's in fact what happened, or they will look for it themselves."[10]

Reagan had campaigned on pledges to free business from the straitjacket of excessive federal regulation, so it can be assumed that the selection of an FDA commissioner was made with some care. Although Hayes's tenure was short, he did not disappoint. On July 18, 1981, in the first major regulatory action of his tenure, Hayes approved aspartame for use as a sweetener in solid foods, thereby disregarding the inquiry verdict as well as yet another internal study that raised alarms about the cancer risk. To buttress his decision, he reached for a new rat study that showed no connection between rat tumors and aspartame. Ajinomoto, a giant Japanese food processor under contract to Searle to produce aspartame, had conducted the study. Reaction of the critics was predictable. Turner suggested that Hayes had walked "through a mass of scientific mismanagement, improper procedures, wrong conclusions and general scientific inexactness." Searle stock, meanwhile, rebounded, followed shortly afterward by the company's credit rating.[11]

Aspartame was marketed as two brands. When used as a food additive it was sold as NutraSweet, while diet-conscious coffee drinkers could tear open little packets of Equal. Sales quickly boomed. Rumsfeld liked to make pious remarks to the business press about not wanting aspartame to be "Searle's savior," but investors were not fooled.[12] The company stock was now assumed to be moving purely in reaction to the success or failure of aspartame in surmounting various regulatory hurdles.

One such hurdle was the necessary extension of the patent. The history of how this was accomplished serves as a fine example of the Rumsfeld management team in action.

It had taken so long to gain approval for aspartame that the all-important patents were due to expire in 1987, thus diminishing profits as well as the price Searle could extract from a buyer if and when the company was put on the auction block. Accordingly, late one evening in October 1982, Senator Howell Heflin (D-Ala.) proposed an amendment to the Orphan Drug Act that would alter the laws covering U.S. patent extensions. Nowhere in the amendment's obscure language did the words "aspartame" or "Searle" appear, but it was all about aspartame nonetheless, having no other effect than to extend the aspartame patent into 1992. The Senate does have a procedure designed to alert senators to such special-interest ploys, but it was mysteriously bypassed in this case. Following five minutes of floor discussion, in which no one uttered the word "aspartame," the measure passed the Senate.

Election spending documents later reviewed by UPI investigative reporter Greg Gordon recorded that Heflin's reelection campaign in 1984 received checks of $1,000 each from Daniel Searle, Mrs. Daniel Searle, Daniel's brother William Searle, Mrs. William Searle, Daniel's sister, Suzanne Searle Dixon, and Suzanne's husband, Wesley. In addition, he later received a further $1,000 from William and $2,000 from the Searle PAC.

Senator Orrin Hatch (R-Nev.), who had closed the Senate floor discussion by describing the measure as an "excellent" amendment, received $1,000 each from Daniel, William, and Wesley shortly afterward.

Senator Robert Byrd (D-W.Va.), who brought the measure up for a vote, had received $1,000 from Daniel the year before.

Congressman Henry Waxman (D-Calif.), who introduced the amendment on the House side, received $1,500 in campaign contributions from the soft drink manufacturers' PAC, including $500 that arrived two days before he brought the measure to the House without, of course, mentioning aspartame.

The "excellent amendment" was worth as much as $3 billion in extra revenue to Searle. Given the comparatively tiny amounts garnered by the relevant legislators' campaign chests—$9,000 in Heflin's case, less for the others—this was a tribute to the generalship of the chief Searle lobbyist, Rumsfeld's old friend William Timmons. The same dexterity was on display in another potentially lethal threat to aspartame's penetration of the $2 billion diet-soda market.

Aspartame was finally cleared for use in liquids—that is, diet sodas—in July 1983, thereby tripling the $200 million aspartame worldwide market.[13] Hayes left it to his deputy to make the announcement, possibly because the army inspector-general's report on his mind-control experiments had leaked to the press just a few days before and he was disinclined to stir up more controversy. Not long afterward he resigned, following news that he had been taking free rides on corporate jets from the food industry. Not all connections with Searle were severed, however, since he soon accepted a consultancy contract from Searle's PR firm, Burson-Marsteller.

Though Searle now had federal clearance to sell its product, opponents were still in a position to cause trouble. One such was Dr. Woodrow Monte, a food scientist at Arizona State University, who argued that aspartame in diet sodas exposed to hot conditions, such as any Arizona summer's day, would degrade into methyl alcohol, a toxic substance capable of inducing everything from dizziness to seizures and amnesia.

Heading off Monte and associated Arizona consumer groups from their effort to get aspartame banned in the state was clearly a matter of urgency. Accordingly, election records depict Searle family checkbooks again pressed into service delivering campaign contributions to relevant Arizona politicians. In no time at all a law glided through the legislature forbidding any state restriction of a federally approved food additive. Displaying a fine sense of irony, the measure's sponsors labeled it as a toxic waste bill.

Meanwhile, Monte himself had unwisely bought "put" options on

Searle stock in the belief that concerns about aspartame would cause the stock to go down. Though he lost money on the deal (the stock went down, but not by enough) his trade was exposed to censorious scrutiny by well-briefed reporters. Shortly afterward, Congressman Bob McEwen (R-Ohio) denounced Monte on the floor of the House for insider trading, since the scientist had previously vented his criticisms in an interview with CBS. In his denunciation McEwen may not have been aware that his senior staff aide, Charles Greener, was the son of Bill Greener, Rumsfeld's old comrade in arms from the White House and Pentagon, and later vice president for corporate communications at Searle. (The SEC found no evidence that Monte had done anything wrong.)

With opposition subdued, if not silenced, Rumsfeld was ready to fulfill the last part of his mandate from the Searle family and sell the company. Although the business press speculated that the company could go for as much as $3.7 billion, thanks to aspartame's ballooning sales, the St. Louis chemical giant Monsanto was eventually able to buy the entire firm for a billion dollars less, $2.7 billion, thereby garnering the Searle family somewhere between $600 million and $900 million (they had initially held out for the higher price).[14] After a decade at Searle, Rumsfeld's own net worth was estimated in Chicago at around $10 million.[15]

Rumsfeld would later run another large corporation, General Instrument, in the early 1990s. *Fortune* magazine noted he was hired because "he knew Washington."[16] He probably made more in that enterprise—he had a paper profit on his stock of over $10 million just two years after starting the job—but Searle and aspartame seemed to have remained closer to his heart.

In 1990, Christopher Meyer, a British diplomat and future ambassador to Washington, was on a five-day river-rafting party through the Grand Canyon. Among his fellow rafters was Donald Rumsfeld. Meyer records that Rumsfeld, in between countermanding the directions of the professional river guide, which he did on a continual basis, "would lecture us interminably on the merits of the artificial sweetener aspartame. . . . His rasping voice would echo from one side of the Canyon to the other." The aspartame lectures ended only when Rumsfeld put his back out hurling buckets of water in an interraft water fight. He finished the trip strapped to a chair on the chase boat that also carried the sealed box containing the rafters' "human waste," being transported out of the canyon by the eco-conscious tour organizers, from which, according to Meyer, "noxious odours began to seep" as the chase boat and its rigid passenger careened down the rapids.[17]

If Rumsfeld could not forget aspartame, neither could the men who had fought him in "hand-to-hand combat," as Jim Turner describes the struggle over FDA approval. In 1996, John Olney asked the National Cancer Institute to send him the data on brain tumors that the institute collects from around the country, covering not only the fifteen years since aspartame had been introduced but also, for purposes of comparison, the ten years preceding approval. The trend revealed in the figures was stark. "I found a steady rise in most subtypes [of brain tumor] in the years following approval before eventually leveling off." Overall, the incidence of such tumors had jumped by 10 percent, corresponding to roughly fifteen hundred extra cases of brain cancer a year in the United States.

Even more chilling, in Olney's view, was the change that had come over the mix of tumors since 1981. "The rate of glioblastoma, the most malignant kind, had markedly increased in the ten years immediately following the introduction of aspartame, while the rate of incidence of less malignant types had decreased." In other words, the types of brain tumor appearing in the population had suddenly shifted to a more aggressive and usually lethal variety.

"Nothing has changed to alter my view," Olney told me in 2006. "The only explanation I can think of is that something has been introduced into the human environment that has caused brain tumors to become more malignant. I don't have direct evidence that aspartame is the cause. But it hasn't been explained in any other way." (He disbelieves in the widely suspected connection between tumors and cell phones.)

Naturally, Olney's conclusion was unwelcome to the aspartame industry, whose worldwide sales had topped the $1 billion mark in 1995, and to its allies in government and commerce. They advanced the counterargument that Olney's increase was merely a statistical anomaly wrought by an improvement in diagnostic technology, though Olney maintains that the relevant technologies had been introduced in the 1970s, well before aspartame, so their effects would have been already apparent in the data for the years preceding Hayes's momentous decision.

In any case, it is unlikely that Rumsfeld has ever given the steady trickle of concerned reports about aspartame's effects—an alarmed study by a distinguished Italian research group was released in 2005—much consideration.[18] Such reports were merely facts, inconvenient ones at that, and Rumsfeld never has a lot of time for those. This could be a serious shortcoming, especially when facts drew attention to themselves in forms that were hard to avoid, such as election results. Long before the bloody statistics of Iraq came to exercise Rumsfeld's powers of denial, he was confronted with awkward truths regarding his appeal as a politician.

CHAPTER FIVE

Politics and Other Games

Late in 1984, G.D. Searle quietly dropped plans to market a newly developed gynecological drug called Gemeprost, one of the few successes in its lackluster drug research program. The company gave no explanation, but the true reason soon leaked out: Gemeprost could be used in performing abortions. Internal documents unearthed by an enterprising *Chicago Tribune* reporter made it clear that Searle feared criticism from antiabortion groups that might, according to the *Tribune,* not only affect prospects for selling the company but also "prove damaging to the political aspirations of Searle's president and chief executive officer, Donald Rumsfeld."[1] Rumsfeld the politician was ever on the mind of Rumsfeld the businessman.

He was now fifty-three, and on superficial examination his future appeared bright, not least to himself. Asked by *Fortune* magazine in 1979 about his political plans, Rumsfeld admitted that "at some point the odds favor my being involved in government again," but that he had absolutely no plans to run for office before his job at Searle was done.[2] Still, as the story of the withdrawn drug indicates, his political ambitions had to be considered along with the Searle bottom line. In 1980, less than a year after he spoke to *Fortune,* he ran for election in the area he had once represented in Congress. The post he sought was merely that of delegate to the 1980 Republican National Convention in Detroit, but some aspects of this forgotten race are instructive.

"He lost," recalls an influential Chicago Republican. "In his old district, where he had been the boy wonder, he managed to lose. He ran 'unattached,' meaning that he was uncommitted to any presidential candidate—think of the arrogance of that. He thought people would vote for him because of who he was; he didn't realize that people in those elections are voting for the candidate. They don't care who the delegate is."

Undeterred by this rebuff, Rumsfeld went to Detroit anyway, nurturing hopes that Ronald Reagan would select him as his running mate. Party leaders did at least permit him to address the convention, along with all the many other candidates angling for a spot on the ticket. The speech fell flat. "The hall was half empty, no one paying much attention," says the Chicago Republican. "It was kind of sad. I think his attitude was 'What does this actor from California know about defense and foreign policy? Reagan needs me.'"

Years later, when Rumsfeld's old friend Richard Allen revealed that he had persuaded Reagan to pick George Bush as his vice presidential running mate and supplied Bush's phone number (Bush had given up hope by the time Reagan called and was getting drunk with James Baker), Rumsfeld called Allen and asked, "Why didn't you tell him to pick me?" To which Allen generously responded, "Because I didn't have your number." His name did surface briefly, at least in the press, as a possible selection. Bill Seidman, Rumsfeld's former colleague from the Ford White House, was asked his opinion. "Don Rumsfeld is an extremely talented and capable man who would do an excellent job," he replied. "And as long as the president has a competent food taster, he'll be fine." This witticism was inevitably repeated to Rumsfeld, who was not amused and never forgave its author.

In the ensuing campaign, Rumsfeld stumped for Reagan and briefly surfaced in the press as a candidate for a senior cabinet post. Nothing happened. Rumsfeld, in the words of one Reagan administration official, "was never going to get anything worthwhile so long as Bush and [White House chief of staff James] Baker were around. Bush hated him and Baker saw him as a possible peer competitor."

These formidable antagonists were, however, willing to permit him a minor role. In 1982 he was enlisted to help kill off the International Law of the Sea Treaty, deemed irksome to U.S. business. The following year, Reagan appointed him special envoy to the Middle East. "Considering the positions he'd held, it wasn't much," said the former Reagan official, "but he was desperate to get back in the game."

As is so often the case, U.S. policy in the region was in something of a shambles. Secretary of State George Shultz's effort to salvage an Israeli-Lebanese peace agreement signed the previous May had just been blown to pieces along with 241 U.S. servicemen when a suicide bomber destroyed the marine barracks in Beirut. "Rumsfeld's appointment was a classic White House maneuver whereby you appear to be doing something even if it doesn't mean much," a former senior State Department official told me.

The record of Rumsfeld's performance as envoy tends to bear out this assessment. Despite his total lack of experience or knowledge of the region's turbulent politics, he was, of course, fully confident that he had the answers. An assistant secretary of state of that era recalls the newly installed Rumsfeld reciting "a long spiel about how his tack would be to get the Arabs to unite against the Soviet threat." As it turned out, Arab leaders, many of whom were on good terms with Moscow, remained unmoved by this specter. Specifically, Rumsfeld was unable to avert America's humiliating ejection from Lebanon, whence the marines were soon "redeployed" to ships offshore before eventually sailing home. He did, however, make the rounds of regional capitals, where he would customarily be lodged with the local American ambassador. He was not always warmly received. Bob Baer, a CIA officer making frequent visits to Syria at this time, told me that whenever Rumsfeld came to Damascus, Ambassador Bob Paganelli would not only arrange to be out of town, but would "lock up the liquor cabinet at the residence and take the key with him, every time." The high point of a visit with King Fahd of Saudi Arabia came when the corpulent monarch held up a packet of aspartame and announced that his wife had told him to use it as an aid to losing weight. "All I could think of," said Rumsfeld later, "was, if I'd had a camera, what an ad!"

There was one country where Rumsfeld found friends who, in the words of that country's foreign minister, liked him "as a person" and praised him as a "good listener." That was Saddam Hussein's Iraq.

In late 1983, Saddam was getting the worst of the war he had foolishly launched against Iran three years earlier. He was therefore desperate for American support. Officially, Washington professed neutrality in the war. Secretly, the administration was determined to go to any lengths to save Iraq from defeat. Thus it was that within a month of arriving in the Middle East, Rumsfeld was photographed shaking hands with the Iraqi dictator in one of the latter's many Baghdad palaces.[3] Both men, conscious of the stakes involved, were careful to exhibit their charming side.

After an hour or so of expressions of high-minded sentiments on the desirability of improving relations between the two countries, curbing Syrian power in Lebanon, cutting off arms supplies to Iran, and bolstering the position of Jordan's King Hussein, Rumsfeld turned to a subject that seemed to interest him deeply: the construction of an oil pipeline westward from Iraq to the Jordanian port of Aqaba. The Bechtel construction corporation, formerly headed by Reagan's secretary of state, George Shultz, was deeply interested in the project. When Rumsfeld raised the subject, Saddam replied encouragingly, according to the classified State Department cable on the meeting, that "in the past Iraq had not been very interested in the Jordanian pipeline because of the threat that Israel would disrupt it. Now that U.S. companies and USG [U.S. government] were interested, Iraq would re-examine it." According to a former Iraqi intelligence officer detailed to monitor Rumsfeld while he was in Baghdad, the pipeline was not the only commercial venture on the visiting envoy's mind. "All he wanted to talk about were business deals," the spook told friends afterward.

Taking his leave of Hussein, Rumsfeld sped straight to London for a meeting with King Hussein of Jordan, who was staying at Claridges hotel. Driving from the airport to the rendezvous, he excitedly informed Richard Viets, U.S. ambassador to Jordan, about both his pipeline discussions with Saddam and his own scheme for a branch running off the main pipeline direct to Israel, thus dramatically breaking the Arab economic embargo against the Jewish state. Viets, an experienced and savvy diplomat, was aghast. "Proposing that is a terrible idea," he said of the scheme, "I will not support it, and in any case the king will never under any circumstances agree to it."

Rumsfeld, scenting a challenge to his authority, reacted in habitual fashion. "Well, we'll see about that," he growled. "You may be looking for another job soon."

Sure enough, when Rumsfeld began to broach the notion of a link to Israel in the meeting, the king made it clear that he was appalled at the idea. Rumsfeld had enough sense to drop the subject, for the moment at least. Uncharacteristically, he later grudgingly conceded to Viets that he had been right.

The following spring, Rumsfeld was back in Baghdad. The day he arrived, March 24, UPI quoted U.N. experts as reporting that Iraq had just used "mustard gas laced with a nerve agent" on Iranian troops. The administration had condemned Iraq's increasingly lavish use of chemical weapons a few weeks before, but, as Shultz explained to Rumsfeld in a secret cable, the condemnation had been more or less pro forma, and that "our interests in (1) preventing an Iranian victory and (2) continuing to improve bilateral relations with Iraq, at a pace of Iraq's choosing, remain undiminished. . . . This message bears reinforcing during your discussions."[4]

Rumsfeld was apparently happy to reassure his hosts that they should not take objections to what would one day be called weapons of mass destruction personally. He was certainly enthusiastic in promoting business deals between Saddam and Israel. Not only was he still pursuing the pipeline idea, now he had a fresh and altogether novel proposal. On his way to Baghdad, he and Lawrence Silberman, a former diplomat and close friend who was assisting him in his mission, had stopped in Jerusalem, where Israeli foreign minister Itzak Shamir had asked them to take a letter to Saddam offering to sell him weapons. Rumsfeld readily agreed and duly tried to hand the letter to Tariq Aziz when he arrived in Baghdad. Howard Teicher, an NSC staffer traveling with Rumsfeld, later submitted an affidavit for a court case in which he described what happened: "I . . . was present at the meeting in which Rumsfeld told Iraqi Foreign Minister Tariq Aziz about Israel's offer of assistance. Aziz refused even to take the Israelis' letter to [Saddam] Hussein . . . [he] told us that he would be executed on the spot by Hussein if he did so."[5]

Two months after his last trip to Baghdad, Rumsfeld resigned, leaving the Middle East no nearer to peace, though the reopening of relations with Iraq now appeared as a positive note on his résumé. Saddam, eager for help against the advancing Iranians, had hardly been a difficult catch, but it sounded good at the time. In any case, now that aspartame was safely launched, there was the important business of selling G.D. Searle to be taken care of. Once that was done, he could again set his sights on the ultimate prize, the White House.

Rumsfeld's presidential run, which formally lasted from May 1986, when he set up a political action committee, to April 1987, has never received much attention in accounts of his career. He is probably happy with that, given the abject failure of his bid and the concurrent victory of the man he had schemed to marginalize in 1975—George H. W. Bush. Yet this campaign was not a casual effort, but the culmination of twenty years of calculation, fueled by ego, ambition, and the constant drip of public comment on Rumsfeld's glowing political prospects. Reviewing those prospects when Rumsfeld first declared his candidacy, a veteran Chicago political reporter wrote that Rumsfeld was a "textbook case" of the "Presidential fever" that "burns in the gut" of ambitious politicians.

For strategic advice, Rumsfeld turned to his old mentor, Richard Nixon. At that time, Republican leaders in Illinois and Washington were looking for someone to run for the Senate against the popular Democratic incumbent Alan Dixon. Party elders in the state assured Rumsfeld he stood a good chance of winning, and that even if he didn't, the publicity would help a presidential bid. One senior official brazenly cited the precedent of Abraham Lincoln, who won the presidency in the aftermath of his narrow loss in his 1858 Senate race against Stephen Douglass.

Nixon disparaged these blandishments. He distrusted gradualist tactics, having long brooded on the losing bid for the governorship of California in 1962 that derailed his political comeback for many years. Did Rumsfeld, he asked, want to be president or a senator? President, responded Rumsfeld promptly. In that case, said Nixon, he should forget about the Senate and aim straight for the White House.[6]

It was advice that fit with Rumsfeld's own inclinations. "Don could never have stood the Senate anyway," one of his former White House colleagues told me, "being one hundredth of a decision wasn't much to his taste." By the end of that year his PAC, Citizens for American Values, had managed to raise $804,000 and Rumsfeld was dutifully commuting to states such as Michigan, Iowa, and New Hampshire, where the early battles would take place.[7] By January 1987, he had already visited New Hampshire seven times and had altogether forayed to thirty states, making 185 "city visits." He rented expensive office space in downtown Chicago to house his headquarters.

Even by those days, the business of electioneering had become highly specialized. Ambitious politicians competed for the services of campaign professionals to guide them through the electoral labyrinth. Rumsfeld saw no such need, building his campaign staff largely out of those who had served him loyally at G.D. Searle. As campaign manager he recruited Bernard Windon, vice president for communications and government affairs at the NutraSweet division of G.D. Searle, where he had worked for the previous fifteen years. Windon's political experience did not extend much beyond a spell on Howard Baker's long-shot presidential campaign in 1979, but he did possess the prime requisite: loyalty to Rumsfeld. In the background were some of the old band of brothers from New Trier, including Ned Jannotta, who had given him a berth at his banking firm, Blair & Co., when he first left Searle.

This tightly knit Chicago group did appreciate that they needed some prestigious outside support. Who better than the man who had stood at Rumsfeld's side in the White House, overseeing the entire federal government, Richard B. Cheney?

With George W. Bush occupying the White House, the precise nature of the relationship between Donald Rumsfeld and Dick Cheney has become a question of global fascination. There has been little dispute that these two men have operated as a partnership in leading the country into unknown and dangerous territory. Few people have known that this fateful relationship has been far more fractious than the world at large has understood.

While Rumsfeld had abandoned Washington for business in

1977, though dreaming that he would one day return, Cheney had stayed in politics. In 1978 he managed to get elected to Congress from Wyoming and had spent the following years crafting a reputation as a forceful and serious-minded right-winger without destroying his credibility among moderates, who did not seem to hold his votes against Head Start and the Martin Luther King holiday against him. Slowly but nonetheless surely, he was making his way up the ladder of the congressional Republican Party. As the senior House Republican on the congressional Iran-contra investigation, he performed valiant service in fending off overly inquisitive Democrats. By the time Cheney left Congress, his peers had elected him minority whip, a leadership post that had remained beyond the reach of Donald Rumsfeld. He even, reportedly, had some wistful conversations about making his own run for the '88 nomination.

Once upon a time, Cheney had been described as devoting his life "to the service of Donald Rumsfeld." When Rumsfeld requested Cheney's assistance for the presidential campaign, he was acting on the assumption that this was still the case.

In spite of the enormous shadows these men would together cast across the United States and the world, this crucial moment has never been revealed or discussed. One of the few Rumsfeld aides privy to the conversation describes what happened, relying on Rumsfeld's subsequent description for Cheney's end of the conversation.

According to this account, Rumsfeld said, "Dick, as you know, I am shortly announcing that I am a candidate for the nomination, and I am counting on your support." "Don," Cheney answered, "there are many things you can ask of me, but I've moved on politically since we worked together in the White House, so I'm afraid I cannot do what you ask."

"Everything you are, I've made you," replied Rumsfeld. "You owe everything to me."

"I've had to make my own way since seventy-seven," said Cheney. "I would do anything for you, but not this."

And that was that. Cheney went on to campaign hard for George H. W. Bush and was ultimately rewarded with the post of secretary of defense in that administration. Rumsfeld, according to a former colleague, was deeply shocked by his former subordinate's rejection. "It was a definite rift, I don't think they even spoke for a number of years. I guess by the time Bush 43 was elected the wounds of yester-year had healed somewhat, but the scar must still be there." For any-one watching, there was a telling indication of the breach during Cheney's tenure at the Pentagon. It is a tradition for secretaries of defense, as well as other high officials, to invite "formers," individ-uals who have had the same job, to come to the Pentagon and offer their support and advice to the current incumbent. Dick Cheney fol-lowed this tradition. Rumsfeld never showed up.

Bereft of the support of his once faithful underling, Rumsfeld set off on his quest. The polls were not encouraging, and did not change. In January 1986, the Gallup poll put his support among Republicans at 1 percent, far at the back of a crowded field led by Vice President Bush. By March he had edged up to 2 percent, his peak, after which he sank back to 1 percent again, and stayed there. There seemed little reason for his standing to increase. While George Bush's campaign style was once memorably described as "Janis Joplin in pinstripes," Rumsfeld on the stump was reported as being "as colorful as a CEO's wardrobe" and in danger of being mistaken for a Secret Service agent.

His themes, so far as they were recorded, seem to have been somewhat pedestrian. He told Republicans that "the biggest single reason" for the Iran-contra scandal, which involved the profits from secret weapons sales to Iran being used secretly to aid the Nicaraguan contras, was that the president had changed national security advisers too often. He promised maximum support for missile defense in a Rumsfeld administration. He was "personally opposed" to abortion, but unsure about sponsoring a constitutional amendment to ban it.[8]

Reality seems to have dawned suddenly. He quit the race on Thursday, April 3, 1987, although Joyce had been campaigning around Iowa on his behalf just four days earlier. Only the week before he had been part of a "cattle call" with other candidates in a New York hotel, and he was due to hold a major fund-raiser in Chicago in early May, for which tickets had already been printed.

His explanation—or excuse—for pulling out was poverty. "For a dark horse," he explained in a letter sent to friends and supporters, "the probable imbalance of revenues and expenses early in the campaign raises the specter of a deficit of several million dollars. . . . As a matter of principle, I will not run a deficit." When Secretary of State George Shultz asked him why he'd quit, Rumsfeld told him, "I concluded that I could either raise money or run for president. I couldn't do both."[9]

"He didn't get any money from the Ford White House people," chortled Bill Seidman, the acid-tongued former economic policy chief, when we discussed the campaign. "No one would give him a single penny." In other interviews he spoke movingly of the five years it took him to pay off the debt of his first congressional campaign—which is surprising, considering the deep pockets of his supporters in the North Shore plutocracy—as well as an affecting conversation he'd held with Senator John Glenn, who spoke of sleepless nights worrying about the debt he still carried from his own abortive White House campaign some years before. Rumsfeld was so moved by Glenn's tale of woe that he and Joyce immediately both wrote checks for $1,000 to help alleviate the famous astronaut's burden.

Others have alternate interpretations of the debacle. Former congressman Ed Derwinski, a power broker in Illinois politics over several decades, suggested that Rumsfeld's size was a contributory factor. "It's a fact," he assured me, "that taller candidates tend to do better than the mini-sized ones. Rummy is relatively short so he looked small on stages alongside all those guys like Bush and Kemp and Dole. Rummy was the runt."

There is a more intriguing explanation of Rumsfeld's failure to make even the slightest impact in the race that he had dreamed about for so long. This version was described to me by one of the few professional electioneers consulted by Rumsfeld in 1986 and 1987.

"Over the years, I must have known thirty guys who wanted the White House," this vastly experienced political operative told me in 2006. "Of all of them, he was the most naive. Most candidates for the nomination really immerse themselves in the nuts and bolts of the process. By the time they get going they can tell you everything anyone needs to know about the Iowa caucus system or building up donor lists. Some of them can tell you more than anyone needs to know, but not Rumsfeld. He just hadn't bothered to study that stuff. I figure that he had decided he was so smart that he didn't need to know the details. It was just shocking."

Asked for an example of such politically shocking naïveté, this individual recalled a conversation in which Rumsfeld had spoken airily of the Illinois primary, which would be held months later in March 1988, in which he expected to "break through." The adviser was amazed.

"'Are you kidding?'" he recalled saying. "'If you're not one or two in New Hampshire, you're dead in the water.' These are the simplest things, and he didn't understand them. He thought he did. He'd been talking about it for so long, he thought he knew it all, and he knew he never made mistakes. I guess it's hard to learn when you've never made a mistake."

Having withdrawn from the race, Rumsfeld was free to endorse one of the other candidates. Among Republicans, George Bush led by a wide margin in the polls. But Senator Bob Dole of Kansas, the man who had secured the coveted slot as Ford's running mate in 1976, scored an upset by solidly defeating Bush in the Iowa caucuses. Rumsfeld promptly endorsed Dole as his choice for the nomination.

Bush went on to win the 1988 election and, as usual, there was ill-informed speculation that Rumsfeld would be offered a senior cabinet post. One of those who paid attention to the rumors was Milt Pitts, the longtime presidential barber, who was summoned to give the president-elect a trim soon after the victory. "Pitts had always liked Rumsfeld," a former White House official explained in recounting the ensuing conversation.

"I've heard that Don Rumsfeld might be secretary of defense," said Pitts brightly as he snipped away. "Have you heard that, Mr. Vice President?"

"No, Milt," said Bush in a low, chilly voice. "I haven't heard that."

Rumsfeld himself was ready to settle for something less. Writing to congratulate Bush on his victory, he stated that he would "like to be your Ambassador to Japan." An official in the Bush transition office processing such requests found that the letter had already been reviewed at a high level. Scrawled across it were the words "NO! THIS WILL NEVER HAPPEN!! GB."

Rumsfeld was offered no position in the administration of George H. W. Bush.

A few months after the inauguration, Donald Rumsfeld was invited to play the role of president of the United States in an exercise devised by a Washington think tank. In this scenario, "President" Rumsfeld was intent on securing congressional approval to go to war. "I don't care what you tell them," he barked at White House chief of staff Ed Markey, "just get over to Capitol Hill and make them do it, and make sure there are no constraints."

"It was an exercise devised by the Center for Strategic and International Studies [CSIS] to study the functioning of the War Powers Act," recalled Markey, a liberal Democratic congressman from Massachusetts. "We acted out roles. I accepted the role of chief of staff because I figured that was my only shot at the job." Rumsfeld may have felt the same way. At the age of fifty-seven he appears to have concluded that if he could no longer realistically aspire to be president, he could at least act the part.

By all accounts "President" Rumsfeld played his role in that 1989 exercise for CSIS with great gusto, raging at the obdurate Congress and deploying the "White House spokesman" (played by the venerable broadcast journalist Daniel Schorr) to maneuver the press into supporting his martial position. But this Washington exercise was a comparatively lighthearted affair compared to Rumsfeld's role in games that were far more elaborate, and deeply secret. Well away from journalists and others lacking highly restricted security clearances, he could perform not merely as a chief executive, but one faced with the awesome responsibility of waging nuclear war.

The games were designed to test a program known as COG, Continuity of Government, and they concerned the ability of the government to continue to function during and after a nuclear attack. Everything about these exercises was secret. "There are seven levels of classification used in the government," one former senior Pentagon official told me when I raised the subject. "You are asking about the most secret level of all." Plans to enable the government to survive a nuclear attack dated back to the early days of the cold war, when vast bunkers were excavated in the countryside around Washington in which the various organs of government could take shelter. At least one of these, in the rural Virginia town of Culpeper, was even supplied with Barbie dolls for the diversion of officials' children sitting out the war underground. Over the years, these efforts became ever more elaborate, and of course vastly more expensive. A major development occurred in the early 1980s, when Ronald Reagan was sold not only on the notion of a missile defense shield, but also on the practicality of fighting a prolonged strategic nuclear war, lasting up to six months. This decision lent added emphasis to the need for keeping the machinery of government going amid the radioactive ruins.

In consequence, the money allocated for COG began to soar to previously undreamed-of heights. A prime architect of the revised system has disclosed to me that the budget hit $1 billion a year by the end of Reagan's first term. Lending intellectual weight to this costly initiative was Andrew Marshall, an influential defense intellectual who had first crossed paths with Rumsfeld when he was secretary of defense. Early in the Reagan years, Marshall predicted that a "weakening" Soviet Union might lash out in a surprise nuclear attack, thus necessitating the extensive facilities in which Rumsfeld was invited to exercise his postapocalypse leadership skills.

Marshall and others had long maintained that the Soviet strategy involved "decapitation" of the U.S. leadership, and that therefore some of the first warheads would land on Washington, very possibly obliterating the president and other senior officials. COG planners therefore began training teams of individuals experienced in national security matters who would be ready to take over and resurrect some sort of government. The teams were divided up by function, one for the Defense Department, one for the State Department, a third for the White House, and so on.

This highly secret program was known as Project 908, and among the individuals earmarked to take power when disaster struck was Donald Rumsfeld. Every so often he would disappear from his Chicago office, leaving no word of where he was headed, or why. Once off the map, he would be moved on a military transport to one of the secret headquarters created as part of the COG network. There, for several days, he would be immured in artificial caverns, staring at electronic displays streaming data of disaster and confusion, sleeping on cots and subsisting on the most austere rations. As often as not, players who had been brought to the locations on planes with blacked-out windows had no idea where they were. A participant in one exercise recalled that "we knew we were in the South, because the people serving the food had Southern accents, but that was all."

Rumsfeld loved these games. There were others who were frequent players in the exercises, notably Dick Cheney. "Cheney and the others often had other priorities," recalls the former Pentagon official. "Rumsfeld always came." He wasn't just trying to organize a devastated country. He was fighting World War III, or at least simulating what nuclear theory suggested such a conflict would be like.

Herein lies an aspect of Rumsfeld's career—and character—that remained deeply buried even after word of his participation in the COG exercises leaked out. Faced with the most awesome choices a simulated environment could present, placed in a situation that was designed and advertised as a rehearsal for what might one day be terrifyingly real, Rumsfeld had one primary response. He always tried to unleash the maximum amount of nuclear firepower possible.

The teams taking part in the game were presented with two main tasks: reconstitution of some sort of working government, and retaliation against whoever had inflicted the disaster. The first of these, reconstruction, was generally considered the most urgent. But this part, according to fellow players, did not interest Rumsfeld. "He always wanted to move on to retaliation as quickly as possible," recalls a former senior official in the office of the secretary of defense, "he was one who always went for the extreme option."

A former participant, enlisted to take the role of a senior national security official, described how his "war" began with a limited Soviet attack in Europe. "It seemed quite possible to defuse the crisis," he recalled, stressing that the State Department "team" was working to avoid an all-out thermonuclear exchange. Rumsfeld, however, had a different agenda. From the outset, this participant remembers, the once and future defense secretary was determined to "launch everything we had left" at the entire communist bloc, Russians and Chinese together.

The individual playing the part of secretary of state, however, a canny retired diplomat, was no less determined to stop Rumsfeld from obliterating several million people. Using every tactic and stratagem he had learned over the course of a long career, the diplomat waged bureaucratic warfare over the postnuclear communications system linking the secret hideouts. As an added note of realism, the State Department official playing the role of deputy to the "secretary" evidently thought that his real-life career would be enhanced by supporting Rumsfeld, and therefore did his best surreptitiously to undermine his notional superior. Even so, the diplomat ultimately prevailed. The northern hemisphere survived. Rumsfeld, deeply chagrined at having lost the argument, never forgave his antagonist.

Of course, immured in the COG bunkers, Rumsfeld and his fellow players were not enacting anything based on real experience (apart from familiar routines of bureaucratic backstabbing). Nuclear conflict existed *only* as a game. In fact, the theorists who worked on nuclear strategy were fond of quoting what they called game theory. No one had the slightest idea of what might actually happen in a nuclear war. Even the known "facts" were anything but. Plans based on tidy predictions of the explosive power or "yield" of various weapons, for example, were belied by tests in which the results often varied wildly from forecasts, as did the accuracy and reliability of intercontinental missiles, which were never tested in operational conditions. Such awkward realities never featured in nuclear war planning, let alone the scenarios concocted by the nuclear theoreticians for the games.

Hopefully, we will never know how any politician, let alone Rumsfeld, would act when presented with the option of launching nuclear weapons in real life. Unfortunately, we do know how Rumsfeld reacted to the option of attacking a country with conventional forces and overthrowing its government. We shall be examining the invasion and occupation of Iraq in later chapters, but it is worth comparing Rumsfeld's behavior in the COG games with his performance in a real war. As we shall see, the casual, maybe even irresponsible decisions taken in that war reflect attitudes and reactions better suited to an elaborate game, from which real-life costs and consequences are excluded.

Insofar as the COG games gave the illusion of reality, they taught Rumsfeld and his fellow players some dangerous lessons, particularly when the fall of the Soviet Union induced some changes in the usual scenarios. Although the exercises continued, still budgeted at over $200 million a year in the Clinton era, the vanished Soviets were now customarily replaced by terrorists. The terrorism envisaged, however, was almost always state-sponsored. Terrorists were never autonomous, but invariably acted on behalf of a government. "That was the conventional wisdom," recalled retired air force colonel Sam Gardner, who has designed dozens of war games for the Pentagon and related entities. "Behind the terrorist, there was always something bigger, and the games reflected that."

There were other changes, too. In earlier times the specialists selected to run the "shadow government" had been drawn from across the political spectrum, Democrats and Republicans alike. But now, down in the bunkers, Rumsfeld found himself in politically congenial company, the players' roster being filled almost exclusively with Republican hawks.

"It was one way for these people to stay in touch. They'd meet, do the exercise, but also sit around and castigate the Clinton administration in the most extreme way," a former Pentagon official with direct knowledge of the phenomenon told me. "You could say this was a secret government-in-waiting. The Clinton administration was extraordinarily inattentive, [they had] no idea what was going on."

When not playing at World War III, Rumsfeld was off making more money. In 1990, Theodore Forstmann, a leveraged-buyout entrepreneur, recruited him to run the General Instrument Corporation, which he had recently acquired for $1.5 billion. The company's principal business was in cable TV equipment, though it had other disparate offshoots. Repeating his Searle experience, Rumsfeld sold off subsidiaries and slashed headquarters staff. By the time he left in 1993, the company's market value, according to a grateful Forstmann, had increased to over $3.8 billion. Rumsfeld's own total take was $23 million before taxes.[10] Thus his reputation as a tough, capable manager was bolstered along with his bank account. Closer examination indicates that his General Instrument experience was similar to his approach at Searle. TV transmission was a regulation-rich environment, especially as the company was heavily invested in its version of the new high-definition TV technology, as were rivals with their own technologies. The decision on which technology should become the American standard lay in the hands of the FCC. Reporting on Rumsfeld's leadership at the company, Crain's *Chicago Business* commented, "Mr. Rumsfeld's connections in Washington, D.C., won't hurt. A master of capital politics, he played a key role at Searle in winning regulatory approval for the smash sugar substitute NutraSweet."[11]

General Instrument's rival in the competition for government endorsement of its HDTV standard was the Zenith Corporation. Rumsfeld solved the problem by arranging a peace pact with his opposite number at Zenith: whoever won the competition would share royalties with the loser. "The two companies," said one trade journal, "are relying, in part, on the high visibility and clout of GI President and CEO Donald Rumsfeld, a former Illinois congressman who held key positions in the administrations of former Presidents Richard Nixon and Gerald Ford."[12] Once again, politics would come to the aid of business.

That was Rumsfeld's last foray as a CEO. He was now extremely wealthy—by the end of the decade he would be worth between $50 million and $200 million. He acquired a private jet and a spread in Taos, New Mexico, where his favorite form of relaxation was to go out and chainsaw the lower branches of trees. "The best time you can have," he once remarked, "is with a chainsaw. I'll come back in, my arms will just be vibrating from it, but I love it."[13]

As a wealthy investor, Rumsfeld was invited to join many boards of directors, sometimes even taking on the job of chairman, as he did with the biomedical firm Gilead Sciences. His government connections would certainly have been an asset to corporations such as the Swiss construction giant ABB. He sat on the ABB board for ten years, starting in 1991, earning $190,000 a year. When the company bid successfully to sell two light-water nuclear reactors to North

Korea, Rumsfeld was reported in news accounts as having lobbied in Washington to get the deal approved. Later, when he was secretary of defense, and denouncing North Korea as a terrorist regime, his spokesman said Rumsfeld "could not recall" the reactor sale being discussed by the ABB board of directors at any time.[14]

In 1990, Rumsfeld had floated a trial balloon for a possible run for the Illinois governorship. It went nowhere, one more failure in the long series of disappointments stretching back to 1976. The Republican Party was in the hands of his antagonists, George Bush and James Baker, and he was nearing retirement age in any case. But in 1994, control changed hands. Led by the seemingly iconoclastic Newt Gingrich, a fiercely partisan right-wing faction seized control of Congress. These were people with whom Rumsfeld could do business. He had watched the rise of Gingrich, to whom he became close, and the general Republican onslaught, with a deep attention that was often expressed in cash. He had always been a generous provider to candidates of his party, but from 1995 onward he began donating considerable sums to the party itself. Over the next five years he pumped $99,000 in soft money donations to the Republican National Committee, quite enough to secure him a measure of influence.[15]

Rumsfeld's accelerating largesse to the Republicans coincided with the fading aura of his former nemesis in the party, George H. W. Bush. In his place, a new Bush was emerging, George W. Bush, who turned from a lackluster career in the oil business and the front man for a baseball franchise to win election as governor of Texas in 1994. The rise of the former president's younger son took many people by surprise, including perhaps some in his own family. As she watched young George's victory confirmed on election night, his mother, Barbara, turned to a friend sitting beside her, and remarked in stupefied amazement, "Can you believe this?"

Gingrich had spelled out his public program in a "Contract with America" before the election. The only clause in the contract addressing foreign or defense policy was a call for the rapid deployment of a missile defense system. There were those who suggested that with the collapse of the Soviet Union, there was no longer any immediate missile threat to the United States, a view endorsed by the

CIA in a 1995 National Intelligence Estimate. This conclusion was highly unpalatable to the defense lobby; without a missile threat, there was no case for missile defense. In 1997, therefore, Congress mandated the creation of a Commission to Assess the Ballistic Missile Threat to the United States. Sponsoring this initiative were a group of congressional staffers closely associated with the neoconservative Project for the New American Century (PNAC), which fused support for Israel with a determinedly hawkish stand on U.S. security policy. Their chosen candidate to run the commission was Donald Rumsfeld.

Assisting him in this work was one of the leading neoconservative defense intellectuals, Paul Wolfowitz. While Rumsfeld had spent the bulk of his time since the Ford administration in business and electoral politics, Wolfowitz had stayed in government, or close to it. Though he always carried the demeanor of an affable, absent-minded academic, this posture masked the personality of an ambitious bureaucrat. In the late 1970s, for example, while occupying a relatively minor post in the Pentagon, he discovered that his secretary was a close friend of her counterpart in the office of Harold Brown, secretary of defense. Wolfowitz employed this intelligence channel to alert him whenever Dr. Brown headed for a workout in the Pentagon gym, whereupon he himself would hasten to the gym for an informal encounter with the boss. Despite this high-level access, his policy proposals were not always taken seriously. Following the detention of American diplomats as hostages by the Iranian revolutionary regime in 1979, Wolfowitz conceived a plan to launch an attack on Iran across the Zagros Mountains from eastern Turkey. "Everyone laughed," a fellow Pentagon official of that era told me. By the time of the 1989–93 Bush administration, when he served as under-secretary of defense for policy, Wolfowitz had developed his passionate interest in Iraq, though his supervisors in the administration rejected his urgings to prolong the 1991 Gulf War in order to destroy Saddam Hussein's regime.

Wolfowitz and Rumsfeld had an opportunity to deepen their bonds during the presidential campaign of 1996, in which President Bill Clinton was running for reelection. As the Republican candidacy of Senator Bob Dole lurched toward defeat, Rumsfeld (who had briefly entertained thoughts of running himself) managed to insert himself into a commanding role in the campaign, enlisting Wolfowitz as an assistant. Almost immediately, candidate Dole adopted an extremely hawkish line on foreign policy and defense issues. This approach found little traction with the electorate, which handed Clinton a resounding victory.

Other members of the commission, with some exceptions, were no less typecast as fervent advocates of an aggressive defense policy. Chris Williams, a congressional staffer who had helped draft the legislation sponsoring the commission, introduced Rumsfeld to a defense intellectual named Stephen Cambone. Taking to the young man, who had spent his career in the crowded national security bureaucracy/think tank field, Rumsfeld appointed him commission staff director. It was the birth of a potent relationship.

As an exercise in policy manipulation, the missile commission was a great success. Its report, submitted in July 1998, concluded that America faced a growing threat from "rogue" nations armed with ballistic missiles that could reach the United States. The principal threats were North Korea, Iran, and Iraq—the trio that would later be notoriously labeled the "axis of evil." In methodology, the commission followed the precedent of Team B, with an overlay of Rumsfeld's customary ill-mannered interruption and dismissal of witnesses whose information he found unpalatable. Rather than unearthing any new intelligence to support their conclusions, the commission simply reinterpreted existing intelligence from a worst-case point of view.

However threadbare its intellectual underpinnings, the operation had the desired effect, partly because the North Koreans cooperated by testing a three-stage missile, the Taepodong I, six weeks after the report's release. (The test was actually a failure, but few paid attention to that.) The conclusions were enthusiastically greeted on Capitol Hill, where the Republicans celebrated by passing the National Missile Defense Act, which President Clinton dutifully signed. The CIA obligingly changed its position and announced that, contrary to its previous estimates, North Korea might test an intercontinental missile "at any time." Such accommodating behavior by the agency would soon become a habit.

Rumsfeld had done such yeoman service for the missile defense business that the beneficiaries soon had him back at work. In 1999, another congressional initiative authorized a Commission to Assess United States National Security Space Management and Organization, with Rumsfeld at the helm. This commission paid even less deference to bipartisan discourse than the previous effort. Commissioners and staff were almost exclusively drawn from the aerospace industry that would benefit from any increase in military spending in space.

For Rumsfeld, this must have been almost a sentimental journey. Over three decades earlier, he had striven to make his mark as a newcomer in Congress by warning of the Soviet drive to dominate "inner space." Now, with Stephen Cambone again serving at his side as staff director, he returned to familiar themes. America, a "spacefaring nation," he reported, must acquire the ability to "project power through and from space in response to events anywhere in the world." Should it fail to do so, the country faced a "space Pearl Harbor."

Rumsfeld's return to space was not the only element of circularity in his life at that time. The day he submitted his report, January 11, 2001, was the same day he sat, once again, in front of the Senate Armed Services Committee for hearings on his nomination to be secretary of defense in the administration of George W. Bush. He was now sixty-eight years old.

Nine days later, at one of the glittering balls held around Washington to celebrate Bush's inauguration, an old friend from Chicago encountered a beaming Rumsfeld. "Can you believe it?" the friend remembers him exclaiming excitedly. "I've got another chance!"

CHAPTER SIX

From Notion
to Bumper Sticker

In the early summer of 2000, a friend asked Rumsfeld his opinion of Dick Cheney, recently unveiled as George Bush's running mate in the presidential election. "He wears easily on you" was Rumsfeld's dismissive answer. Clearly, relations between the former colleagues were still comparatively distant. Nine months later, Rumsfeld had vaulted from the political fringe to secretary of defense designate and outsiders assumed that one of the old partners from the Nixon and Ford White Houses had reached out for the other, reaffirming a bond that had existed since 1969. As we know, that bond had been strained for some years. Old friend or not, Donald Rumsfeld got the job by default.

The Bush team had initially settled on former senator Dan Coats (R-Ind.) as their choice for the Pentagon. Coats had served on the Armed Services Committee, giving him at least the pretense of defense expertise. This, and more important, his Christian fundamentalist credentials and other ties to the Republican right, were considered adequate qualifications for the post. But just when all was set for an official announcement, a meeting between Coats and the president-elect went badly enough for Bush and Cheney to start looking elsewhere for a secretary of defense.[1]

It is commonly believed that the former senator failed the job interview only because he gave the impression that he would be little match in internal debates with Colin Powell, already nominated for secretary of state. Equally significant, according to sources close to the former senator, Coats wrecked his chances by letting drop that he did not consider missile defense an urgent priority. As an afterthought he indicated unhappiness with the presence of women in combat-related roles, which he intended to curtail.

For Bush and Cheney, such thoughts about missile defense were rank and unacceptable heresy. Rumsfeld's missile commission had helped restore the concept to priority status. Deployment of missile defense would remove constraints on U.S. power supposedly imposed by third-world missile powers such as North Korea. Bush had campaigned on a pledge to build a Star Wars system as soon as possible, regardless of any international treaties. So far as Bush and Cheney were concerned, Coats had talked himself out of the administration. They had little quarrel with the man's views on women, but they could foresee these would inevitably whip up an unnecessary political storm.

With less than a month to go before the inauguration, they needed to find a defense secretary quickly, and in this crisis, Cheney's thoughts turned to his former friend and colleague who, until then, had been under consideration for the directorship of the CIA. It was not an automatic choice. "I remember Cheney called me to talk about Don in the context of the Pentagon," a former senior national security official told me. "He was quite dispassionate about him, I certainly got no impression that he was making a special effort for an old friend."

On December 28, Rumsfeld responded to an invitation to visit the president-elect at his temporary headquarters in the Madison Hotel in Washington, apparently unaware of the central role he was about to be offered in the new government. It was an extraordinary moment in the lives of the two men. Fourteen years apart in age, they belonged to different generations. There is little indication that their paths had crossed much before.

For George Bush Jr., a salient fact about the man walking into his hotel suite was that he and his father hated each other. Bush would have known all the stories of that relationship, dating back to

Nixon-era rivalries and Rumsfeld's attempt to sabotage his father's political career in 1975. Rumsfeld, on the other hand, was almost certainly well aware that the two Bushes had a difficult relationship. Stories abounded of confrontations between the two, as in the episode when the son offered to go "mano a mano" with his father during an altercation over the young man's drinking.[2] Presumably in consequence, job seekers in the new administration who sought help from the father got no joy. "A phone call from me wouldn't do you any good," the forty-first president told one old friend who had sought his intercession with the forty-third. "You might have more luck with Barbara."

Distanced from his actual father, the younger Bush had evinced a pattern of adopting father figures. Back in Texas, Lieutenant Governor Bob Bullock had occupied this role. Despite being a Democrat, he had nurtured and guided George W. Bush even before Bush became governor and continued to serve as a mentor until his death in 1999 at the age of seventy. That was around the same time that "W" forged his bond with Richard Cheney, who was to play Bullock's part on a far larger stage. Now he was embarking on a close relationship with Rumsfeld, one that was perhaps warmed by the tensions in the triangular relationship.

Close acquaintances of both Rumsfeld and George W. Bush agree that they share a gift for "emotional intelligence," an ability to size a person up and, in an instant, discern their weaknesses and vulnerabilities. This gift had served Rumsfeld well since the days when he had befriended first his wealthier contemporaries in high school, and then their fathers. He had used it to good effect in maneuvering Richard Nixon into accepting him as a protégé. Now, in the most important encounter of his life, he played to the younger man's most important underlying feature, his insecurity. Rumsfeld perceived that Bush above all things needed reassurance that despite his previous lack of experience or accomplishment, he was fit for command. In return, Bush could give what Rumsfeld customarily exacted from close associates: loyalty and obedience. One person familiar with both Bush and Rumsfeld suggested that the younger man may have been "intimidated" by Rumsfeld. "He's a very strong personality, with that way of putting you down, putting you off-balance."

So perceptive was Rumsfeld in his assessment of Bush that the bond he established at the dawn of the administration, which would only be strengthened by the trauma of 9/11, would endure through years of disaster and embarrassment. It was a relationship that would enable Rumsfeld to change the president's mind on issues in public, to ignore decisions that he found inconvenient, and to survive repeated attempts by powerful enemies seeking to bring him down.

In the Middle Ages, they used to call people in this position "over-mighty subjects." Rumsfeld, a failure as a democratic politician, should be remembered as one of history's great courtiers. His success in this capacity was highlighted by the failure of a rival who had hitherto enjoyed a brilliant career in palace politics. Colin Powell had risen to great heights in previous administrations thanks to his efficient deference in the service of powerful patrons, most importantly defense secretary Casper Weinberger, whose executive assistant he had been in the 1980s. Having scaled those heights, Powell believed that his poll ratings as "the most respected man in America" had made his position unassailable. So, on December 16, 2001, when President-elect Bush introduced him to the press as his choice to lead the State Department, Powell felt free to launch into a lecture on the state of the world and what he was going to do about it. The story of Powell's relations with the White House over the following four years is prefigured in the tape of that event. As Powell happily proceeds with his lengthy discourse, Bush's expression gradually shifts from respectful admiration to bored irritation while his supposed subordinate dominates the stage as if he, not Bush, were the newly elected president. Powell always had difficulty disguising his assessment of the younger Bush. The distinction was summed up by one observant Washington power broker: "Powell worked *for* forty-one. He worked *with* forty-three."

Rumsfeld, on the other hand, was careful to ensure that Bush Jr. would never for one instant wonder which of them was supposed to be president.

Twenty-two years earlier, following another meeting at the Madison Hotel to discuss aspartame, attorney Jim Turner had concluded that Rumsfeld was "a fixer, an operative, you assign him a job and he does it." Now Rumsfeld was being assigned a job, not just to oversee the Pentagon but to execute policies on defense already spelled out by Bush early in the campaign. In September 1999, the candidate had given a speech at the Citadel in Charleston, South Carolina. Stage-managed by Cheney, the speech had been designed to establish Bush's national security credentials by announcing a plan to transform the U.S. military. After invoking the allegedly threadbare condition of the military under Democratic rule, the candidate outlined the defense policy of a future Bush administration. He would deploy an antiballistic missile system "at the earliest possible date." He promised an "immediate, comprehensive review of our military" that would "challenge the status quo" and "replace existing programs with new technologies and strategies" that would "skip a generation of technology," rendering U.S. forces "agile, lethal, readily deployable" and able to "strike from across the world with pinpoint accuracy" and even fight in space. All this was made possible by a recent "revolution in the technology of war."[3]

Anyone familiar with the jargon of defense theory could have detected the influence of Andrew Marshall, the former Rand analyst who had displayed a genius for bureaucratic durability in heading up the Pentagon's Office of Net Assessment ever since 1973. He had impressed Rumsfeld when the pair first encountered each other in 1975, and at his ceremonial welcoming to the Pentagon on January 26, 2001, Rumsfeld went out of his way to acknowledge two old associates: "Doc" Cook, the defense secretaries' internal watchdog, and Marshall.

Marshall had long perfected the knack, pioneered by his peers at Rand, of proposing what appeared to be wildly unconventional ideas but which somehow ended up bolstering military budgets in one way or another. Hence his long survival in the bowels of the Pentagon, where his tenure would have been abruptly terminated had he posed any serious threat to military service missions and programs. His argument that if the Soviets were in terminal decline, the nuclear war budget (i.e., COG) should be boosted, serves as a case in point. As the Soviet Union vanished from the pages of history, Marshall had obligingly promoted a new threat, China, and Bush's Citadel speech duly included an allusion to the nefarious designs of the People's Republic.

Early in the 1980s, Marshall began talking about "the Revolution in Military Affairs." The notion was that newly developed technologies in surveillance, communication, and missile accuracy had fundamentally changed the nature of warfare, making it possible to wage war around the world by remote control, striking at will at enemies far away who could be located, identified, and eliminated at the touch of a button, as in a—very expensive—video game.

This prospect was alluring enough to obscure the real-world performance of these vaunted new technologies, which tended to be unimpressive. Task Force Alpha, an early experiment consisting of an electronic fence of computer-linked sensors deployed across the Ho Chi Minh Trail during the Vietnam War, had no effect on the southward flow of North Vietnamese troops and supplies and was quietly terminated $2.5 billion later.[4] Complex systems such as the F-117 stealth bomber and precision-guided bombs proved far less effective in the 1991 Gulf War than advertised, with the more expensive delivery systems providing no better results than cheaper alternatives.[5] As recently as 1999, the Serb army in Kosovo survived seventy-eight days of precision-guided bombardment virtually unscathed. Smiling Serbs retreated home, having neutralized the billion-dollar sensors deployed to seek them out by such stratagems as wooden decoy tanks and strips of black plastic laid out to look like roads. The countryside stank of rotting chicken corpses, as heat-seeking missiles had tended to mistake chicken coops for enemy vehicles. NATO commanders claimed to have destroyed over one hundred tanks. The verifiable figure turned out to be closer to thirteen.[6]

Such unwelcome realities found no place in Bush's rhetoric, or in that of Marshall's many disciples strewn across the defense establishment, and particularly among the ranks of martially minded neoconservatives. One such disciple was the principal author of the speech, Richard Armitage, a veteran of the Defense and State Departments in previous Republican administrations, who had expectations of moving into the deputy secretary of defense's office in a Bush administration. The assumption among Bush's advisers had been that he would supply the expertise on defense matters necessary to complement Coats's political connections, but that scheme fell apart when the senator's lack of faith in missile defense was exposed, along with his potential feebleness in the face of Colin Powell, and he was summarily discarded from consideration. Once selected in Coats's stead, Rumsfeld had no desire to have Armitage, who was known to be Secretary Powell's closest friend, in the office next door. Furthermore, as aggressively domineering characters, he and Armitage had a mutually repulsive effect. Thus Armitage, who prided himself on having helped chart the new administration's defense policy, would have to watch from the outside as Rumsfeld adopted the Citadel program as his own. "Armitage had spent years preparing to be deputy secretary of defense," one of his friends told me. "It was a bitter, bitter disappointment that he didn't get it." As consolation, he took the job of deputy secretary of state under Powell.

The post of deputy defense secretary is traditionally reserved for a managerial figure, in effect a chief operating officer, who supervises the day-to-day functions of the department and also maintains the all-important relationships with industry. Even so, the leading candidate, thanks to his support from the powerful neoconservative faction in the new administration, was Paul Wolfowitz. Wolfowitz infamously lacked managerial skills in general and experience of the defense industry in particular, apart from service as an intellectual enabler for increased defense spending in forums such as Team B. (Such service was not without reward. In 2000, for example, Hughes Electronics paid him $300,000 for his unstrenuous labors on the Nunn-Wolfowitz Commission, a Hughes damage-control effort following revelations of the company's thriving missile guidance technology trade with China.)

Wolfowitz's supporters, most importantly Vice President Cheney and his highly influential chief of staff Lewis "Scooter" Libby (who had been deputy to Wolfowitz in the Pentagon ten years before), assumed that his management deficiencies would be offset by Rumsfeld, the man whom everyone believed to be an efficient, no-nonsense administrator. One person who had his doubts about this arrangement was Rumsfeld himself, who hesitated on accepting the affable academic as his deputy. Wolfowitz, however, had a fallback offer from Cheney to go to New York as ambassador to the

United Nations, which he used to force a decision. "You have to decide now," he announced in a phone call, "or I'm going to the U.N." Pushed to the wall, Rumsfeld agreed.

This arrangement had a dangerous flaw. Wolfowitz anticipated a cerebral role in which he could chart high policy and grand strategy while Rumsfeld busied himself with more mundane tasks such as budgets and weapons procurement decisions. But Rumsfeld considered himself fully qualified to supervise the grander themes, and had no intention of ceding the role to Wolfowitz. The net result was that neither man paid the requisite attention to routine tasks of management and decision making, although Wolfowitz did make an effort to perform both. "Paul would stay until ten at night or later, doing the job that he should have been doing during the day," one of his former aides told me. "That meant his staff had to stay, too, so no one ever got to go home."

"Rumsfeld and Wolfowitz were always uneasy with each other," an official who had frequent contact with both men explained to me. "There was a cold atmosphere in meetings and they didn't see each other outside of working hours, didn't socialize." Wolfowitz, who is not short of intellectual arrogance himself, was conscious that Rumsfeld's attitude to him was fundamentally patronizing. Armitage grew used to receiving calls from Wolfowitz after their bosses had attended a Principals Committee meeting at the White House to ask what had happened, since Rumsfeld refused to tell him. Adding to the awkwardness was a decree enforced by Rumsfeld that the secretary and deputy secretary could not both be away from Washington at the same time. Hence Wolfowitz was frequently forced to cancel long-planned trips because Rumsfeld suddenly decided to take himself off, thus forcing his subordinate to stay behind and mind the store.

Things might have been different if Richard Perle had needed a paying job. The position of under-secretary of defense for policy, ranked third in the Pentagon hierarchy, was initially reserved for Perle. Perle shared Wolfowitz's neoconservative ideology, but Rumsfeld also had great respect for the ruthless cold warrior who had fought by his side in the long-ago battles over détente. "Most of these relationships go back in history," a former colleague of Perle's told me. "You have to look at the 1970s to see how Rumsfeld and Richard got together."

Rumsfeld accepted few people as his intellectual equal. Those to whom he was prepared actually to defer were fewer still. One of them was Perle. It was a relationship rarely displayed in public, but sometimes exhibited in more exclusive surroundings, such as think tank seminars on policy and similarly important topics, or other gatherings where all in attendance were assumed to be of like mind. In February 2001, just weeks after his installation as secretary of defense, Rumsfeld was guest of honor at a lunch hosted by newspaper proprietor Conrad Black. Black was a socially ambitious Canadian, later indicted on multiple fraud charges, who sought to enhance his stature by recruiting an "International Advisory Group" of eminent people. On this occasion they were summoned to honor Rumsfeld in Decatur House, a historic building across Lafayette Square from the White House. Perle was one of the two dozen celebrity guests, joined at the table by Margaret Thatcher and Giscard D'Estaing.

Throughout the entire event, Rumsfeld showed no reserve in exhibiting deference toward the man nicknamed "The Prince of Darkness" by the Soviets during the cold war. In the course of an informal talk to his fellow diners, "he paid homage to Richard several times," one of the other guests told me, "almost as if he was some kind of a guru—I would even describe Rumsfeld's attitude as obsequious. There was a lot of 'Richard, what do *you* think?'"

The episode illustrates how closely Rumsfeld was prepared to hitch himself to the neoconservative wagon, certainly a politically opportune move at that time. Perle was still very much identified with the issues that fostered neoconservatism in the first place: undeviating support for Israel and a prosperous U.S. military-industrial sector. In 1996, he had been the moving spirit, along with fellow neoconservatives such as Douglas Feith and David Wurmser, behind a policy memorandum submitted to newly elected Israeli prime minister Benjamin Netanyahu with the portentous title "A Clean Break, a New Strategy for Securing the Realm."[7] The paper proposed jettisoning the ongoing Israeli-Palestinian peace process, and instead adopting a more aggressive attitude toward the Palestinians as well as preemptive military action against Lebanon and Syria. "Israel can shape its strategic environment, in cooperation with Turkey and Jordan, by weakening, containing, and even rolling back Syria," urged the authors. "This effort can focus on removing Saddam Hussein from power." In addition, the authors urged a right-wing economic policy for Israel of selling off state assets and cutting taxes, as well as promoting U.S.-Israeli cooperation on missile defense.

Netanyahu chose not to act on these suggestions, many of which were soon to become familiar themes in U.S. foreign policy. The following year, Perle played an important role in founding the Project for the New American Century, a group that inherited the mantle and objectives of the old Committee on the Present Danger, fused with more recent themes that had bubbled up in the well of neoconservative thinking. Perle, along with Rumsfeld and Wolfowitz, was one of the eighteen signatories to the January 26, 1998, open letter to President Clinton proposing the overthrow of Saddam Hussein, thus ending "the threat of weapons of mass destruction against the U.S. or its allies." Later, in 2000, the Project had published its prescriptions for rearmament, Rebuilding America's Defenses, reiterating well-worn themes, especially the obsession with missile defense: "Effective ballistic missile defense will be the central element in the exercise of American power and the projection of U.S. military forces abroad." In spirit, the document very much echoed the sentiments of a Defense Planning Guidance policy document crafted by Scooter Libby in the dying days of the Bush 41 administration that had been shelved after public exposure in the press.

Shortly after Rumsfeld received the nod from Bush, he reached out for his "guru," offering Perle the post of under-secretary for policy. But Perle refused, not because he had any ideological differences with the administration, but because of money. As one close adviser to Rumsfeld told me, "Perle was making far too much to take a government job." Just one of his income streams, his earnings as CEO of a company controlled by Black called Hollinger Digital, had generated more than $3 million in 2000 alone. (In 2004, an investigation prompted by outraged Hollinger stockholders would label Perle a "faithless fiduciary" and demand the return of millions of dollars.)[8]

Instead of taking the policy job, Perle negotiated an alternative arrangement by which he became chairman of the Defense Policy Advisory Board, a nonsalaried position that allowed him untrammeled access to the inner workings of the Pentagon and its highly classified secrets. Pentagon officials, both civilian and military, confirm that Perle took full advantage of this privilege. One senior general, who had daily access to Rumsfeld's office, goes so far as to describe Perle as "one of Rumsfeld's principal military advisers." A civilian official recalled to me how Perle would often spend hours closeted alone with Wolfowitz "at least once a week." Thus Perle was able to maintain his income while exercising enormous influence at the Pentagon, not only through his direct interventions but also because the job he had turned down went to someone on whose total loyalty he could rely, Douglas Feith.

Feith had first arrived in Washington in the Reagan era to work as a staffer on the NSC under the sponsorship of his Harvard professor Richard Pipes, a committed cold warrior who had played a leading role in the Team B exercise of the mid-1970s. In 1982, however, he abruptly left the NSC and went to work for Perle, who then had an influential post at the Pentagon. Moving to the private sector in 1986, he teamed with Israel-based lawyer Marc Zell to found the law firm of Feith and Zell. A few years later, he joined Richard Perle in Perle's International Advisory Group, a lobbying firm whose principal client was the government of Turkey. The Turks were attracted by Perle's pitch that he could deploy the lobbying clout of the pro-Israel lobby on behalf of Turkish causes, such as quashing attempts in the U.S. Senate to commemorate the Armenian Holocaust, as well boosting U.S. military aid.[9]

Like Perle, Feith did not let commercial activities keep him from active involvement in public affairs, as he commented frequently on issues relating to Israeli and U.S. security. He was active in preparing the notorious Clean Break initiative addressed to Netanyahu in 1996. Earlier he had denounced the extension of Geneva Convention protections to insurgents. When the Project for the New American Century opened its doors in 1997, Feith was prominent in its activities, eagerly promoting favored PNAC causes such as missile defense and the need for increased military spending.

Perle's suggestion that Feith be appointed in his stead as under-secretary for policy predictably encountered little opposition from the incoming administration. The office handling routine business associated with personnel appointments did, however, get a curious reaction from Judge William Clark, who, as Ronald Reagan's national security adviser, had been Feith's boss prior to the latter's abrupt departure in 1982. Responding to a routine query from the personnel office seeking a reference on Feith, Clark replied that he could give only an "emphatic non-endorsement," adding a cryptic remark about "some papers that were transferred, if you know what I mean"—which the official took to be a reference to Feith's allegedly casual attitude to sharing classified information with friends.

Two days later, however, according to this same official, Clark rang back to register a totally different judgment on Feith. "Doug had never done anything that was unpatriotic," he emphasized. Then the conversation grew even more curious. "Have you ever seen that marvelous book *Ronald Reagan in His Own Words?*" said Clark suddenly. The official thought Clark had lost his mental faculties, but the former national security adviser was trying to convey a message. "I don't have a copy, but I was looking at one yesterday in Paul Wolfowitz's office," he continued. The penny dropped. Clark was signaling that Wolfowitz wanted Feith waved through regardless. "I understand you perfectly," said the personnel official, and hung up.

Not long after Feith moved into his capacious office—there were eighteen hundred people in his department—military officers being interviewed for assignment to the policy "shop" started complaining that they were being quizzed on their views regarding unrelated topics, such as the International Criminal Court (a neoconservative bête noire) and their personal opinions on missile defense. "I took an oath to defend my country," said one colonel irked at such intrusive probing, "and that's what I will do. I shouldn't be asked these questions." Feith himself made it clear that he was prepared to work only with the ideologically committed. "He's not one of us," he would declare in rejecting the advice of one of the career staff he had inherited. Colonel Pat Lang, a retired Defense Intelligence Agency specialist who had formerly served as the chief DIA officer for the entire Middle East, was interviewed by Feith for a possible position.

"I see you've spent a lot of time in the Middle East," said Feith, leafing through Lang's résumé. "Do you speak Arabic?"

"Yes, fluently," replied Lang, happy to have this asset noted.

"Too bad," said Feith, apparently convinced that such a skill automatically damned Lang as a biased "Arabist."

By all accounts, Rumsfeld was entirely happy to have the man on his team who would later be immortalized by Tommy Franks, the commanding general in the Afghan and Iraq wars, as "the fucking stupidest guy on the face of the earth."[10] "He liked Feith *because* he was stupid," explains one former Pentagon official who worked closely with Rumsfeld, Wolfowitz, and Feith. "Rumsfeld didn't want anyone else going over to the White House and making decisions. So he would send Feith, knowing that Feith would argue endlessly in a meeting and no one would be able to come to a decision."

Another former senior official, who described Feith to me as a "disorganized nutcase," also offered a vivid recollection of the policy under-secretary's relative lack of status at the Rumsfeld court. "I actually sympathized with him," this official told me, "because while Doug had to make an appointment to see Rumsfeld a week ahead of time, Stephen Cambone was wandering in whenever he felt like it at all hours of the day or night, to shoot the shit with Uncle Donald!"

Cambone had broken out of the pack of bureaucrat-intellectuals in constant orbit among think tanks, defense contractors, and government, thanks to his attentive service on Rumsfeld's missile commission. Starting as a special assistant to the defense secretary, Cambone was soon promoted to principal deputy under-secretary for policy. In theory this made him subordinate to Feith, but as his easy access demonstrated, his connection to their master was far more potent. His peers in the administration would eventually note a more physical display of fealty by the younger man. "Steve's beginning to walk and talk like Rumsfeld," a White House official remarked to me not long after Cambone had secured another promotion.

Rumsfeld had even admitted Cambone to the first meeting he held in the secretary's office on January 21, 2001. The others around the table were men he had known and worked with in earlier phases of his career. Martin Hoffman, who was overseeing decisions on personnel, had been a member of the same Princeton class and eating club, and subsequently secretary of the army from 1975 to 1977. Tom Korologos, a veteran of the Nixon and Ford White Houses, was an eminence among Washington lobbyists and long the partner of G.D. Searle's master lobbyist, Bill Timmons. William Schneider Jr., whom Rumsfeld had known since the 1970s, and who had written the final report of the missile commission, was the man he turned to for advice on technological matters. Ray Dubois had met Rumsfeld back in the 1960s and had worked under him in his 1975–77 Pentagon incarnation. Paul Wolfowitz was there, too. He was, after all, the deputy secretary.

According to accounts from some of those present, the meeting was not concerned with planning an invasion of Iraq, or any other favored neoconservative project. Instead, they discussed how Rumsfeld could gain control of the Pentagon bureaucracy in order to pursue the major goal of his administration: the reform, or transformation, of the U.S. military.

Few people inside and outside the Pentagon could deny, at least in public, that the Defense Department needed an overhaul. The U.S. military, with its aircraft carriers, heavy armored divisions, and long-range nuclear bombers, was still organized and equipped to confront the now-defunct Soviet enemy. Even new weapons under development, such as the air force's F-22 fighter, the army's Crusader artillery gun, and the navy's Virginia-class nuclear submarine, had all been conceived and commissioned to fight the now-vanished Soviets. These, along with practically every other system under development, cost far more than the systems they were replacing, took longer to develop, were more difficult and more expensive to maintain, and as often as not performed either little better or sometimes worse than older models. Invariably, they entered service years late and in far fewer numbers (thanks to their inflated cost) than originally advertised. The professional military, which had managed to survive unscathed the loss of the enemy that had long justified their size and budgets, had been left largely unsupervised during the Clinton years. Individual services remained dedicated to their own parochial concerns, fiercely defending their bureaucratic prerogatives and budget share. Despite military complaints of poverty, and a decline in the number of combat units, the defense budget itself remained close to cold war levels. Defense spending for 2001, at $291 billion, was as much as that for the next eight biggest-spending nations combined.[11] While the armed forces could be relatively precise in identifying sums of money urgently required to save America from ruin—the figure was $50 billion at the time of the inauguration, according to a plea from the Joint Chiefs—the books of DoD were in such disarray that no less than $2.3 trillion in transactions could not be accounted for.[12]

To the outside world, it seemed that Rumsfeld, the tough, efficient manager, the no-nonsense CEO, was just the man to use modern business methods that would force the American military machine into the twenty-first century. Rumsfeld himself was fond of talking about "changing the culture" of the Pentagon and the need to implement new "tactics, techniques, and procedures." It was to be his legacy, his final contribution to his country. The only problem was that neither Rumsfeld nor those he chose to consult had any clear idea of what "transformation" actually meant. Among those not consulted were the various officers and civilian defense officials, many with combat experience, who had been arguing for years that the Pentagon culture was wholly dominated by a corrupting imperative to "feed the machine" with budgets and contracts. This attitude, argued those dissidents, led to the neglect of the real needs of U.S. defense, and the ostracism of any would-be reformer who challenged the status quo.

No one talked like that at the January 21, 2001, meeting in Rumsfeld's office. In fact, accounts from some of those present suggest a rather mundane conversation.[13] Topics discussed included a possible overhaul of the military personnel system, the need to close more military bases around the country, and a drive to promote "jointness" between the services. "You have to gain control of promotions," said someone at the table. That last point was something Rumsfeld could fasten on to. Resolved to beat back what he considered an unwarranted usurpation of authority by the uniformed bureaucracy, he determined that he would personally vet all promotions in the upper ranks of the military. To help him do this he summoned eighty-five-year-old Staser Holcomb, who had been his military aide back in the mid-seventies, out of retirement. Holcomb, a former navy admiral, began interviewing all officers of three- and four-star rank. The interviews, according to some who experienced them, were "polite" but nonetheless unsettling—this was an unprecedented intrusion into the tribal customs of the services. Rumsfeld's own rambling cross-examinations of aspiring three- and four-star generals and admirals were more abrasive.

No secretary of defense had ever intervened in the process in this fashion. Previously, the services had exercised a great deal of control over senior appointments, even when they were nominally the responsibility of the defense secretary. Officers who had negotiated the tortuous route up the promotion ladder suddenly found there was a new factor in the game, a politically minded civilian. For example, Admiral Dennis Blair, commander of the Pacific Fleet, was deemed a rising star by his peers, a strong candidate for chairman of the Joint Chiefs of Staff. But he did not share the new official orthodoxy that China was emerging as a threat, and said so in public. Blair's service career promptly withered and he retired soon after. Rumsfeld took an especial delight in disturbing the delicate minuet of service politics. "Stir the pot," he would urge his closest civilian staff, "stir the pot." Following his unprecedented appointment of a marine general to command U.S. strategic nuclear forces, he commented gleefully to a Pentagon official, "That really stirred them up, didn't it?" and shook his fists in celebration.

The immediate effect of Rumsfeld's intervention in the military's rites and procedures was to boost the degree of pusillanimity among the general officer corps. If their chances of promotion now rested more with the defense secretary and his minions than with their own direct superiors, they were going to be that much more careful in speaking truth to power. "I remember going to my first meeting with Rumsfeld and the Joint Chiefs," said a former defense official who had been part of many such meetings under previous secretaries of defense. "I was astonished to find the chiefs all sitting there quiet as mice, not speaking unless spoken to."

General Hugh Shelton, the Joint Chiefs chairman inherited by Rumsfeld, caused irritation early on by taking a week to respond to a request for the military's plan for a U.S. response to an Iranian-

sponsored terrorist attack. The plan that Shelton eventually produced three weeks later called for an invasion of Iran by half a million men following a six-month buildup, a scheme that Rumsfeld
derided as ludicrously ponderous, firming his conviction that the military were absolutely incapable of inventive thought. Shelton, despite
his bluff exterior as a former Special Forces commander, rarely
challenged the secretary directly, but Rumsfeld nevertheless sought
a successor—Shelton was due to retire in the fall of 2001—who
would be even more amenable.

He found him in the head of Space Command, air force general
Richard Myers, whom even a friendly former high-ranking colleague
on the joint staff referred to as "not a man who looks for or enjoys
confrontation." Under Rumsfeld's contemptuous bullying he came
to be viewed as "an abused puppy," the "sycophant to end all
sycophants" who shrank from facing up to his master, though his
visceral hatred of Feith would occasionally erupt during meetings. As
deputy to Myers, Rumsfeld settled on an ambitious marine, Peter
Pace, then heading up southern command in Miami. The two generals had served together in the early 1990s in Japan, where Myers
was the commander of all U.S. forces in the country, with Pace as his
deputy. "It's interesting how little Pace liked Myers," a former Pentagon official who often visited Tokyo recalled to me. "Myers big-
footed him all the time, while Pete did all the work."

Pace, known without affection among his peers as "Perfect Peter,"
was considered a "political general," ever attentive to any shifting
winds at higher levels that might affect his career. When offered the
vice chairmanship of the Joint Chiefs, he played a canny game, telling
Rumsfeld that he would rather wait and become commandant of
marines. To secure his acceptance, Rumsfeld was obliged to guaran-
tee that Pace would succeed Myers as chairman.

Though they chafed under Rumsfeld's aggressive rudeness, the
more savvy officials gradually began to notice that for all the vicious
intimidation, and the threat of career oblivion, there was very little
follow-through on substance. Rumsfeld's "snowflakes," peremptory
memos that he dictated and dispatched around the Pentagon in
manic quantities, would reduce recipients to dread when they saw
the secretary's military aide advancing with snowflake in hand.

These missives usually set a date, often within a day, for confirmation that the assigned task had been completed. "In the beginning," said one formerly high-ranking individual routinely in receipt of scores of snowflakes, "I'd work late to get the job done and respond by the set time. Then I started letting it slide for a week, and no one seemed to notice." Eventually he stopped responding altogether, and still heard nothing.

The same phenomenon recurred even when fundamental policies were at stake. For example, the director of operations on the joint staff, known as J3, was traditionally responsible for consolidating all requests for satellite reconnaissance by different regional commanders, or "combatant commanders" as Rumsfeld had renamed them, before passing the list on to the satellite operators. Rumsfeld seized on this as an example of military inefficiency. It made no sense, he fumed, simply to make up the list on the basis of individual requests. There should instead be an overall assessment of priorities on a global basis. It was accordingly decreed that the secretary of defense and his staff, which in this instance meant Stephen Cambone, would survey the world every month and hand down the order of priorities for tasks allotted to the billion-dollar satellites circling the heavens. "Never once," a former senior officer on the joint staff told me, "did the secretary's staff ever come up with their promised strategic vision." As the satellite operators waited in vain for orders, the military's system of strategic intelligence fell into chaos. After a few months, the military quietly reverted to the old system. "That was the whole story of transformation," the former staff officer told me. "It was all just slogans, notions translated into bumper stickers."

Key to Rumsfeld's initial scheme for controlling the military were the politically appointed civilian secretaries of the air force, army, and navy. "Don always likes to run things by setting up a group who take care of the management side, kind of a board of directors, leaving him to fly along above the clouds," a former official who worked for Rumsfeld both in the White House and the Defense Department explained to me. "That was his initial idea this time. He thought that he could run the services through the service secretaries."

The individuals who eventually moved into their handsome

offices down the E Ring corridor from Rumsfeld's quarters were certainly well versed in military matters. Gordon England, navy secretary, had previously been a senior executive at General Dynamics, a major contractor. James Roche, secretary of the air force, who stepped over from his previous post as a senior vice president of the Northrop Grumman Corporation, was in addition already trained in neoconservative ideology through his involvement with think tanks such as the Center for Security Policy, founded in 1987 by a group that thought Ronald Reagan had become dangerously dovish. On the other hand, army secretary Thomas White, a former one-star army general who had found a new career as a senior executive with the Enron Corporation, was foisted on Rumsfeld from above. "Tom was a 'must hire' from the White House," a former Rumsfeld aide explained to me. "Ken Lay," the late Enron chief executive and Republican fund-raiser who enjoyed close relations with President Bush, "personally lobbied Bush."

Rumsfeld optimistically billed the secretaries as his "change agents" who would execute his master plans and enforce his will. Before long, however, these officials reverted to the traditional role of their offices in supporting their particular service against higher authority, rather than the other way around. "Jim Roche was the first to go native. When I saw him arrive for a meeting wearing an air force flight jacket, I knew he was gone," a former senior aide to Rumsfeld told me. "They were all soon pimping for their services," recalled another former official.

That left Stephen Cambone as the point man on transformation. As special assistant to Rumsfeld in the early months, Cambone's principal assignment was to oversee preparation of the Quadrennial Defense Review, an analysis that the Pentagon is legally required to produce every four years detailing the nation's long-term defense requirements, and the structure of forces needed to meet them. This was the perfect opportunity for Rumsfeld to lay out his transformation policy and set it in stone as an official planning document. The next QDR was due in the summer of 2001, so the task was urgent.

One indication that Cambone might not necessarily be the best man for the job came early on when he summoned a group of "three-stars"—lieutenant generals and vice admirals—to a nine o'clock Saturday-morning meeting to discuss transformation and the QDR. He himself, according to one of those present, arrived at 9:30. "So, guys," he began, "what's transformation?" Walking around the table, he quizzed each of the senior officers on their understanding of the term. At their exalted rank, each of these men at some stage in their careers had commanded bases or ships where they had been minor gods, their every whim catered to. They were not used to being treated "like morons." Reconvened by Cambone a week later, they signaled their feelings by remaining utterly mute, refusing to respond to the powerful Rumsfeld aide's rhetorical queries, or even look him in the eye. Stymied, Cambone stormed out. Before long a three-star's witticism that "If we were being overrun by the enemy and I had one round left, I'd save it for Stephen Cambone" began circulating up and down the building to an appreciative military audience.

Back in his early days at Searle, Rumsfeld had relied heavily on outside consultants to tell him what needed to be done to reorganize the company. Now he reached for the same device again, instituting a series of "strategic review" panels "to stimulate and inform" his thinking. Despite what was promoted as a mandate to operate untrammeled by preconceptions, these panels were not about to stray very far from prevailing orthodoxies. Doug Macgregor, an iconoclastic army colonel who had written *Breaking the Phalanx,* a stimulating rethink of land-warfare doctrine, was summoned to give his thoughts to one of the panels. There was an urgent need, he told them, to reorganize and reform conventional forces, which might well be called on to intervene in the Middle East. The panel members, unmoved by his argument, expressed their overriding concern with missile defense. "If just one warhead reaches the U.S.," a retired air force general heading the group pronounced somberly, "it's all over."

Four months after the panels had set to work, Rumsfeld, with Cambone's assistance, issued a "Terms of Reference" paper intended to guide planners who would assemble the Quadrennial Defense Review. The twenty-four-page document dutifully headlined the notion that "networked" technology (systems linked by computers) would ensure U.S. superiority on the battlefield and allow for the retirement of more old-fashioned hardware. However, the thirteen "priorities for investment" identified in the paper, which was laced with fashionable transformation buzzwords such as "information operations" and "pre-conflict management tools," collectively catered to the hopes and dreams of almost every single existing Pentagon interest group, and therefore offered no change at all.

The reference paper quickly spawned seven "integrated product teams" to conduct additional analysis, and these teams in turn gave birth to further spin-offs. In no time, there were no less than fifty study teams, "breeding like drunken muskrats," according to one official, in many cases duplicating one another's work. Rumsfeld's instructions were expressed vaguely enough to allow special interests to use them as justification for massive raids on the taxpayer's wallet. A team with strong naval attachments, for example, used a clause in the reference paper calling for forces stationed overseas to be able to defeat the enemy with minimal reinforcement to urge that the navy's fleet of aircraft carriers (each of which cost roughly $4.5 billion without planes or escorts) be tripled to thirty-four. Although the entire process was becoming what one official described as a "reality-free zone," Rumsfeld himself may have been oblivious to the true situation, as Cambone was overheard assuring him that everything was going "swimmingly."[14]

Meanwhile, the services were working hard to protect their assets, reaching out to allies on Capitol Hill and in the press, spreading word of imminent threats to key constituencies. Shipbuilding states, such as Maine, got the word that Rumsfeld was contemplating severe cuts in the navy's shipbuilding program. Senators from Kansas were reduced to apoplectic fury when they read in the papers that the B-1 bomber force based in Kansas might be cut by a third. Other legislators rushed to battle stations on word that national guard units were candidates for demobilization. The army put out the word that Rumsfeld was thinking of cutting two divisions out of the active force of ten divisions. These leaks were not coincidental. "There was a concerted and well-organized effort inside the joint staff to stop Rumsfeld in his tracks at that time," a senior career bureaucrat assured me. "They were orchestrating the leaks at a very high level."

Had they but known it, legislators standing guard to protect big weapons development programs had less to worry about than they feared. There might have been frequent talk of canceling major cold war "legacy" projects such as the F-22 fighter and the Joint Strike Fighter, as well as the army's treasured Crusader artillery system. But weeks and months went by and nothing happened. No decisions on these systems emerged from Rumsfeld's office. There were many reasons why he might not have wanted to take on the formidable military-industrial coalitions supporting these programs, but few outside his inner circle knew that the secretary of defense was refusing even to take part in discussions about them. The reason was simple: he still held stock in companies that stood to profit from these systems.

During his January confirmation hearings, Rumsfeld told the Senate Armed Services Committee he owned "a large number of investments and activities that would have to be characterized as 'conflicts' were they to be maintained during service as secretary of defense" and pledged to get rid of them as soon as possible. But he did not sell them that week, or for some months afterward. He argued that the complexity of his portfolio made it impossible for him to unwind his positions quickly. To avoid blatant violation of the conflict-of-interest laws, he therefore opted out of what would normally be a major responsibility of his job.

The F-22 "Raptor" air force fighter, for example, was an obvious candidate for cancellation. Vastly expensive—even in 2001 it was already a $62 billion program—it had lost its mission with the fall of communism and the disappearance of the Soviet air force from the skies of central Europe. It was rife with technical problems, and despite the air force's fanatical defense of the project, the program was a strong candidate for cancellation. Yet when the issue arose at high-level meetings, officials were astonished to hear Rumsfeld announce, "I've got this problem, I can't get involved." This policy raised eyebrows among the few who were aware of it. "I had a bunch of stock options in my company," a senior official who had moved to the Pentagon from a major contractor told me. "I sold them all, took a loss on it. Beats me why he couldn't have done the same."

With Rumsfeld on the sidelines, ultimate responsibility for deciding whether weapons programs would live or die, or at least have their financial rations adjusted, fell to Wolfowitz. "Normally it is the deputy secretary's day job to deal with weapons acquisition anyway," the official who had lost money by speedily divesting his holdings pointed out to me, "but in this case we're talking about Paul Wolfowitz. He just never could make up his mind."

Rumsfeld appears to have completed his divestments by August 2001, though when he forwarded the relevant financial disclosure report to the Office of Government Ethics he attached a petulant note. "Dear Ms. Comstock," he wrote the ethics office director, "Attached is my disclosure report. . . . I have read it. I find it excessively complex and confusing. To be able to attest to every word, or the checks in every box, would take days and probably weeks of reviewing mountains of records. I do not have the time." He therefore devolved responsibility for the accuracy of the document. "If there are questions or problems, please contact my accountant. . . ."

I read the note to the former official who had complained of having to dump his own stock options. "That's Rumsfeld all over," he observed. "He found a lot of things excessively complex and confusing. We'd go in to give him a detailed budget briefing and he'd say, 'I'm the secretary of defense, I don't have time to get immersed in this sort of material. Give me a summary.' He just refused to bend his brain around these sorts of details. He had little patience in making the intellectual effort to master an area he was not already familiar with."

Even when he had completed his divestiture, Rumsfeld continued to display a reluctance to make hard decisions on weapons programs. As we shall see, his one major initiative in this area, canceling the army's Crusader artillery gun, was something less than a profile in courage. He was probably aware from the beginning that trying to kill a major program was a titanic endeavor, and even then the effort might be wasted. One of the projects ripe for cancellation, for example, was the marines' V-22 "Osprey" transport, a plane that could take off and land like a helicopter. Unfortunately, the Osprey showed a persistent tendency to crash, while its cost had soared to over $100 million each. The Pentagon's own testing office unequivocally recommended in 2001 that it be canceled. But ten years before, Secretary of Defense Dick Cheney had tried to do the same thing, cutting it from the budget every year he was in office. Every year the marines, in alliance with the Boeing and Bell Corporations, prime contractors for the Osprey, successfully lobbied Congress to restore the money.[15]

By the middle of August, eight months after he had returned to the Pentagon, it appeared that the military had Rumsfeld on the run. At a Pentagon press conference he announced that the services could decide for themselves what to plan for the future. "It would be foolhardy to try to micromanage from the top of this defense establishment every aspect of everything that's going on."[16] He would be happy, he indicated, if the services simply agreed to abide by some priorities and requirements that would be set in the defense review. There would be no slashing cuts. Unsurprisingly, at a long-delayed Principals Committee meeting to discuss Osama bin Laden's al Qaeda on September 4, 2001, he "looked distracted" throughout the session, and dismissed the notion of al Qaeda as a threat.[17]

Rumsfeld had lost, and he was bitter about it. On September 10, 2001, he opened what was billed as the Defense Department's Acquisition and Logistics Excellence Week, 2001, with an angry speech castigating the Pentagon bureaucracy as "an adversary that poses a serious threat to the security of the United States . . . with brutal consistency, it stifles free thought and crushes new ideas." Bravely, he spoke of the far-reaching transformations he had in mind, such as privatizing the vast military health system, as well as military garbage collection and janitorial services. To implement these and other far-reaching changes, he said, he would be setting up a "senior executive council" composed of himself, Wolfowitz, the service secretaries, and a few other high officials.[18]

The council was indeed set up, and for a while held regular monthly meetings. Rumsfeld never bothered to turn up. But by then he had a new role to play.

CHAPTER SEVEN

Warlord

Thanks to 9/11, everything changed for Rumsfeld. The military high command's escalating whispering campaign was suddenly halted in its tracks. The Congress, which had been growing increasingly resentful of his evident disdain, had no option but to offer wholehearted support. The press, recently competing to relay the latest speculation on the defense chief's ineffectiveness and imminent dismissal, was now a supportive chorus.

It was as if all those years of political disappointment—the failed effort to get on the 1976 ticket, the abortive presidential campaign, the trial balloons for races for governor and senator that always somehow deflated—had been wiped away and his dreams of political triumph had finally and brilliantly come true. Now, when he addressed Pentagon staff in a "town meeting," he found himself mobbed afterward by effusive Pentagon employees asking to shake his hand or have their pictures taken with him. Tourists reacted the same way when they encountered him leaving Capitol Hill after testifying to respectful congressional committees. In January 2002, Ginia Bellafante, a *New York Times* fashion writer, suggested that "the post–Sept. 11 world has caused a certain kind of woman to re-evaluate what she is looking for in a man. . . . She has seen the valiant efforts of rescue workers and remarked to herself that men like Donald Rumsfeld make big, impactive decisions in the time it would take any of her exes to order lunch."[1]

Even more gratifying were the reports from his polling office, a secret operation buried in the Office of Public Inquiries, an obscure offshoot of the Office of Public Affairs. As well as sampling public opinions on military operations and matters pertinent to defense policy, these surveys also charted the public approval of Rumsfeld relative to other leading administration figures such as Secretary of State Powell. "He was *very* interested in that number," recalled one former public affairs official.

Rumsfeld's suddenly stratospheric standing was, of course, gratifying to Victoria "Torie" Clarke, the public relations professional who had taken over as Rumsfeld's spokesman and Pentagon public affairs chief in May. Suddenly her client, previously loath to make public appearances, was eager to go on the road, or, as she delicately phrased it for me, "he recognized the need to have a sustained level of engagement" with the public.

Clarke, who had worked on political campaigns for John McCain and George Bush Sr., was keenly interested in the concept of "information dominance," which she explained as "flooding the zone with information." This was originally a military term, succinctly defined by Martin Libicki of the National Defense University as "superiority in the generation, manipulation, and use of information sufficient to afford its possessors *military* [emphasis in the original] dominance." In pursuit of this dominance, Clarke saw her first priority as keeping the media well enough fed with material to leave them little incentive, or time, to go out and seek their own. "The idea was to leave no vacuum available for other sources of information to fill," one of her former Pentagon colleagues told me. "We intended to be the Ground Zero for all information." At the height of their success, Clarke's team were not only guiding almost all expert military analysis, at least on television, but also molding most news reporting from the battlefield thanks to the invention of "embedding."

"It's about much more than the news media," Clarke told me. "There are a whole variety of tools that can be used; the Internet of course, but also face-to-face meetings." So it was that under her supervision, Rumsfeld, once derided in the press as having the campaign style "of a CEO's wardrobe," went out on the road again, talking to "everyone from universities to chambers of commerce, business groups. I took every opportunity I could [to have Rumsfeld speak]," Clarke told me. "It was never as much as I wanted." Though he had wars to supervise, his schedule was sometimes as intense as that of a candidate for office. On one visit to Atlanta in 2002, for example, he started the day giving back-to-back interviews to local press and TV, then moved on to address the Atlanta Chamber of Commerce, then a meeting with the editorial board of the *Atlanta Constitution,* followed by a speech to university students.

In speeches and press briefings he was relaxed, self-assured, on top of his material, bantering with the press, tartly correcting reporters who fumbled a question, sprinkling ostentatiously antique terms of speech into his remarks—"Henny Penny, the sky is falling!" (A quote from the nursery story of Chicken Little.) Many of his pronouncements were opaque to the point of incomprehensibility, though some may have regarded them as profound. "There are known knowns. These are things we know that we know," he observed at a February 2002 Pentagon press briefing. "There are known unknowns. That is to say, there are things that we know we don't know. But there are also unknown unknowns. There are things we don't know we don't know." He himself was sufficiently impressed with the sagacity of this concept that he repeated it on several occasions, though he never got around to mentioning that it was not his original thought. Old Pentagon hands recall it circulating in the Office of Defense Research and Engineering in a Xeroxed compilation of similar maxims as long ago as the 1960s.

While reveling in his newfound status, Rumsfeld made sure to keep a firm grasp on the real source of his power, his position as sole controller of the Defense Department, along with everyone and anything in it. He drove that point home to those who needed to know within days of the 9/11 attacks. On Friday, September 14, President Bush spoke at a memorial service in Washington National Cathedral. His address was carried live on television, and thus millions of viewers watched and wondered as a uniformed officer paced urgently up the long aisle and sought out General Hugh Shelton, chairman of the Joint Chiefs of Staff. The general listened briefly to the officer, and then got up and left the cathedral. At a time when

Americans were fearful of further attacks, the sight of the nation's highest-ranking officer interrupted during such a solemn occasion seemed an alarming development, though after a few minutes Shelton returned to his seat.

The episode was a brief public glimpse of a tense backstage drama. Immediately following the service, Bush was due to fly to New York on *Air Force One* to visit the still-smoking ruins of the World Trade Center. Earlier that morning, someone on the NSC staff had taken an apparently innocuous call from the Pentagon. The caller was a lieutenant colonel on the joint staff checking to confirm that the White House did not want an air force fighter escort for the presidential jet during the short flight.

The question made its way all the way up the White House bureaucracy to Chief of Staff Andrew Card, who in turn called deputy defense secretary Paul Wolfowitz. "Just want to make sure you guys are comfortable with no fighter escort for *Air Force One* today," said Card.

Wolfowitz had difficulty coming to a decision, as was frequently the case, and took the question to Rumsfeld, who exploded in anger at the officer's innocent inquiry. "He went nuts," one senior official privy to his outburst told me later. "He was yelling and screaming, 'I am the chain of command between the White House and the Department of Defense. I want to know who has been speaking to the White House behind my back. Those bastards,' meaning the military, 'are trying to cut out civilian control. I won't have it.' And he starts tearing apart the Pentagon, hunting for the poor dumb colonel who made the call."

The question was still reverberating as the military and civilian high command gathered in prayer at the cathedral, which was why General Shelton had to leave to take yet another call on the issue. In Rumsfeld's mind, this was a vital matter. He, and only he, would speak for the Pentagon in the White House and to ram home the point, he refused to say whether *Air Force One* would have its escort until just fifteen minutes before the president was to take off. Only then did he give the order approving the escort. "It was all simply so he could show everyone that he's in control," one embittered White House official told me later.

While asserting his position through such backstage maneuvers, Rumsfeld used the media's thirst for news to become the public face of the wartime government and the major source of news on the war. In the ninety days following 9/11, he gave 111 press briefings and interviews, more than one a day. No longer did he have to talk about transformation and discuss "sets of connectivity and interoperability that totally change outcomes and capability." In fact, transformation, previously billed as the defining mission of the Rumsfeld Pentagon, almost vanished from his lexicon. "After 9/11, he was gone," recalls one former senior Pentagon official who had spent many hours briefing the secretary on transformation issues before the attacks.

The Quadrennial Defense Review, on which so many man-hours had been expended, was finally unveiled at the end of September 2001. In his foreword to the seventy-one-page document, Rumsfeld claimed that though the report was largely completed before 9/11, "the attacks confirm the strategic direction and planning principles that resulted from this review." In reality, the review as it stood in draft form on September 10, 2001, signaled little change in the plans and structure of the Defense Department, a reflection of Rumsfeld's defeat at the hands of entrenched Pentagon special interests. The numerous references to terrorism sprinkled throughout had been hurriedly added by a pair of analysts from the Office of Plans, Analysis and Evaluation working under a draconian deadline.

To insiders in the office of the secretary of defense, the last-minute adjustments to the review merely demonstrated the state of disorganization under their current management. But the outside world now had a different image of the defense secretary, the brave leader who had rushed to rescue his people on 9/11. "It's ironic," one former senior official remarked in the midst of describing the chaotic state of Pentagon management at that time. "While all this is going on, Torie Clarke was projecting the public image of Rumsfeld as this no-nonsense leader, making tough decisions."

War freed Rumsfeld from the irksome constraints of the Pentagon military bureaucracy. So long as his principal responsibility was the overhaul of the U.S. military, Rumsfeld had little option but to deal with the Joint Chiefs of Staff and their attendant military service organizations. But the chiefs and their staffs were charged with equipping and preparing the armed forces, not commanding fighting forces in combat. Actual combat was the responsibility of the regional commands spread around the world. The four-star generals who headed them were formerly known as commanders in chief, or CINCs. In their regions, they had the status of viceroys. "When the Pacific commander went to call on the leaders of South Korea or Japan, they knew he had aircraft carriers, legions of troops at his command," Colonel Larry Wilkerson, special assistant to Colin Powell, once pointed out to me. "An American diplomat had only a briefcase." Rumsfeld, determined to assert civilian control, in the form of himself, over the military, sought to reduce the power of the CINCs, in the first instance by rechristening them combatant commanders, relishing the irritation this caused the military hierarchy. In wartime, the chain of command ran directly from the secretary of defense, via the chairman of the Joint Chiefs, to these regional commanders. Since the chairman who took office within weeks of 9/11 was the compliant General Myers, Rumsfeld would have direct and unfettered access to the general commanding Central Command, or Centcom, Tommy Franks.

This arrangement allowed ample scope for Rumsfeld's management style. By law, any movement of any U.S. military unit outside the United States requires the signature of the secretary of defense. Normally, this would be a pro forma exercise, with the actual management of the movement supervised and monitored by the joint staff with final authorization from the chairman. But Rumsfeld had already developed the habit of intervening in such routine matters. Earlier in 2001, he had deeply involved himself in the redeployment of a twelve-man Special Forces unit overseas, holding the movement of this tiny group for two weeks while he questioned the justification for the move, as well as its $80,000 cost. Deployment of forces for the Afghan campaign obviously presented far greater opportunities for micromanagement. By the time the relevant units were in place for the Afghan campaign, Rumsfeld had, according to a staff officer who prepared the orders, scrutinized and signed no less than 280 separate movement orders. The military staff that had to accommodate the secretary's seeming obsession with obscure details grew increasingly resentful of Rumsfeld's reliance on nonmilitary advisers, particularly Richard Perle as well as Newt Gingrich and former CIA director Jim Woolsey, whom they derisively nicknamed "the plastic Rambos."

The plan for the conquest of Afghanistan eventually produced by Franks and his staff at Centcom and accepted by Rumsfeld required extensive use both of airpower and Special Forces—lightly armed soldiers trained to operate with a minimum of support and in unconventional situations. Rumsfeld loved the whole concept of undercover operations derring-do. "Have you killed anyone yet?" he would eagerly ask General Charles Holland, head of Special Operations Command, whenever they met.[2]

Key to the Afghan strategy was the Northern Alliance, an opposition group composed mostly of Tajik tribesmen that had been holding out against the Taliban from a shrinking enclave in northeast Afghanistan. In the past, this group had garnered little or no support from the United States, receiving the bulk of their meager supplies of weapons and finance from the Chinese. As it so happened, General Chen Xiaogong, the Chinese intelligence officer in charge of supplying the Northern Alliance —"he knew the location of every arms cache in Northern Afghanistan and a lot else besides," according to one former U.S. diplomat—had recently been posted to Washington as chief military attaché for the People's Republic. Eager to assist the Americans in their Afghan operation, the Beijing authorities instructed General Chen to offer to share his extensive knowledge with the American military. But Rumsfeld had frozen all contact with the Chinese military the previous spring after a Chinese F-8 interceptor had collided with a U.S. Air Force E-P3 electronic spy plane off the Chinese coast, forcing it to make an emergency landing on the island of Hainan, where the crew was interned. (These espionage flights had recently been stepped up for no better reason than that the air force had finally stopped monitoring the former Soviet cold war enemy and had E-P3s to spare.) As a result, the general could not get access to the Pentagon. "We'll talk to him if he asks to come," was the best the Defense Intelligence Agency could offer. General Chen, who was only trying to help, felt it would be an unacceptable loss of face to beg in this way. In a final effort to resolve the impasse, Brent Scowcroft, former national security adviser to Presidents Ford and George Bush Sr., personally called Rumsfeld to suggest that the Chinese general be asked to come over with his trove of vital information. "I don't want to talk to him," snapped Rumsfeld, and that was the end of that.

Despite this attitude, the initial campaign to wipe out the terrorist lair in Afghanistan was a triumphant success, with the Taliban pulling out of Kabul just thirty-eight days after the first airstrikes. It appeared that a combination of small units of elite U.S. troops and precision-guided airpower had provided a successful demonstration of the Revolution in Military Affairs. Rumsfeld himself was in no doubt that this combination had been the key to victory. Two months later, in a speech on "21st Century Transformation of the U.S. Armed Forces," he gave a lyrical account of the "transformational battle" of Mazar-e-Sharif, the first major victory over the Taliban, won by "a combination of the ingenuity of the U.S. Special Forces, the most advanced precision-guided munitions in the U.S. arsenal, delivered by U.S. Navy, Air Force and Marine Corps crews, and the courage of valiant one-legged Afghan fighters on horseback." (Rumsfeld had been highly taken by reports of one Northern Alliance fighter charging the enemy despite a prosthetic limb.)

There was a certain amount of truth in this. Resistance to the U.S.-supported Northern Alliance did collapse when the Taliban lost the northern city of Mazar-e-Sharif. But most of their casualties came after they surrendered, when prisoners were crammed into shipping containers and left to suffocate. Had the airstrikes really had the devastating effects as claimed in Rumsfeld's exultant history, there would have been a large number of wounded. Yet even in the north, where the bombing had been most intense, there were very few fighters to be found among the casualties at local hospitals even within days of the fighting. At Ghazni, which had been heavily bombed thanks to the large number of Taliban tanks based there, the total number of casualties, according to postwar local testimony, was three.

More decisive than the airstrikes were the orders to the Taliban from their longtime sponsors and overseers in Pakistan not to resist the Americans, but to retire and wait for a better day. The Taliban had been organized and controlled by the Pakistani intelligence service, ISI, since the very beginning. Originally composed of young Afghan refugees ideologically molded in Pakistani fundamentalist religious schools, the group had taken over most of Afghanistan in a lightning campaign in 1996 with the help of ISI cash, weapons, and advisers. Thanks to Taliban control of the country, save for a small segment in the northeast where the opposition Northern Alliance held out, ISI commanders were effectively in control. Hence the most effective move to displace the Taliban came not in the form of the Special Forces linked to B-52s, but in the blunt demand by Deputy Secretary of State Richard Armitage to the head of ISI, General Mahmoud Ahmad, that Pakistan either help the U.S. or itself be "bombed back into the stone age."

Though General Ahmad was even then loath to give up Afghanistan, and in fact urged the Taliban to resist, his superior, President Pervez Musharraf, wisely made sure that Pakistan's surrogates were ordered to retire from the field, which with some exceptions they did. Whole provinces, particularly in the Pashtun areas of the country where Pakistani influence was particularly strong, changed hands without a shot being fired, though the healthy quantities of $100 bills distributed by the CIA to encourage defections by regional warlords allied with the Taliban played a significant role.

Rumsfeld must have been aware of this background, but he was not about to let such complexities cloud the widespread impression that Operation Enduring Freedom had been a triumph for "new thinking" and the substitution of light, flexible forces operating very much under his personal supervision. So far as the outside world was concerned, this had been Rumsfeld's war, as reported by Rumsfeld himself in those daily live TV briefings. In the 1991 Gulf War, Americans had looked to three military authorities for direction on events: Secretary of Defense Cheney, Joint Chiefs chairman Colin Powell, and battlefield commander Norman Schwarzkopf. Now Rumsfeld had combined all three into one star turn. Powell himself, meanwhile, was being increasingly marginalized as public attention fastened on Rumsfeld the warlord.

Though eager to inform the public, Rumsfeld was no less assiduous in attending to President Bush, whom he described at the time as "a president who handles a set of very tough, complicated issues . . . an exceedingly skillful executive . . ." Sometimes he would literally clear the stage, brusquely ordering lower-ranking officials out of the room while he conferred with the president on sensitive topics, though he did permit the national security adviser, Condoleezza Rice, to stay. Beyond those morning meetings, he would talk to Bush every evening and perhaps have further discussions several more times during the day. When not catering to these important audiences, the defense secretary was in constant contact with his military commander. "I talked to General Franks today maybe two or three times already, and I'll probably visit with him again before I talk to the president," he told an interviewer in December, when the tempo of action had already slowed.

Meanwhile, thanks to the video links from missiles and other munitions, Franks could watch trucks blowing up in the middle of Afghanistan from his office in Tampa, Florida. On the first night of the war, the commanding general and his own staff, along with other senior generals sitting in their operations room in the Pentagon, as well as further numbers of officials at the CIA, were able to follow the progress of a convoy of vehicles possibly containing Taliban leaders as it drove at night into the city of Kandahar, where the passengers entered what might have been a mosque. Unsure whether to order the building destroyed along with those inside, Franks consulted Rumsfeld, who in turn turned to the president of the United States, who gave his assent. The building was accordingly obliterated, though the chief of staff of the U.S. Air Force called to say he personally had spotted some of the intended victims making their escape. This was the Revolution in Military Affairs in action: complex in technology and organization, muddled in execution. But few in the high command saw it that way.[3]

Close command and control of faraway events from the Pentagon was not limited to the targeting of bombs and missiles. Thanks to breakthroughs in communications, the interrogation and torture of prisoners could be monitored in real time, too. The first prisoner to experience such attention from Rumsfeld's office, or the first that we know about, was an American citizen, John Walker Lindh, a young man from California whose fascination with Islam had led him to enlist in the Taliban. Following a Taliban defeat at Kunduz in Northern Afghanistan in November, he and several hundred others surrendered to the Northern Alliance warlord Abdu Rashid Dostum in return for a promise of safe passage. Dostum broke the deal, herding the prisoners into a ruined fortress near Mazar-e-Sharif. Lindh managed to survive, though wounded, and eventually fell into the hands of the CIA and Special Forces, who proceeded to interrogate him. According to documents later unearthed by Richard Serrano of the *Los Angeles Times,* a Special Forces intelligence officer was informed by a navy admiral monitoring events in Mazar-e-Sharif that "the secretary of defense's counsel has authorized him to 'take the gloves off' and ask whatever he wanted." In the course of the questioning, Lindh, who had a bullet in his leg, was stripped naked and blindfolded, handcuffed, and bound to a stretcher with duct tape. In a practice that would become more familiar at Abu Ghraib prison in Iraq eighteen months later, smiling soldiers posed for pictures next to the naked prisoner. A navy medic later testified that he had been told by the lead military interrogator that "sleep deprivation, cold, and hunger might be employed" during Lindh's interrogations. Meanwhile, his responses to the questioning, which ultimately went on for days, were relayed back to Washington, according to the documents disclosed to Serrano, every hour, hour after hour.[4] Someone very important clearly wanted to know all the details.

Lindh was ultimately tried and sentenced in a U.S. court, but Rumsfeld was in no mood to extend any kind of legal protection to other captives. As the first load of prisoners arrived at the new military prison camp at Guantánamo, Cuba, on January 11, 2002, he declared them "unlawful combatants" who "do not have any rights under the Geneva Convention." In fact, the Geneva Conventions provide explicit protections to anyone taken prisoner in an international armed conflict, even when they are not entitled to actual prisoner-of-war status, but no one at that time was in a mood to contradict the all-powerful secretary of defense.

While Washington celebrated the defeat of the Taliban, other Americans on the ground in Afghanistan foresaw a bumpy road ahead. Anne Wright, the deputy chief of mission who reopened the long-shuttered American embassy in Kabul that December, told me, "The moment we arrived, we were hearing from around the country, 'Where is the U.S. military? We need to have the U.S. military here because the warlords are reasserting themselves.'" The warlords were the provincial strongmen whose fratricidal and viciously criminal behavior in the early 1990s had destroyed much of the country and left the people too exhausted to resist the Taliban takeover. Many of the warlords had made their peace with the Taliban, though they resented the curbs eventually imposed by the fundamentalist regime on their opium production. The huge cash rewards proffered by the CIA to change sides again in the winter of 1991 had boosted their strength, enabling them to rebuild their private armies.

Wright, who joined the Foreign Service after retiring as a colonel from the U.S. Army, recalls the urgent messages to Washington pleading for more troops, which, "because Rumsfeld had the ear of the President," were not answered. Instead, the harried diplomats in Kabul were told that security would be in the hands of the International Security Assistance Force that had just been authorized by the United Nations. As it stood, this force of some five thousand troops was far too small to police Afghanistan, but Wright was astonished to learn from British colleagues that the force was being kept at this ineffectual size at the express wish of the United States. "Our government did not want troops outside Kabul," she told me.

The ejection of the Taliban, so Rumsfeld believed, had been a triumphant vindication of all his arguments for transformation. The mission that remained, exterminating or capturing the remnants of the bin Laden gang, could be safely entrusted to teams of Special Forces and their CIA paramilitary colleagues, backed by U.S. airpower. The U.S. Army, though subsequently eager to blame all unfortunate decisions on the secretary of defense, was happy to accept this policy. As one former high-ranking officer on the joint staff explained to me, "This was the mentality the army had carried over from Somalia and the Balkans," two major peacekeeping operations entrusted to a resentful military in the 1990s. "Added to that, they were completely casualty averse, which was why they retreated into bunkers on those operations. So for them, Afghanistan in prospect was an extension of the Balkans and Somalia. To get over that, you needed transformation, sure, but a transformation in thinking, not simply a shopping list of platforms [weapons systems] and pork. Rumsfeld could have done something, but only if he's really had an overall strategic view, which he did not."

As it was, the policy inevitably cleared the way for the return of the warlords, just as long-suffering Afghanis had feared. The apparent success of the Northern Alliance, one-legged or not, had generated a belief in Washington that with enough cash and other inducements, any Afghan strongman could be relied on to hunt down the remnants of Osama bin Laden's al Qaeda, and perhaps even lay their hands on bin Laden himself. Supervising the policy, first as the NSC official responsible for Afghanistan and later as ambassador, was Zalmay Khalilzad, who had left his native Afghanistan for the United States as a high school student and never returned until 2001. During the administration of the elder Bush he had worked in the Pentagon under Paul Wolfowitz and Scooter Libby, for whom in 1992 he had written the initial draft of the Defense Planning Guidance, later an iconic text for neoconservatives.

Afghans first felt the impact of Khalilzad's authority during a conference of various factions held in Bonn, Germany, at the end of the war against the Taliban. Despite competing claims from better-known candidates, Khalilzad, the presiding U.S. official, insisted on the selection of the previously obscure Hamid Karzai as interim leader of Afghanistan. Afghan politicians of all stripes concluded that Khalilzad had purposefully picked someone with little internal support to ensure that his own authority remained unchallenged. This authority he exercised by operating as the supreme warlord, rewarding or threatening the inferior strongmen with grants of aid or threats of airstrikes from the bombers and unmanned Predator drones at his disposal.

Afghans who could foresee the inevitable consequence of this laissez-faire policy toward the warlords did their best to persuade Khalilzad to change course. "You should put ten of them in handcuffs and ship them off to the International Court at The Hague for crimes against humanity," suggested one.

"I'm going to bring them in and demobilize them," countered Khalilzad confidently.

"No, Zal," replied the Afghan sadly, "you're going to legitimize them."

So it transpired. While the handpicked Hamid Karzai held forth in his self-designed costume of furry hat and cape—"No Afghan ever wore such a thing," snorted one veteran anti-Taliban politician—large swathes of Afghanistan fell under the control of characters like Hazrat Ali, a sinister ruffian of pliable loyalties who used American support to gain control of the eastern city of Jalalabad, installing himself with Khalilzad's approval as security chief of Nangarhar Province. Here he developed various profitable income streams, including the delivery for reward of several hapless Afghans to the Americans as al Qaeda suspects, these unfortunates being thereafter incarcerated in the Guantánamo internment camp. By 2005, according to Afghan officials and Western diplomats interviewed in Kabul, Ali was vying with fellow warlord Sher Mohammed Akhundzada, hereditary ruler of Helmand province in the south, for the title of world's largest heroin trafficker. In interviews, both men vigorously denied the charges. (In December 2005, Akhundzada was removed from his post by President Karzai, an old family friend, and appointed to the upper house of the new Afghan parliament.)

Long before that, Ali played a leading role in an episode that dramatically exposed the shortcomings of the Special Forces/airpower/local allies combination in a most dramatic way. As the Taliban retreated in November 2001, Osama bin Laden and a large group of his followers took shelter in his mountain lair at Tora Bora, not far from Jalalabad and close by the Pakistani frontier. Word of his presence soon spread and the United States began intense bombing while summoning special operations unconventional warfare specialists both to pinpoint bombing targets and also to organize locally recruited troops for a ground assault. Hazrat Ali, who was then in the process of consolidating his power in Nangarhar, was happy to offer his militia to the Americans, and the attack on the snow-clad al Qaeda redoubt gradually got under way.

However, the siege of the "most wanted man alive" was certainly not airtight. There was much complaint later on about the failure to place U.S. troops between Tora Bora and the Pakistani border as a blocking force to prevent Osama fleeing that way, but the exits were open in many directions. On December 3, for example, an American reporter overheard Ali negotiating a deal in a Jalalabad hotel lobby to allow safe passage for three of bin Laden's Arab followers. All the evidence suggests that bin Laden himself had left as much as a week earlier. Ali's ill-clad troops began a somewhat halfhearted attack up the snowy mountain slopes on December 5, preceded by a hail of U.S. bombs, and most of the remaining al Qaeda fighters made their own way through the permeable cordon five days after that.[5]

The most vivid account of how it was possible to escape the bombs came from bin Laden himself just over a year later. His main recommendation was to dig in: "We were three hundred mujahideen [at Tora Bora]. We dug one hundred trenches spread over an area no more than one square mile—one trench for every three brothers—so as to avoid heavy human casualties from the bombing. The American forces barraged us with smart bombs, bombs weighing a thousand pounds, cluster bombs, and bunker busters. B-52 aircraft were flying every two hours over our heads and dropping twenty to thirty bombs at a time." Despite this inferno, bin Laden proudly recounted how his little group, huddled in their foxholes in temperatures of ten degrees below zero, survived relatively unscathed. "We suffered only about six percent casualties in the battle, and we ask God to accept them as martyrs. As for those in the trenches, we lost only about two percent, thank God. So use trenches as much as you can," he told others facing the same situation. "As the Caliph Umar, may God be pleased with him, said, 'Use the ground as your shield.'"[6]

Bin Laden's escape from Tora Bora was a touchy subject, a deflating counter to all the brave talk of "dead or alive" that had launched the war on terror. Rumsfeld's solution was to cast doubt on the possibility that bin Laden had been there at all, telling the press some months later that he was unaware of "any evidence that he was in Tora Bora at the time, or that he left Tora Bora at the time, or even where he is today."[7]

The rationale for supporting characters like Hazrat Ali to operate unmolested was their supposed value as intelligence assets in the hunt for bin Laden and the rest of al Qaeda. While happy to hand

over the occasional hapless victim—in exchange for cash—for interrogation or worse in one of the expanding network of secret American prisons in Afghanistan, the warlords failed to produce any
notably useful intelligence. Operation Anaconda, an elaborate
attempt to trap an al Qaeda force in the Shah-i-Kot Valley in eastern Afghanistan in March 2002, turned into a near disaster for U.S.
forces partly because the enemy were in a different place (the mountains rather than the valley floor) and five times as numerous than
as advertised by local Afghan intelligence sources.[8]

Despite such failings, Khalilzad and U.S. military teams liaising
with warlords carried out their part of the bargain, which included
a hands-off policy so far as drug trafficking was concerned. Opium
production, suppressed by the Taliban in their last year of power,
soared to just over twelve hundred tons in 2002, doubled in 2003,
and doubled again in 2004. State Department officers involved in
narcotics control reacted with horror and proposed plans to erad-
icate the harvest by aerial spraying, but any efforts of this kind were
strongly resisted not only by Hamid Karzai, but also by Khalilzad
and Rumsfeld himself. Feith succinctly summed up the prevailing
Pentagon policy during a meeting in the White House situation
room in 2002. "Counter narcotics," he told NSC official Flynt
Leverett, "is not part of the war on terror." When Robert Charles,
assistant secretary of state for international narcotics and law
enforcement, protested this approach, he was told that National
Security Adviser Condoleezza Rice found him "inconvenient."

Ultimately, Colin Powell himself took the matter to George Bush.
Despite repeated objections from Rumsfeld, who was monitoring the
meeting via a video link, Bush emphatically agreed that the opium
plague had to be stopped, even stating that he would "not waste
another American life on a narco-state." But as was often the case,
the president's views counted for little compared with the wishes of
his secretary of defense. Despite the clear pronouncement from the
Oval Office endorsing the view of the secretary of state, Rumsfeld
made no move to carry out the president's injunction. Finally, he
secured a private meeting with the president for Khalilzad, who
managed to persuade the president to allow him "flexibility" on the
issue.

Momentous though the consequences may have been not only for Afghanistan but also millions of future heroin addicts, Rumsfeld's drug policy was not the only area in which he ignored, or on occasion reversed, presidential decisions he found inconvenient. "He could talk to the president in a way that no one else could," one former White House official recalled, still awed at Rumsfeld's behavior. "He breathed different air from anyone else in the administration. I saw him hijack meetings again and again."

As an example, this official described one gathering at the White House that included not only the president but a mass of officials from various departments to discuss the proposed creation of military tribunals to try the increasing number of prisoners at Guantánamo. Attorney General Ashcroft had been urging the creation of some quasi-legal mechanism for these men for fear that, as the official termed it, "our clocks would get cleaned" if any prisoner's appeal reached the appeals court. Rumsfeld, however, opposed putting the prisoners under any sort of legal framework at all. He turned up late for the meeting, accompanied by a slew of aides—he was noted for always bringing more aides than anyone else—and launched straight in. "Mr. President, I haven't had time to read these [briefing] papers, but let me tell you I don't think this is a bad idea. These are bad men, Mr. President, and I think we ought to let people know that."

"Yeah, these are bad guys," said Bush, quickly falling under Rumsfeld's thrall. "We need to get the communications machinery working, to get the word out." And so, for better or worse, the proposal was put on hold for a period. Condoleezza Rice, at the time still national security adviser, had been presenting the case for tribunals when Rumsfeld appeared, but neither he nor the president seemed to care what she thought. Had Vice President Cheney been present, it would have made little difference, since he never expressed his views in such gatherings anyway.

Because Afghanistan was a war zone, and Guantánamo was a military base, it might seem almost reasonable for Rumsfeld to dictate policy on these issues. But by early 2002, his reach extended even farther than that. "He has exclusive control of a domain where he gets to spend half of the entire discretionary budget of the

United States government," one White House official explained to me, "*and* he's got a veto on all foreign policy decisions. How powerful is that?"

Rumsfeld was now legally entitled, among other manifestations of power, to hold American citizens under lock and key without trial, as José Padilla, a Puerto Rican former gang member, discovered in June 2002, when he found himself incarcerated in a naval brig in South Carolina on the direct authority of the secretary of defense. Padilla was one of three prisoners accused of terrorism held in the jail who were subjected to a carefully designed regime of isolation and sensory deprivation. Padilla, according to his attorneys, would ultimately spend 1,307 days in a nine-by-seven-foot cell, often chained to the ground by his wrists and torso and kept awake at night by guards using bright lights and loud noises. In repeated legal arguments, administration lawyers maintained that Rumsfeld was entitled to hold anyone deemed an "enemy combatant" in his rapidly expanding prison system.[9]

When Bush was absent, Rice would preside over meetings of the so-called Principals Committee—the secretaries of state, defense, and treasury, the chairman of the Joint Chiefs, and the CIA director. Traditionally, areas of disagreement in this powerful group were decided by a show of hands, but voting gradually ceased because, as one participant in such gatherings explained to me, "it's too embarrassing for Condi when Rumsfeld votes no and that decides the issue, regardless of how anyone else votes. Sometimes he can be stopped, but it takes a full-court press by the rest of the government to do it. The P-3 incident [when the Chinese forced down a U.S. spy plane in April 2001 and Rumsfeld unsuccessfully argued for a belligerent response] was about the last time that happened." That may have been a pity, because the Rumsfeld veto was to have some serious consequences around the world, particularly in the Middle East and the Korean peninsula.

Historically, the Middle East "peace process," as U.S. policy regarding Israel is quaintly termed, has been the preserve of the president and his National Security Council staff along with the State Department and, on occasion, the CIA. Rumsfeld, however, was able to insert himself and his department into all high-level discussions on this topic by securing agreement from Rice and Powell that the Pentagon be admitted to all "interagency" discussions on the topic. According to Flynt Leverett, Richard Haas, director of policy planning at the State Department until 2003, "begged Powell to go to Rice and threaten to fall on his sword unless she stopped this. But Powell told him, 'Don't worry, I can handle it.'"

Even so, for a time, the State Department enjoyed small victories. In November 2001, George Bush spoke in positive terms to the U.N. about the prospect of "two states, Israel and Palestine [living] peacefully together." However, in December 2001, the tide turned at an interagency meeting at the White House. The diplomats had come with a proposal to offer the Iranians and Syrians a deal by which in exchange for cooperation with the United States, they could expect specified concessions in return. But Powell's representatives now paid the price for his fatal acquiescence in a Pentagon presence at such meetings. Feith, representing Rumsfeld, insisted that there should be no spelling out of the benefits that Iran and Syria might receive for good behavior. That would be a "concession to terror," and a "reward for bad behavior."

Throughout the first half of 2002, as violence between Israelis and Palestinians continued to escalate, it became increasingly clear that Rumsfeld's Pentagon was far more influential than Powell's State Department. On occasion, President Bush made gestures of even-handedness in the Middle East conflict, calling for an Israeli pullout from Palestinian areas it had recently reoccupied. But the text of a major presidential address in June lost language deemed favorable to the Palestinian cause following review by Rumsfeld and Vice President Cheney. Finally, on August 6, at a "town meeting" of Pentagon staff, Rumsfeld, in the course of a somewhat muddled historical summary, declared that Israel had every right to keep the land it had conquered in 1967 and colonize it with settlements: "My feeling about the so-called occupied territories are that there was a war, Israel urged neighboring countries not to get involved in it once it started, they all jumped in, and they lost a lot of real estate to Israel because Israel prevailed in that conflict. In the intervening period, they've made some settlements in various parts of the so-called occupied area, which was the result of a war, which they won."

Rumsfeld and his team were hardly alone in promoting hard-line pro-Israel policies. Given the political influence of Israel supporters, there were huge domestic political stakes involved; Bush's June 24, 2002, speech laying out his vision for a Middle East peace was also vetted by political adviser Karl Rove, not to mention Vice President Cheney.

North Korea was a different matter, with fewer domestic political stakes involved. Although the neoconservatives in the Pentagon leadership did not have quite the same long-standing emotional investment in Korean issues as with Israel, there may have been exceptions. According to Chas Freeman, then deputy chief of mission in the Beijing embassy, early in the Reagan years, when Paul Wolfowitz was assistant secretary of state for Asian affairs, the Chinese leadership made repeated efforts to foster peace negotiations between North and South Korea. Freeman reports that in September 1983, Chinese leader Deng Xiaoping suggested to visiting U.S. defense secretary Caspar Weinberger that China could host talks involving the two Koreas and the United States in Beijing, but Wolfowitz, who was accompanying Weinberger, removed all reference to Deng's suggestion from the official report that was sent back to Washington, maintaining that he had not heard the offer.

Freeman told me, however, he had no doubt about the overture: "Senior Chinese foreign ministry officials made a particular point of asking whether we had heard and understood Deng's initiative on Korea. We said we had and subsequently reported that the Chinese had underscored its importance. Everyone in Washington was baffled because there *was* no apparent initiative. Wolfowitz then had our cable reporting the reiteration of the initiative recalled from distribution." The following year, Freeman maintains, Wolfowitz acted again to persuade Secretary of State George Shultz not to relay the details of a Chinese proposal to the South Koreans. Had such Chinese overtures been successful, it is possible that North Korea might have emerged from isolation or at least never have proceeded with its nuclear weapons program.

As it was, ten years later, the Clinton administration, horrified by North Korea's progress on a plutonium-based nuclear weapon, seriously considered taking military action. However, direct negotiations fostered by former president Jimmy Carter in 1994 yielded a North Korean agreement to halt their plutonium production in exchange for supplies of oil, economic assistance, and two light-water nuclear-power reactors (unsuitable for making bomb material). Both sides lived up to the bargain, more or less. The Koreans put their plutonium reprocessing facilities under seal and the United States delivered oil, although one Clinton administration official admitted to me that "we did screw around with the fuel shipments." Construction of the reactors finally began only in 2002, with key components to be supplied by the Swiss firm ABB, which prior to 2001, it may be remembered, had board member Donald Rumsfeld to lobby on its behalf for the $200 million contract. Rumsfeld, of course, was simultaneously using the specter of intercontinental North Korean missiles as the centerpiece of his missile commission report. The threat was key to the marketing of an accelerated U.S. missile defense program, further diminishing any appetite in the Pentagon or White House for any kind of negotiation with Pyongyang.

In reality, Rumsfeld assumed that North Korea posed little threat. He and his advisers firmly believed that the communist regime was, as one former Rumsfeld aide closely involved in Asia policy told me, "a bankrupt regime close to imploding and if we put pressure on them, that would hasten the implosion. Of course," he added ruefully, "the imminent implosion of North Korea has been imminent for the past decade."

One irritating complication, however, was that the South Koreans, led by new president Kim Dae Jung, were ardently pursuing a "sunshine policy" of negotiations with North Korea. When Kim arrived in Washington for an official visit in March 2001, President Bush, his mind-set bolstered by a Defense Intelligence Agency briefing (arranged by Rumsfeld) on the persecution of North Korean Christians, told him sharply that the United States emphatically disagreed with his policy. This humiliation of Kim, a former political prisoner and Nobel Peace Prize winner, written off by Bush as a "naive old guy," represented a major victory for Rumsfeld over Powell. At the beginning of the visit Powell had announced that the Clinton policy on Korea would continue. Now he was forced to make a groveling public admission that he had leaned "too far forward on my skis." The secretary of state, as one former Pentagon official summed up the consensus view within the bureaucracy, had suffered "a major defeat."

The following month, two events occurred that were to have a significant effect on the power game. The first of these began on April 1, when the Chinese forced down the American E-P3 spy plane. Rumsfeld, a devout student of Andrew Marshall's thesis that China was the emerging "peer competitor," immediately urged confrontation with the People's Republic. "He was pushing for sanctions, a major demarche," one former deputy assistant secretary of defense told me. Powell and Deputy Secretary of State Armitage, on the other hand, counseled a diplomatic approach, and for once they won the argument. After eleven days of delicate negotiations the aircrew was released, followed sometime later by the disassembled plane. But for the senior State Department duo, this was a Pyrrhic victory. "The incident fooled Powell and Armitage into thinking they had command of foreign policy," explained the former defense official, "but that was the last time they were allowed to do things their way."

Ever attuned to the prevailing wind, Feith's clique in the policy office now began referring to China as "the enemy" or "the next threat." Defense intelligence assessments, according to a career official, routinely described the world's most populous country as "the adversary."

Even though Rumsfeld had failed to seize overall control of China policy, he continued to do what he could to disrupt relations, principally by continually encouraging the nationalist government of Taiwan to expect unqualified U.S. backing regardless of its actions. "Almost every week," Colonel Larry Wilkerson, Powell's former special assistant and later State Department chief of staff, told me, "we'd hear that some DoD emissary had been trying to convince the Taiwanese that the State Department was talking with a forked tongue and that U.S. policy really was to support Taiwan whether or not they declared independence from China. That was entirely contrary to what we were telling them—and what President Bush was saying." So far as the Beijing regime was concerned, Rumsfeld decided that if he could not entirely rupture all diplomatic relations with China, he could at least do so as far as the Pentagon was concerned. Accordingly, all Defense Department personnel were thence-forth banned from any contact with the Chinese military, an edict that had severe consequences, as we have seen, during the Afghan war.

In Rumsfeld's world, China was isolated. France was to follow. When the French government began raising serious objections to U.S. plans for Iraq, all travel by Pentagon employees to Paris was forbidden.

As Rumsfeld aggressively inserted himself into the diplomatic sphere, it should come as no surprise that he also asserted an ever-increasing role in areas traditionally assigned to the CIA. Although the Pentagon accounted for most U.S. intelligence resources, he was irritated that these were dispersed through multiple agencies. He wanted "one dog to kick," he complained, but "right now I have a whole kennelful." Accordingly, he sought to create one powerful defense intelligence czar, who would have overall control of the kennel, an under-secretary of defense for intelligence. This ambition was spurred by the experience of the Afghan war, where he found to his irritation that all too often the military depended on help from the CIA even to operate in the country. Determined that this should not happen again, he relentlessly pushed for the expansion of Pentagon intelligence assets into spheres hitherto dominated by the agency, deploying "Defense Liaison Element" teams of undercover operatives around the world. Old agency hands resented and mocked this intrusion by what they considered inexperienced neophytes, citing as confirmation incidents such as a bar fight in the Paraguayan capital, Asunción. On that occasion a "DLE" four-man team, present in the country without the knowledge of the U.S. ambassador, murdered a man in a bar fight and then hurriedly exited the country, leaving a gun behind in their hotel.

In the hierarchy of power, CIA director George Tenet was no match for the master of the Pentagon, and could only watch as Rumsfeld encroached on agency territory. "It looks as if you are trying to do my job," said Tenet plaintively when a Pentagon emissary explained the secretary's plans for the consolidation of intelligence power. But while involving himself ever more deeply in intelligence matters, Rumsfeld was willingly immersing himself in very dark affairs indeed. A year after his counsel had passed the message that interrogators should "take the gloves off" when questioning the hapless John Walker Lindh and report the results on an hourly basis, Rumsfeld was personally deciding on whether interrogators could use "stress positions" (an old CIA technique) like making prisoners stand for up to four hours, or exploit "individual phobias, such as fear of dogs, to induce stress," or strip them naked, or question them for twenty-eight hours at a stretch, without sleep, or use "a wet towel and dripping water to induce the misperception of suffocation." These and other methods, euphemistically dubbed "counter-resistance techniques" in Pentagon documents that always avoided the word "torture," were outlined in an "action memo" submitted on November 27, 2002, for his approval by William Haynes, the Department of Defense's chief counsel. The lawyer noted that Wolfowitz, Feith, and Myers had already agreed that Rumsfeld should approve all but the most severe options, such as the wet towel, without restriction. A week later, Rumsfeld scrawled his signature in the "approved" box but added, "However, I stand for 8–10 hours a day. Why is standing limited to 4 hours?"[10]

The answer, of course, was that he could always sit down if he felt like it, and in any case wore specially made shoes, built up and filled with extra padding. His staff called them the duck shoes.

According to a sworn statement by Lieutenant General Randall Schmidt, U.S. Air Force, appointed in 2005 to investigate charges by FBI officials that there had been widespread abuse at Guantánamo, Rumsfeld's signature was merely for the record; he had given verbal approval for the techniques two weeks before.[11] In any event, sitting down at will was not an option available to Mohammed al-Qahtani, a Saudi inmate in Guantánamo, who soon began to feel the effects of Rumsfeld's authorization in a direct way. Qahtani, alleged to have been recruited for the 9/11 hijackings only to fail to gain entry into the United States, had been under intense questioning for months. There is no more chilling evidence of just how closely connected Secretary Rumsfeld was to the culture of torture so defiantly adopted by the Bush administration than Schmidt's fifty-five-page statement, which at times takes on an informal, almost emotional tone.

Schmidt is adamant that Rumsfeld intended the techniques "for

Mister Kahtani [sic] number one."[12] And so Qahtani's jailers now began forcing him to stand for long periods, isolating him, stripping him, telling him to bark like a dog, and more. "There were no limits put on this and no boundaries," Schmidt reported. After a few days, the sessions had to be temporarily suspended when Qahtani's heart slowed to thirty-five beats a minute. "Somewhere," General Schmidt observes, "there had to be a throttle on this," and the "throttle" controlling the interrogation was ultimately Rumsfeld, who was "personally involved," the general stressed, "in the interrogation of one person." Bypassing the normal chain of command, the secretary called the prison chief directly on a weekly basis for reports on progress with Qahtani. Years before, a G.D. Searle executive had remarked on Rumsfeld's practice of "diving down in the weeds" to check on details, but this was new. The secretary of defense of the United States was supervising the torture of a single man.

At one point in Schmidt's description of an interview with the secretary during his investigation, it appears that Rumsfeld expressed bemusement at the practical consequences of his edicts: "Did [I] say 'put a bra and panties on this guy's head and make him dance with another man?'" Schmidt quotes him as remarking defensively. To which Schmidt, in his statement, notes that Rumsfeld had indeed authorized such specific actions by his broad overall approval.[13]

The same day he signed his formal approval for Qahtani's interrogation methods, Rumsfeld welcomed President Bush to the Pentagon for the more public signature of the following year's $396.8 billion defense authorization bill, which awarded the Pentagon a $46 billion increase over the previous year's budget. At the ceremony, Bush thanked Rumsfeld for doing "a fabulous job on behalf of the American people." Victorious, or so he thought, in Afghanistan, his rivals crushed at home, a White House obedient to his will, Rumsfeld, through 9/11, became master of the stage. Now it was time to go massive, as he had mused on the afternoon of that fateful day, and "sweep it all up."

CHAPTER EIGHT

A Game of War

Why the United States of America, the most powerful nation on earth, attacked Iraq and how it failed to occupy the country successfully once its military had routed Saddam Hussein will be a subject of argument for decades to come. Whether the fullest historical truth will ever be revealed remains to be seen, however, for there are many facts that the people who made the decision to go to war would rather not remember, or have actually forgotten, or were never told in the first place. Veterans of the prewar Pentagon and White House, for example, even those who lament the disaster of the war they launched, often remark that "the intelligence I saw on Saddam's WMD at the time was convincing." At this point in the conversation I ask if they knew, as did Dick Cheney et al., what Hussein Kamel had revealed in the summer of 1995. Too often they have answered no, they had not been briefed.

What should they have known? On the night of August 7, 1995, Hussein Kamel, the son-in-law of Saddam Hussein, fled Baghdad and sought asylum in Jordan. Two weeks later, he sat down in an Amman villa with senior U.N. inspectors who had spent years trying to ferret out details of Iraq's nuclear, chemical, and biological weapons programs. Now they had the ultimate source, one who had no reason to lie. Kamel had been the second most powerful man in Iraq until he fled in fear of Saddam's psychopathic son Uday. More important, he had been directly in charge of all military industry.

The key question, of course, for the U.N. as well as the American and allied intelligence agencies anxious to talk to Kamel, was the location and quantity of Saddam's remaining stocks of the so-called weapons of mass destruction. There were none, he replied, none at all. In 1991, following some initial successes by the inspectors, on Saddam's instructions he had "ordered destruction of all chemical weapons. All weapons—biological, chemical, missile, nuclear were destroyed" and the programs for producing them dismantled.[1] He told exactly the same story to the CIA and Britain's MI6.

In addition, Kamel disclosed details of the huge amount of lethal chemical and biological weapons his former organization had produced before his 1991 destruction order. These revelations were to be repeated and publicized by Western officials for years to come. Testifying to a Senate committee in September 1998, Richard Perle bemoaned Saddam's supposed success in continuing to conceal his weapons, and alluded to "the intelligence supplied by Saddam's defecting son-in-law [which] brought us briefly closer than we could have hoped."[2] In the buildup to the 2003 invasion, President Bush invoked the defection of "the head of Iraq's military industries" as a crucial factor in forcing the Iraqi regime to admit to the production of a "massive stockpile of biological weapons that has never been accounted for, and capable of killing millions."[3] Vice President Cheney said Kamel's story should serve as a reminder to all that we often learned more as a result of defections than "we learned from the inspection regime itself."[4] Meanwhile, Kamel's authoritative but inconvenient testimony that all stocks of these weapons had been destroyed years before was not only ignored, but kept a closely guarded secret.

In January 1998, Rumsfeld, just then setting up shop with his missile commission, was faxed a letter from the Project for the New American Century with a request that he add his signature. The letter was addressed to President Clinton and demanded that his administration proclaim a new strategy aimed "above all, at the removal of Saddam Hussein from power" on the grounds that "experience had shown that it is difficult if not impossible to monitor Iraq's chemical and biological weapons production." Leaving Saddam in place, according to the letter, would endanger "the security of the world in the first half of the 21st century." Rumsfeld duly signed and faxed it back to the PNAC for onward transmission to the White House and media. It was Rumsfeld's first direct intervention in Iraqi affairs since his last visit to Saddam fourteen years before.

The seventeen additional signatories to the letter included such right-wing heavyweights as Richard Perle, Paul Wolfowitz, and Richard Armitage as well as others who were soon to find a place in the Bush administration. In October 1998, Congress passed the Iraqi Liberation Act, which made Saddam's overthrow a declared policy of the United States, and authorized $97 million for the Iraqi opposition.

The Iraqi opposition that the moving spirits behind this legislation had in mind was the Iraqi National Congress, a group headed by Ahmed Chalabi, the Iraqi exile raised in Lebanon and convicted in Jordan as a swindler after the 1989 collapse of his Petra Bank. Following the first Gulf War, Chalabi had been recruited by the CIA to head up the exiled Iraqi opposition. The agency selected him not only because he seemed efficient, but also because, as one senior agency official explained to me, "he was weak" and would therefore keep his fellow exiles in line without causing too much trouble. This turned out to be a misplaced assumption. Chalabi managed to cause a great deal of trouble thanks to his attempts at provoking a U.S.-Iraq war by launching attacks against Saddam's forces with his tiny militia, along with Kurdish allies, from their safe haven in Kurdish-controlled northern Iraq.

Eventually abandoned by his exasperated paymasters, and driven from northern Iraq in 1996, Chalabi began intensively lobbying for his cause in Washington, where he found a nurturing welcome among the neoconservatives. He already enjoyed a relationship with Perle that reportedly dated back to their days at the University of Chicago. With this master manipulator to advise him, Chalabi rapidly expanded his circle of influential connections. Among other selling points he advertised his readiness, as soon as he took over the government of Iraq, to open relations with Israel and even fulfill Rumsfeld's old dream of opening an oil pipeline running directly between the two countries, from Mosul in northern Iraq to the port of Haifa on Israel's Mediterranean coast. As Doug Feith's onetime law partner Marc Zell later told a reporter, "He promised a lot of things."[5] Scott Ritter, formerly a high-profile U.N. weapons inspector, told *The New Yorker* that Chalabi offered him Iraqi oil concessions. "He told me that, if I played ball, when he became President he'd control all of the oil concessions, and he'd make sure I was well taken care of. I guess it was supposed to be a sweetener." Chalabi's office strenuously denied Ritter's account, calling him a "liar."[6]

Chalabi's blandishments regarding Israel were music to the ears of the neoconservatives. Feith, when appointed to the Pentagon, even sent a cable to the Israeli foreign ministry expressing enthusiastic support for the pipeline idea. No less swayed by Chalabi's arguments was Wolfowitz, who had long been brooding about the lost opportunity to overthrow Saddam in 1991, when the elder George Bush had halted the war once the Iraqi army had been driven out of Kuwait. While sitting out the Clinton years as dean of the Paul H. Nitze School of Advanced International Studies in downtown Washington, he spent many hours discussing Iraq with his friend and neighbor, Swedish ambassador Rolf Ekéus. The diplomat had headed the U.N.'s Unscom WMD inspectors until 1997 and had been one of those who debriefed Hussein Kamel. When Rumsfeld recruited Wolfowitz to his missile commission, both men consulted Ekéus for his insights into Saddam's missile arsenal, though Kamel's categorical report that all WMD had been destroyed was somehow not reflected in the commission's final report.

However, despite the array of well-briefed neoconservatives in its ranks, the new administration did not, as many of them had hoped, move instantly to prepare to attack Iraq in early 2001. The military high command believed Saddam was steadily losing 10 percent of his military capability every year, as equipment that he could not replace wore out and troop quality deteriorated for lack of training. One former senior officer on the joint staff recalled that discussions of Iraq at pre-9/11 Principals Committee meetings, usually consisting of Cheney, Powell, Tenet, General Shelton, and Rice, were concerned with "smart sanctions"—a Powell scheme to readjust the crippling economic sanctions on Iraq so as to cause less suffering to civilians—as well as the cost of maintaining the no-fly zones over southern and northern Iraq. "Rumsfeld was questioning the cost of

Southern and Northern Watch" (the code names for the no-fly patrols), this officer told me. "He argued for what he called a 'more robust and punitive retaliation to stop [Saddam] challenging our aircraft,' but the British wouldn't go along."

In those early days, Rumsfeld had not yet come to dominate such meetings. Sitting inconspicuously with other aides along the wall, the joint staff officer concluded that Rumsfeld didn't really know much about world affairs, about which he would ramble at length while the others listened with weary patience. "The vice president would support him, which signaled 'don't interfere,' but there would be a general shifting of seats as he launched off. Eventually Powell would say something like 'Well, Donald, I'm not sure that's really the case.' Of course, everything changed with 9/11. Rumsfeld moved from being just one of the actors in the play to center stage, and Wolfowitz moved with him."

But the pair did not move in harmony. Rumsfeld was distrustful enough of his deputy to refuse to brief him on what had happened in those meetings, while Wolfowitz, according to sources who were in a position to observe him in action, had his own agenda to pursue, a quest that was marked in the daily logs of his phone calls preserved in "OSD Cables," the Pentagon communications center. An official who had occasion to review the logs on a regular basis recalled to me how "every night, there were a lot of calls to Richard Perle, calls to Scooter Libby, calls to Robin Cleveland [Wolfowitz's influential ally in the White House budget office]. I always felt that the Perles of this world knew where Paul was coming from, and could get him to do what they wanted."

Whatever encouragement he may have had, Wolfowitz was by all accounts eager to push the idea of using 9/11 as an excuse to attack Iraq when he was invited to join other high officials at Camp David the following weekend. However, at that point his superiors were not ready to accept unreservedly the idea of assaulting Iraq, even though Rumsfeld's mind had turned in that direction on the day of the attack. Wolfowitz was asked to drop the subject for the time being. Powell and the senior military man present, Hugh Shelton, had argued against any attack on Iraq. Rumsfeld, hedging his bets, was equivocal.

But others were working hard to generate momentum for an assault on Saddam. While Feith, deemed Perle's "catspaw" by other officials, was telling senior military officers that they should already be working on Iraqi war plans, Perle himself invited Ahmed Chalabi to speak before the Defense Policy Advisory Board. On September 19, 2001, with the stench of fire and smoke still pervading the building, the Iraqi, accompanied by his ubiquitous American assistant Francis Brooke, arrived to make his case. Coincidentally, that very month the State Department's inspector general issued a disobliging report on Chalabi's stewardship of funds he had been allotted under the Iraqi Liberation Act.[7] Preceding him as speaker was Professor Bernard Lewis of Princeton University, an icon among neoconservatives thanks to his assessment of Islamic culture and societies as chronically backward and resistant to modernization. Lewis not only endorsed the liberation of Iraq, but also confidently asserted that neighboring Arab countries would support the use of force to bring this about.

When it came Chalabi's turn to speak, he suggested that the United States avoid the distraction of an attack on Afghanistan in favor of going for Iraq right away. Touting a scheme he had been advocating since 1993, he explained how armed insurgents under his command could easily overcome Saddam's threadbare military—so long as he had the protection of U.S. airpower and Special Forces advisers. There would be no postwar guerrilla resistance and a government could be easily and quickly set in place. The end result, he asserted with practiced fluency, would undoubtedly be a stable, free-market, and democratic Iraq, a reliable U.S. ally.[8] The proposal to use insurgents against Saddam had been scorned three years earlier as a potential repeat of the failed 1961 Bay of Pigs Cuban invasion by Centcom's then commander, General Anthony Zinni, when he heard Perle propound it to a Senate committee. "Before we sign up the American military to little short term [projects] like 'airpower to defend'—'a few special forces in there to just control the region'—be careful," warned the four-star marine general. "Bay of Pigs could turn into Bay of Goats."[9]

For the finale of Perle's post-9/11 policy board show, Rumsfeld himself made an entrance and addressed the group. Avoiding specifics, he expounded a grander vision of the U.S. demonstrating its invincible power in a manner that would draw the world's attention. Swatting the Afghan Taliban regime would not be enough; there had to be a blow to some government that was sponsoring terrorists. It was the same theme that had sprung to the Rumsfeld mind on 9/11—"Go Massive"—and even before, when he was first bonding with George W. Bush and had urged the need for the United States to be "leaning forward." Talking to visiting journalists in his office a few months after 9/11, he invoked François de Rose, the French ambassador to NATO whom he had befriended all those years before. This "wonderful old gentleman" had told him in the Clinton years that he was "concerned about America" because of a growing habit of "reflexive pull-back" when attacked or threatened. "The capability of the United States and the will of the United States," Rumsfeld recalled his mentor telling him, "helped discipline the world . . . by virtue of the fact that people recognized that we had capabilities and we were willing to use them. And to the extent that we were not willing to use them, we had a reflexive pull-back. It encouraged people to do things that were against our interest." In other words, the United States had to hit someone bigger than the Taliban, just to show who was in charge.[10]

Bush had secretly authorized Rumsfeld on November 21 to go ahead and begin planning for an attack on Iraq, stressing that he should not tell anyone else, such as the head of the CIA. But it was not only the president who had an appetite for something bigger. That same day the *New York Times* had asserted, "With the defeat of the Taliban perhaps only days away and the hunt for Osama bin Laden intensifying, the force of the American destruction of Afghan targets has sent an unambiguous warning far beyond the war theater to a number of nations that continue to provide bases and training to terrorist groups. The warning is: this could happen to you."[11] In other words, it had been easy. There seemed every reason for the Bush team to believe that defeating Saddam would be easy, too.

Early in December 2001, General Gregory Newbold, director of operations on the joint staff, "J-3" in military shorthand, received a request direct from Rumsfeld's office to deliver a briefing on the military's current plan for invading Iraq.

Newbold, a three-star marine general whose job made him the key link between the Pentagon and all U.S. combat forces around the world, was surprised at the request. Like anyone who was paying attention to unbiased intelligence from the Middle East, he understood that Saddam was at most a minor irritant who had anyway gone "supernaturally quiet" since 9/11. It also struck him as strange that he, rather than his colleague the director of operational plans, had been asked to deliver the briefing. Clearly, this was intended to be more than a routine update.

On arriving with his charts and slides, Newbold found not only Rumsfeld himself, but much of the Pentagon's senior management in attendance. Wolfowitz was there, as well as his direct superiors, Joint Chiefs chairman Richard Myers and Vice Chief Peter Pace. William Haynes, general counsel to the Defense Department, was also in the room. Haynes was not merely the Pentagon's lawyer, he was also the protégé of the immensely powerful David Addington, counsel to Vice President Cheney, who supervised a government-wide chain of command through fellow members of the ideologically hard-line Federalist Society.

The plan, as explained by Newbold, called for a force as large as the one that had reconquered Kuwait from Iraq ten years before—half a million men. Merely getting that huge assortment of men and supplies to the Middle East would be a massively time-consuming undertaking. The planners had calculated that keeping the entire force equipped and provisioned would require moving 60,000 tons, the equivalent of 3,500 truckloads, every day. Overall, the buildup was expected to take as long as six months.[12]

Newbold's careful iteration of the troop levels called for in the plan soon drew a disobliging response from Rumsfeld. "Absurd," he called them. "We don't need nearly that many."

"What number would *you* think to be appropriate, Mr. Secretary?" asked Myers.

"Not very many," responded Rumsfeld offhandedly. "Certainly no more than 125,000."

"I was stunned," Newbold told me. "The group was in a position of fixing numbers of troops before there was a strategy in place to use them."

However startled they may have been by these theatrics, none of the high-ranking military professionals in the room raised a protest. "Shame on us," Newbold commented to me afterward. "Here was a man with absolutely no concept of what was involved in mounting an operation of this kind. I wish I'd said, 'Mr. Secretary, this is wrong.'"

The military believed such an offhanded dismissal of years of professional planning must have emanated from Rumsfeld's private brain trust of outside advisers, Perle, Gingrich, and Woolsey. "Like Wolfowitz and his acolytes, they would make dismissive remarks about 'Clinton generals' who believed that the military was governed by 'old think,' addicted to 'mass,' and so could only come up with a plan for a six months buildup and half a million men. Wolfowitz liked to talk about 'maneuver,'" one senior officer commented to me later.

Ironically, although Saddam was marketed as a threat to the national security of the United States, Rumsfeld's experts privately believed that his regime was a house of cards, needing only a nudge—"Special Forces with air support, maybe just ten thousand or fifteen thousand troops," according to one experienced military spectator of these events as they unfolded. "The faith in technology was boundless."

There was less faith in the people who would use the technology. "Where did all these stupid generals come from?" Wolfowitz asked an old friend who came by his office in the summer of 2001. The friend asked if he was talking about anyone in particular. "Shinseki," answered Wolfowitz, "Franks."

Tommy Franks at least managed to secure and retain Rumsfeld's confidence by deferring to his whims on the proper means to invade countries. With Eric Shinseki, the chief of staff of the U.S. Army, it was a different story. There was something about the general, who had lost half a foot to a mine in Vietnam, that brought out the domineering bully in the defense secretary. "Are you getting this, are you getting this?" he would snarl contemptuously at the soft-spoken soldier in meetings.

He may have been especially galled that Shinseki had been using the word "transformation" before he got there. Shinseki had announced in 1999 that he planned to reorganize the army's ten divisions into smaller, more adaptable "Stryker Brigades" that would discard heavy tanks for lighter, supposedly more mobile wheeled armored vehicles called Strykers. To demonstrate his determination to shake up the system, Shinseki also decreed that in future every soldier should wear a black beret. Headgear of this color had previously been exclusively reserved for the elite Rangers, who forthwith launched a campaign of outraged protest. Soon, the entire service was embroiled in a passionate debate about the color of its hats, with important announcements on the dispute carried live on television. The crisis was ultimately settled when the Rangers accepted the offer of a tan beret for their exclusive use, and other elite units opted for maroon or green, leaving black for the less distinctive formations.[13] Clearly, the army was a difficult institution to transform.

Shinseki might have been prepared to show flexibility on berets, but he made no effort to move on other traditions, such as the steady increase in cost and complexity of new weapons systems, particularly Crusader, the army's prized new artillery gun then under development, each of which weighed eighty tons and cost, as of 2001, $23 million. To the eager revolutionaries in military affairs who arrived with the Bush administration, the rifled artillery piece was a prime example of hidebound "old thinking." The Project for the New American Century had marked Crusader for death in 2000, listing it among the "Roadblock" programs soaking up money that might be better used to "spur the process of military transformation."[14]

Unfortunately for the army, powerful officials at the White House, notably Robin Cleveland in the Office of Management and Budget, had made cancellation of the Crusader their special cause and continually prompted Rumsfeld and Wolfowitz to carry out the execution. In response, Shinseki and the rest of the army staff mobilized to defend their gun. "In the winter of 2001 I spent more and more of my time looking at truly egregiously stupid slides prepared by the army to justify Crusader," one former very senior civilian Pentagon official later groused to me.

Shinseki had no direct responsibility for combat preparations, that being the responsibility of Franks and his staff at Central Command.

But there is no record that he tried to intervene at any point in 2002 as Rumsfeld used his familiar techniques to grind down any qualms Franks might have had about invading Iraq with a stripped-down force. By the time Shinseki did express an opinion, three weeks before the war began, it was far too late. In contrast, Shinseki and the rest of the army's Pentagon staff fought hard for Crusader, and at times it seemed they might be victorious.

As noted, Rumsfeld had disengaged himself from weapons programs decisions, so the burden of Crusader fell to Wolfowitz, who kept changing his mind. "Paul had so many meetings on Crusader," sighed one civilian veteran of the struggle. "Every meeting he would ask, 'What's it for, in what scenarios would we use Crusader?' Every meeting, the army would change its story, and ask for time to make another study that would prove their case. One time they said, 'We need it for Korea,' so Wolfowitz said, 'O.K., let's buy some just for Korea.' Shinseki rejected that, said it was 'unacceptable.'"

Steve Herbits, the former liquor company executive and gay rights activist who had served Rumsfeld in 1976 and returned again to advise his friend in 2001, was one of the army's more determined foes. He made no secret of his belief, as he later wrote, that "for too many years" the service had "simply not produced the talent" for critical positions on the joint staff.[15] Hence his role in a maneuver that earned Rumsfeld the undying enmity of the army general officer corps, the details of which have not been previously disclosed. At a Saturday-morning meeting with Rumsfeld and Wolfowitz at the Pentagon early in April 2002, Herbits proposed undercutting the obstructive chief of staff by leaking the name of his successor. As the three of them knew, Shinseki was not due to retire for over a year. Naming the man who would succeed him so far in advance would inevitably cripple his authority.

Outsiders have assumed the purpose of the leak, which duly appeared in the *Washington Post* on April 11, was to emasculate leadership of the army for the next fourteen months. However, that was not Herbits's intent, nor that of Rumsfeld or Wolfowitz when they agreed to his scheme. "He calculated that Shinseki would inevitably resign in the face of such a public humiliation," a former high-level Pentagon official, one of the few who knew about the Saturday meeting, told me later. "Steve can be such a prick some-times."*

Despite Rumsfeld's cruel declaration of no-confidence, Shinseki did not resign, remaining doggedly at his post. Meanwhile, after wavering back and forth for months, Wolfowitz finally determined once and for all that there would be no more studies. He was definitely going to terminate Crusader, and so informed Rumsfeld. "Who's going to tell White?" asked the secretary, referring to the secretary of the army, who had long since placed himself in the generals' camp.

"You?" said Wolfowitz hopefully.

"No, you do it," ordered Rumsfeld.

Wolfowitz summoned White and told him point-blank, "We're canceling Crusader."

"Please give me thirty days to make one more study," countered White.

"O.K.," said Wolfowitz.

After White had left, one of the Wolfowitz aides who had been

---

*Herbits himself was to be forced out into exile, at least temporarily, not long afterward. Despite his affection for Rumsfeld and his endorsement of the neocons' schemes for overseas initiatives, Herbits parted company with the administration on domestic social issues, specifically gay rights. This put him at odds with the immensely powerful Senator Trent Lott, who had earned a reputation as a homophobe among the gay rights community. Thus it was that when one of Lott's aides, Sam Adcock, put his own name forward to become the navy's assistant secretary for acquisition, he got a dusty reception from Herbits, Rumsfeld's adviser on high-level civilian appointments. Herbits told Adcock that he was doing his best to kill the aspiring official's chances of getting the job, but if the application nonetheless succeeded, he would make his life miserable. Adcock duly reported this conversation to his boss, who reacted with potent outrage, placing a "hold" on all Pentagon appointments that were subject to Senate approval. This restriction, the senator made clear, would remain in force until Herbits not only left the Pentagon, but departed Washington altogether. Rumsfeld bridled at this injunction. He despised Congress in any event, and such malign intrusion into his office was almost beyond endurance. Still, Lott made it clear his demands were nonnegotiable. "The only way Lott could be satisfied," a former senior Defense Department official told me, chortling at the memory, "was for Marty Hoffman [Rumsfeld's Princeton classmate and kitchen cabinet member] to drive Steve to the airport, watch him board, and then call the Lott office and report 'the eagle has flown.' Only then would Lott remove the 'hold.'"

listening to the conversation pointed out, "Now you're going to have to go and tell Rumsfeld that you've changed your mind and given the army another thirty days." An unhappy Wolfowitz trudged off to break the news.

Meanwhile, the army scrambled to make use of the reprieve, faxing one and a half pages of "talking points" to every office on Capitol Hill, claiming that soldiers would die in combat if the program was canceled.[16] This was too much for Rumsfeld. Before the thirty days were up, he canceled Crusader and made Wolfowitz explain the decision to the press with White standing by his side.[17] After all the heady demands of the neoconservative and other defense studies that had fueled Bush's campaign Citadel speech, this was the single program that Rumsfeld, the domineering bully so detested by the uniformed military, actually managed to kill. An army helicopter named Comanche was indeed terminated the following year on the instructions of Shinseki's successor, but as a member of Rumsfeld's civilian staff told me, "That didn't count, the 'uniforms' did it by themselves."

At that point the army had received some consolation for the Crusader defeat, having been authorized to press ahead on the Future Combat System, a project originally promoted by Shinseki. This was a notion that took the revolution in military affairs to new extremes, not least in terms of expense. Whereas the terminated gun was supposed to cost $11 billion in total, the FCS, as it was familiarly known, was projected to consume at least $128 billion by 2014, and would consist of manned and unmanned air and ground vehicles all tied together by computer networks that would automatically identify targets and instantly destroy them with precise firepower. So rapidly would it destroy enemies, proponents boasted, that U.S. troops would no longer need armor on their vehicles. Two years after development work began, and with $4.6 billion already invested, so an official from the Government Accounting Office told Congress in March 2005, "requirements are not firm and only one of over 50 technologies are mature,"[18] another way of saying that no one yet knew if or how the system would work.

Rumsfeld loved Future Combat Systems, and would list its development as one of his major accomplishments at the end of his six years at the Pentagon. At that point the overall lifetime cost, as estimated by his own office, had climbed to $307.2 billion.[19] Despite its extraordinary complexity, FCS was only one aspect of a truly esoteric concept of war fighting that flourished under Rumsfeld's patronage. It was dubbed Effects Based Operations, or EBO, a theory that emerged from the experience of a group of targeteers on the air staff in the first Gulf War. They believed that precision guidance techniques had made it possible to gauge, and therefore anticipate, the ultimate effects of a bomb targeted on a specific location, which of course could be identified and located thanks to the wonders of the latest surveillance technology. So the destruction of a few critical targets, such as power stations and communications centers, would bring the entire enemy society to a halt. In practice, the bombing campaign against the Iraqi infrastructure in 1991 did little to affect the military situation, though it did disable the water-treatment system, guaranteeing a life of deepening misery for ordinary Iraqis.

Notwithstanding these unintended consequences, which were generally ignored or glossed over in official circles, the concept became more refined over the following decade, the classic example being the "crony targeting" of the Kosovo war in 1999. On the assumption that the Serbian leader Slobodan Milosevic depended on the support of a specific group of business cronies to rule, and on the further assumption that these individuals could and would pressure him into withdrawing from Kosovo if they themselves suffered economic damage, the targeteers rained bombs on specially selected factories and other businesses across Serbia.[20] There was no indication that the approach had anything to do with Milosevic's ultimate cave-in, but the doctrine of EBO had taken root, not least in a complex of architecturally challenged low-rise buildings across the street from a Wal-Mart in Suffolk, Virginia. This was the home of the Joint Forces Command, or JFCOM.

At Rumsfeld's meeting with intimates at the Pentagon the day after the inauguration, someone had mentioned that he should pursue "jointness" as a goal. While individual services defended their traditional customs and practices like tigers, JFCOM, which had been created only in 1999 and drew its staff from all four services,

was charged with coming up with new ideas about military organization and strategies. From 2001 on, the organization proved to be
an enthusiastic source of upbeat commentaries on transformation,
a sure way to the secretary's heart. "It was kind of his pet command," pointed out Jim Warner, who, as a one-star general, served
a two-year tour at the command during the Rumsfeld years. "For
example, he sent his M.A. [military assistant] [Admiral] Ed Giambas-
tiani down there as commander and then brought him back as vice
chief."

Given Rumsfeld's sources of military inspiration, not least
Andrew Marshall, it is hardly surprising that he should have been
so attracted to JFCOM. The concepts being explored here accepted
the premises of the revolution in military affairs and took them to
new heights. As with Marshall's original suggestions about the revolution, the doctrines preached at the Suffolk center took as a fundamental assumption the idea that it was possible to purge warfare
of uncertainty and ambiguity, and that war could become simply a
mechanistic procedure, in which actions and reactions of the enemy
could be effortlessly programmed, anticipated, and dealt with.
Along with EBO, which, as explained, grew out of the experience of
air force targeteers in the 1991 Gulf War, the bright young officers
assigned to the command were also developing the concept of rapid
decisive operations (RDO), as facilitated by the wonders of operational net assessment (ONA), described in the command's in-house
glossary as "A continuously updated operational support tool that
provides a JTF [joint task force] commander visibility of effects-to-
task linkages based on a 'system-of-systems' analysis of a potential
adversary's political, military, economic, social, infrastructure, and
information (PMESII) war-making capabilities."[21]

In plain English, they believed that it was possible not only to
know everything about the other side's society in all its ramifications
and connections, but also to forecast the enemy's reaction to any
action against any component of that society, and how that would
affect all the other components. Rumsfeld liked this kind of thinking. In December 2001 he sent Franks a snowflake commending a
study called "Shock and Awe" by two defense intellectuals that
argued the case for disorientating the enemy's capacity to resist with

devastating salvos of munitions precisely targeted at command centers.[22]

Among other effects of interest to JFCOM were those induced by prolonged sensory deprivation and other forms of psychological pressure on interrogation subjects. The South Carolina naval brig in which José Padilla was being held fell under JFCOM control, so it should be of little surprise that their treatment involved all the most refined techniques.

Toward the end of the following July, Rumsfeld made a special trip down to Suffolk.[23] He was there to survey preparations for Millennium Challenge 2002, an enormously elaborate war game that its designers—the JFCOM commanders—confidently expected would fully vindicate the arcane theology of EBO, RDO, ONA, and PME-SII that they preached so enthusiastically. It would also give Rumsfeld something to show, as he said during his visit, "the progress that we have made this far in transforming to produce the combat capability necessary to meet deep threats and the challenges of the 21st Century." Viewing the arrays of computer terminals and esoteric communications equipment, he may well have been reminded of happy times in the COG exercises, waging nuclear war.

Escorting Rumsfeld around the premises, the commanding general, William Kernan, took care to keep his distinguished guest away from a tall, bald-headed man in civilian clothes, for this was the enemy. A retired marine general and Vietnam combat veteran, Paul Van Riper had been asked to command the Red Team in the Millennium war game. In such exercises, the enemy is always red; the U.S. side is always blue. But General Van Riper was a twofold enemy. Not only was he playing the role of an opponent, but he made no secret of his derisive opinion of the concepts underpinning JFCOM's approach to war.

"The hubris was unbelievable," he told me, after delivering a droll recitation of the full range of acronyms pumped out by the command. "They claimed to be able to understand the relationship between all nodes or links, so, for example, if something happened to an enemy's economy, they could precisely calculate the effect on his military performance. They talked about the Milosevic crony-targeting a lot."

In the scenario designed by the exercise planners, Van Riper was playing the role of a rogue military commander somewhere in the Persian Gulf who was willfully confronting the United States. Though there were more than thirteen thousand troops, as well as planes and ships taking part in the game across the country, much of the action was to occur in computers and be displayed on monitors. It was to be the ultimate video game.

Thanks to their enormous operational net assessment databases, the Blue Team thought they knew all they needed to know about their enemy, and how he would behave. But they were wrong. For a start, they did not know what he looked like. The Blue commander, a three-star army general, worked in full uniform, surrounded by his extensive staff. Van Riper, dressed in casual civilian clothes, took a stroll, unrecognized, through the Blue Team headquarters area to get the measure of his opponent. With his own staff, he was informal, though he forbade the use of acronyms. "We'll all speak English here," he told them.

In the first hours of the war, the Blue Team knocked out Van Riper's fiber-optic communications, confidently expecting that he would now be forced to use radio links that could be easily intercepted. He refused to cooperate, quickly turning to motorcycle couriers and coded messages in the calls to prayer from the mosques in preparing his own attack. He was no longer performing an assigned part in a scripted play; Van Riper had become a real, bloody-minded, Middle Eastern enemy who had no intention of playing by the rules and was determined to win.

Just a month earlier, the Bush administration had unveiled a new national security policy of preemptive attacks, justified by "our inherent right of self-defense." So, when a Blue Team carrier task force loaded with troops steamed into the Gulf (at least on the computer simulation) and took up station off the coast of his territory, Van Riper assumed they were going to follow the new policy and attack him without warning. "I decided to preempt the preempter," he told me. Oddly enough, the Blue general sensed this, saying, "I have a feeling that Red is going to strike," but his staff was quick to assure him that their ONA made it clear that this could not happen.

Van Riper was well aware of the U.S. Navy's "Aegis" antimissile capabilities, and how many missiles it would take to overwhelm them. "Usually Red hoards its missiles, letting them out in dribs and drabs," he told me in retracing the battle. "That's foolish. I did a salvo launch, used up pretty much all my inventory at once." The defenses were overwhelmed. Sixteen virtual American ships sank to the bottom of the Gulf, along with twenty thousand virtual servicemen. Only a few days in, the war was over, and the "transformed" military had been beaten hands down.

For General William Kernan, the JFCOM commander, there could be only one solution to this crisis. Van Riper was informed that the sunken ships had magically refloated themselves, the dead had come back to life, and the war was on again. But this time there would be no surprises. He was not allowed to shoot down Blue Team V-22 troop transports, though these are highly vulnerable planes. The Red Team was ordered to switch on their radars so they could be more easily destroyed. The umpires announced that Red's missile strikes had been intercepted. In short, the game was now unashamedly rigged to ensure that the United States won and all the new theories were proven correct. Van Riper resigned as Red leader, but stayed on to monitor the predictable rout of his forces under these new conditions. Afterward he wrote a scathing report, documenting how the exercise had been rigged and by whom, but no outsider could read it because it was classified secret.

Asked by reporters when Van Riper's report would be declassified and released, an embarrassed General Kernan said that it would remain under wraps "until I've had an opportunity to brief my boss."[24] His boss, of course, was Donald Rumsfeld, who showed no interest in the report, still less of releasing it to the public. Once again, as lawyer Jim Turner had discerned years before, Rumsfeld was interested less in facts or fundamental realities than, "by will and force," pulling all the resources that he could possibly pull together to achieve his goal.

At that time the goal had been getting aspartame on the market. Now his aim was to show that he could conquer Iraq with a small light force, a truly rapid and decisive operation. This would prove that he had indeed carried out the mandate for transformation, confounding the generals who had dragged their feet and mocked his efforts the year before. His inspiration had already defeated the Taliban; now he would prove his case on the banks of the Euphrates. It did not seem to occur to him that there might be an equally bloody-minded Van Riper, worse, many Van Ripers, waiting on the other side, all equally determined to ignore the rules. Six months later, as the Americans advanced on Baghdad, one of the commanders, General William Wallace, made a plaintive admission. "The enemy we're fighting," he told reporters, "is a bit different from the one we war-gamed against." The remark came close to costing the general his job.[25]

Among Rumsfeld's sources of inspiration was the gifted military theoretician, Colonel Douglas Macgregor, who led an armored squadron and fought a victorious tank battle in the 1991 Desert Storm operation. Macgregor had long brooded on what he considered the outmoded organization of army combat units into twenty-thousand-man divisions and had proposed the divisions' reorganization into smaller, more flexible units capable of more agile deployment and maneuver. Forthright in his judgments of superiors, Macgregor had suffered the traditional fate of innovative military thinkers, his radical ideas exciting fear and distrust among a high command inherently nervous of change. Though Shinseki had appeared receptive to Macgregor's concepts, the colonel concluded that the chief of staff was less an agent of change than a narrow-minded defender of the status quo.

Outside the army, Macgregor attracted attention from amateurs with an informed interest in military affairs, notably former House Speaker Newt Gingrich. Gingrich was attracted by Macgregor's thesis that it would be possible to take Baghdad with a fast-moving armored force as small as fifty thousand men. Jumping off from Kuwait—without any attention-getting preliminary air campaign ("We have already been bombing Iraq for twelve years," he correctly pointed out)—this expeditionary force would race directly across the desert to the Iraq capital, bypassing all towns and cities on the way. On arrival, the attackers would locate Saddam, hand him over for execution to whatever Iraqi army general had been selected to take over, and then leave. This scheme certainly had the attraction of novelty, dash, and excitement, even if it left a few questions, such as the possibility of Saddam removing himself elsewhere until the Americans had departed, unanswered. Macgregor emphasized, on the basis of his Desert Storm experiences, that "putting American soldiers in close conjunction with Arabs was a bad idea," and therefore the less time the U.S. Army remained in-country the better. Such finer points may have been lost in transmission somewhere between Macgregor and Rumsfeld, via Gingrich. The principal effect was to confirm Rumsfeld's belief that the generals were consumed with "old think," but that if he held the line, he could yet force them into executing an operation employing relatively few troops, a showcase for a transformed, slimmed-down army.

In Franks, by wide report himself a temperamental bully to his staff, Rumsfeld found an acquiescent underling willing to carry out his master's bidding. The plan bequeathed by Zinni had called for 400,000 troops overall. Rumsfeld remorselessly nagged him to cut this, using his favored technique of relentless cross-questioning, as the compliant commander gradually shaved numbers and units. To encourage Franks to think along the right lines, Rumsfeld sent Macgregor down to Centcom headquarters early in 2002 to brief Franks on his ideas. The general listened politely to his visitor's enthusiastic arguments. However, his inclusion of a vigorous bombing campaign in the ultimate plan, along with large numbers of light infantry despite Macgregor's emphasis on a purely armored force, suggested that he had not listened that carefully to the bold colonel's scenario.

Once Rumsfeld had achieved his goal of a smaller invasion force, he turned his attention to reducing what he regarded as the excessively ponderous supporting "tail" that would attend the combat formations. Over decades, the U.S. military had developed a computerized planning system when preparing for large overseas operations. Called the Joint Operational Planning System (JOPS), it systematically prepared the logistical and deployment plans needed to actually carry out any approved operational scheme. So if the plan was to attack with, for example, a brigade of six thousand troops and a hundred tanks, the JOPS delineated how much fuel needed to be shipped, how many spare tires for the trucks, how much ammunition, emergency rations, laundry detergent, etcetera. The key component of this system was the Time-Phased Force and Deployment List, reduced inevitably to the acronym TPFDL, which in turn entered spoken military language as Tipfiddle. This list automatically calculated the order and dates for the shipment of all these items so they would arrive when needed. It was absolutely key for ensuring that any operation ran smoothly, and Rumsfeld tore it apart. Presented with the military's carefully itemized list, he decreed that he would decide which of the units requested by Centcom would be sent, and when. In addition, he arrogated to himself the right to strike from the deployment list parts of units that did not take his fancy. "This is an interesting exercise of power," commented Colonel Pat Lang, formerly defense intelligence officer at the DIA for the Middle East, South Asia, and terrorism, "for someone who has no experience of ground warfare and, in fact, little experience of military affairs other than his two stints as secretary of defense, isolated in the ivory tower of his Pentagon offices."

As hammered out by Rumsfeld and Franks, the Iraq invasion plan bore the heavy imprint of the legend of the Afghan war, supposedly won by elite Special Forces using unconventional tactics to achieve the same effect as whole divisions of conventional forces. As indicated earlier, the contribution of these specialized units was probably less than advertised, and the chaos into which Afghanistan gradually subsided thereafter was hardly a model for other operations. Nevertheless, Rumsfeld's faith in these elite units was apparently undiminished. The plan as it stood in October 2002, for example, called for the stationing of a full division in western Anbar province. By January, under further whittling by Rumsfeld, that division had disappeared from the blueprint, to be replaced by Special Forces units. Such deletions from the battle plan would come back to haunt the secretary in the years ahead, although, as we shall see, it is open to question whether the stationing of more troops in Anbar and elsewhere would have delayed or accelerated the insurgency.[26]

It must be said that Rumsfeld did not undertake this task in any lighthearted fashion. Hour after hour, he would pore over the three-ring binders presented by the staff, ruminating on whether a particular unit really needed that size motor pool, or that much ammunition. "He abandoned the system," said General Van Riper. "He was striking out National Guard companies. He confused acronyms. It was chaos." As a result of the acronym confusion, Rumsfeld struck off a medical unit in the belief it was a transport unit, leaving doctors needed to treat the wounded stranded back in the United States. Though retired, Van Riper watched this shambles with less than detachment. His son, a company commander in the marines, flew to Kuwait with his men. Normally, his company's amphibious vehicles, arriving by sea, would have been shipped in time for overhaul and final training. "They finally turned up just five days before he crossed the border into Iraq," scandalously delayed, as Van Riper bitterly remarked, thanks to Rumsfeld's capricious abandonment of the well-tried system. Long before his son's reports confirmed Van Riper's opinion of Rumsfeld's interventions, the general had received authoritative confirmation that the war was based on a lie. A few weeks after the debacle of Millennium Challenge he went fishing with his old friend and fellow marine general Tony Zinni, the former Centcom commander who had so eloquently ridiculed Richard Perle and his Bay of Goats. As they cast their lines, Zinni had explained the facts of life on Saddam's deadly arsenal. "He told me, 'Rip, there are no weapons of mass destruction programs in Iraq,'" Van Riper later recalled. "He said there might be some isolated ones here and there, but no programs the way we would think of them."

That, of course, was not the official view of the administration. Rumsfeld himself would tell anyone who asked that Saddam certainly had WMD programs, and even on occasion confidently specified their location. Wolfowitz gave every indication of believing in their existence. But this apparent unanimity masked the swirling currents of feuding and rivalry that characterized the higher management of Rumsfeld's Pentagon. Early on, Wolfowitz had backed Feith in the creation of an intelligence "shop" known as the Office of Special Plans. The OSP provided a ready market for anyone with information supporting the case against Saddam, and there was no more assiduous a supplier than Ahmed Chalabi, who by this and other means had forged close bonds with Wolfowitz, Perle, and Feith, but not Rumsfeld.

The secretary, always inherently distrustful of news brought by others, and no less keenly aware of the importance of controlling intelligence, had taken steps to strengthen his own intelligence resource by creating the new post of under-secretary of defense for intelligence and nominating his loyal subordinate Stephen Cambone for the job. Cambone was not among those beguiled by the wily Chalabi. "Steve thought Chalabi was a bad guy, he would rail against him," another senior Pentagon official recalled, "complaining about the amount of money we were paying him, saying that he was not telling us the truth, so Chalabi was certainly not Rumsfeld's guy."

Close though he was to Cambone, Rumsfeld was unwilling or unable to enable him to win all his fights. Thus Cambone fought hard to divest Feith of his in-house intelligence operation, a move fiercely contested by Wolfowitz, who feared and distrusted him. "That was one fight Steve didn't win," recalled one observer to the contest. "There were so many webs being woven. Cambone was in charge of intelligence, yes, but Perle would be feeding in stuff; Chalabi was feeding in stuff; the CIA had their own bunch of bullshitters. Everyone had their favorite guy who would tell them what they wanted to hear."

In any event, the intelligence was essentially irrelevant. As the report on a July visit to Washington by the head of British intelligence noted, "Bush wanted to remove Saddam . . . the intelligence and facts were being fixed around the policy." The war would go on, and Rumsfeld would use it to prove his points about military policy. By late in 2002, when this process of winnowing the troops' numbers was well advanced, news of what was going on had spread well beyond Franks's harried staff at Centcom. Finally, there were intimations of disquiet among the joint staff and the chiefs in the Pentagon. In accordance with tradition, the grumbles found public form as anonymous leaks to the press regarding the plan for a fast charge across the desert without pausing to wait for slow-moving supply columns to catch up. These concerns were attributed to Shinseki, who was apparently unwilling publicly to declare his views, and General James Jones, commandant of marines, who did state that he didn't align himself "with folks around town who seem to think that this is preordained to be a very easy military operation." In rebuttal, Wolfowitz stated that "It would be a terrible mistake for anyone to think they can predict with confidence what the course of a war is going to be" and that in discussing the war plans he had repeatedly emphasized the risk of Hussein "using his most terrible weapons."[27]

But the complaints were focused merely on the form of the proposed operation. In general, the high command were loath to critique the underlying premises of the invasion. Instead, the Joint Chiefs of Staff chose explicitly to endorse the overall rationale for invasion, sketched out a year before by Rumsfeld on the afternoon of 9/11, that Saddam Hussein was in some fashion linked to Osama bin Laden, and that therefore the upcoming invasion was a justifiable extension of the war on terror. An official directive to this effect was accordingly dispatched to all senior military commanders around the world.[28] When the directive was first circulated in draft form, a significant number of officers wrote back to complain, pointing out the obvious truth that there was no evidence of any such link. Such dissent was dismissed, and the directive was issued without reservations.

Only one high-ranking officer concluded that he could no longer be part of this exercise. In November, General Greg Newbold, who had been so surprised that Rumsfeld and colleagues were suddenly interested in invading Iraq the year before, quietly resigned, ending a thirty-two-year career in the marines. Newbold had clashed with the secretary on occasion, unwilling to accept the officially mandated assumption that Saddam Hussein was a threat to the United States, despite warnings that his career would "not be interesting" if he continued to talk that way. Rumsfeld can only have been relieved at his departure and assumed, wrongly, that General Newbold was at last out of his life.

Afterward, those who knew Rumsfeld well looked back on his ruthless pruning of the invasion force and noted that in one sense it was out of character. As a former colleague from the Nixon White House had noted, Rumsfeld had an acute sense of "incoming lethality." He applied this principle in the selection of subordinates, who were chosen not only for their loyalty, combined when possible with intelligence and efficiency, but also because they would not make what he called "the big mistake." Asked early on what he saw in Stephen Cambone, for example, Rumsfeld told an associate, "He won't make the big mistake." He would frequently repeat the idea as an admonition to subordinates, "Don't make the big mistake." Yet in the years to come, as critics sourced the cataclysmic disaster of Iraq to the shortage of troops in the occupation army, it seemed it was Rumsfeld who had made the big mistake.

Yet he was not alone in mandating the limit on troop levels. Wolfowitz was no less insistent on ensuring that the expeditionary force remain small. But while Rumsfeld was anxious to demonstrate that a punitive expedition should not and need not lead to the despised "nation building" and other internationalist commitments, Wolfowitz was pursuing a different agenda, one in which Iraq would be handed over unencumbered to Ahmed Chalabi. Early in 2003, the deputy secretary had a revealing conversation with James "Hoss" Cartwright, a senior general on the joint staff. Cartwright was explaining that a total of 400,000 people would be involved in the forthcoming operation. "How can that be?" said Wolfowitz with surprise. "I thought we were only sending 150,000 or so." That might be the case, the general replied, but to keep a force of 150,000 in Iraq for anything longer than a very short amount of time required far more people both in the region and back up the supply chain in the United States. There would be large numbers of personnel, for example, in the pipeline as they rotated in and out of the country. A significant number would be tied up in manning the logistics operation in Kuwait and other resupply bases around the Gulf and elsewhere in the Middle East. Wolfowitz was aghast, and instructed the staff to work up a schedule for a rapid withdrawal of forces once Saddam had been removed from power. They dutifully obliged, giving Wolfowitz the comforting assurance that the numbers involved could be pared down to no more than 34,000 in a matter of weeks.

Late in February 2003, General Shinseki shared his thoughts on the proper number of troops required in Iraq. Asked at a Senate Armed Services Committee hearing if he could give "some idea as to the magnitude of the Army's force requirement for an occupation of

Iraq following a successful completion of the war?" Shinseki replied that "something on the order of several hundred thousand soldiers" would be about right. This somewhat vague response, which elicited little interest from the senators, ignited outrage elsewhere. Wolfowitz called the assessment "wildly off the mark." Perle derided it as "an absurd number," while Rumsfeld, who had just embarked on a scheme to cut the service chiefs' terms of office in half, misquoted Shinseki's statement, saying that the answer to the question posed to the chief of staff was "not knowable" and finally stated that "any idea that it's several hundred thousand [troops stationed in Iraq] over any sustained period is simply not the case."[29]

Though Rumsfeld and Wolfowitz shared an interest in keeping the Iraq expeditionary force as small as possible, they had different motives. Rumsfeld, as we have seen, was determined to prove that the Afghan success story was a model for future operations. His scheme for the Iraq campaign seemed designed to be a lightning raid, at the conclusion of which the raiders would return to base. He showed little interest in what would happen to the country once the regime had been destroyed. His main concern was that American forces should not remain to put down roots as part of some Clinton-style nation-building exercise, as had happened in the Balkans. In many respects, Rumsfeld was an isolationist. It is certainly the case that Bush signed National Security Presidential Directive 24 in January 2003 at Rumsfeld's request, giving the defense department exclusive control of postwar Iraq, but that was at a moment when the State Department was making efforts to secure the postwar portfolio for itself, a bureaucratic gambit that Rumsfeld felt the need to crush summarily. Powell, outmaneuvered yet again, threatened retaliation.

Wolfowitz, on the other hand, along with Perle and the platoons of neoconservatives nestling in the Pentagon, was very interested indeed in what happened to Iraq after the war. The man they trusted to fulfill their hopes and dreams for post-Saddam Iraq was of course Chalabi, whom they expected would assume power in Baghdad as soon as the Baathist regime had been chased away. There was much talk about the overall objective of bringing democracy to Iraq. Years later, the wisdom or otherwise of adopting this goal was still being debated. Yet at the time, the U.S. commitment to democracy was less clear-cut. In February 2003, Zalmay Khalilzad, the expatriate Afghan who at this point had been detailed as White House liaison to the Iraqi exile opposition, informed his clients that Iraq would remain under American military occupation for a year, at least, and strictly forbade them to set up a government-in-waiting before the war started, as they had planned. Despite furious complaints from Chalabi and the Kurdish leaders (who, in contrast to Chalabi, really did have a base of popular support inside the country), the injunction stood.[30] Asked years later about the initiative so abruptly dismissed at that time, a former senior White House official replied vaguely, "I think it was a plan that was too hard to explain and got shelved."

Democracy, or at least Iraqi self-government, might have been shelved, but Chalabi's supporters were still promoting their man. At a White House meeting shortly before the invasion, with Bush presiding and Rumsfeld present, Feith spoke confidently of the leadership role of Ahmed Chalabi in postwar Iraq. However, the president then suddenly spoke up. According to one of those present, he declared forcefully that Chalabi was not "my man" and that the United States would not be imposing a leader on the Iraqis. Chastened, Feith beat a retreat. Rumsfeld said nothing.

A few days later, a similar meeting convened at the White House. This time Wolfowitz was present instead of Feith, but arguing the same case for Chalabi. Again the president refused to endorse the Iraqi, and again Rumsfeld made no demurral—not his normal behavior if he disagreed with a pronouncement from Bush.

It was an extraordinary moment. For years, Ahmed Chalabi had been a key factor in the neoconservative plan for Iraq and the Middle East as a whole. They had poured millions of dollars of taxpayers' money into his pockets. The imminent war would almost certainly not have taken place without him. Only those close to the pinnacle of power would have understood that Rumsfeld himself cared little for the Iraqi intriguer, and the significance of his silence as the president pronounced his judgment. The keystone of the neoconservative plan for Iraq had just been removed, and as time would tell, they had no constructive plan to replace it. Rumsfeld might still

CHAPTER NINE

Reality Intrudes

Contrary to later recriminations, there *was* a postwar plan for Iraq. It worked. Unfortunately, the plan belonged to the other side. Shortly before American forces launched Operation Iraqi Freedom, one of Paul Wolfowitz's aides was handed a document courtesy of Indian intelligence. The document was in Arabic but already translated by the Indians, who had obtained it from their own sources in Iraq. In three pages it outlined Iraqi plans for a postinvasion resistance, complete with instructions to organize resistance cells, destroy government infrastructure, collect arms, and target occupation forces. The Indians, via their intermediary, swore it was genuine.

According to a senior Pentagon official familiar with the episode, those who reviewed this blueprint for insurgency—Wolfowitz, Cambone, and Di Rita—were not impressed. "They looked like this was one of those Nigerian e-mails offering to pay $20 million into your bank account," the official told me. "Their attitude was, 'These people aren't capable of putting something like this together.'" The official does not know if the document ever got passed to Rumsfeld, but in light of later events it is unlikely that the secretary would have paid any more attention to it than did his deputy. Neither of them could believe, as Wolfowitz remarked in response to Shinseki's offhand comment about a postwar requirement for "several hundred thousand" occupation troops, that occupying Iraq might require a bigger force than conquering it in the first place.

As it turned out, Rumsfeld was right about the one thing that would later earn him unending vilification: his insistence that invading Iraq and crushing the regime of Saddam Hussein would not require the enormous force called for in the original war plans. As one of the Kurdish leaders eloquently put it just before the war, Iraq was a "bankrupt emirate with sixty percent of the population on U.N. rations"—a reference to the lifesaving U.N. oil-for-food program. The society had been successively ravaged by the bloody war of attrition with Iran in the 1980s, the brief but destructive war with the United States in 1991, and the crippling economic sanctions imposed and maintained by the victors following that war. Saddam's military forces were as worn down as every other institution in the country. A small but telling example of their disarray was visible at a 1998 military parade in Baghdad, where the elite unit marching past Saddam wore on their hands not white gloves, but white *socks*. Perhaps the billion-dollar satellites high above could not discern this detail, but anyone paying close attention could reasonably conclude that a regime unable to find an adequate supply of gloves was unlikely to have a secret nuclear weapons program.[1]

Nevertheless, the U.S. military planners had done their best to proceed along traditional lines. The air force, for example, insisted on cratering Iraqi airfields to prevent the barely existent Iraqi air force from taking off, as well as pounding "command and control" targets with great determination in unavailing efforts to kill Saddam. The senior ground commanders were mesmerized by Saddam's Republican Guard, which they expected to put up a staunch and bloody defense of Baghdad. Even so, in the absence of significant opposition, the invading forces did move rapidly northward, at least initially. The 3rd Infantry Division, for example, crossed the Euphrates River two days after the start of the war, and then raced three hundred miles in ninety-six hours to within fifty miles of Baghdad at a cost of two American dead. On the other hand, an ill-advised attempt to use massed Apache helicopters in a night assault behind enemy lines failed dismally, with the battered force beating a hurried retreat in the face of enemy rifle fire. This minor setback to the campaign had a depressive effect on American commanders. As General William Wallace told a reporter at the time, "We're dealing with a country in which everybody has a weapon, and when they fire them all into the air at the same time, it's tough."[2] When the 3rd Infantry Division lost all of two tanks and a Bradley fighting vehicle three days later, the mood turned even bleaker, leading to calls to Washington for a halt in the advance while the air force dropped more bombs on the tattered units of Saddam's army. On what was described as the "worst day of the war," an ill-trained and ill-equipped American transport unit ran into a rear-area ambush, losing eleven killed, nine wounded, and seven taken prisoner. Tragic as these casualties were for those affected, overall losses remained extraordinarily light, certainly as compared with conflicts in the past. Suicidal attacks on the heavily equipped U.S. forces by lightly armed "fedayeen" partisans, though causing little damage, were entirely unexpected, leading to the first complaints that Rumsfeld's insistence on a light invasion force had produced disaster.

Doug Macgregor, the military theoretician and combat veteran who made no secret of his contempt for hidebound generals, sent Rumsfeld, via Newt Gingrich, a fiery memo on March 25 pointing out that the "massive" force had taken "almost no casualties" and urging there be no delay in the advance. "Thanks for the Macgregor piece," Rumsfeld replied to Gingrich a day later. "Nobody up here is thinking like this." But on the same day he agreed to a temporary halt in the advance north.[3] His public response to these rumblings was characteristic. Queried on all too accurate reports that he had mandated a far smaller invasion force than that requested by the military, he quickly shifted responsibility onto the shoulders of his faithful combatant commander, Tommy Franks, roping in the Joint Chiefs and the rest of the senior military for good measure. "Tom Franks and the chairman and I, when the president asked us to prepare a plan, looked at the plan that was on the shelf and to a person agreed it was inappropriate," he told George Stephanopoulos on ABC's *This Week* ten days into the war. "Franks then sat down and began planning. The plan we have is his . . . and it is his plan and it has been approved by the chiefs. Every one of the chiefs has said it's executable and they support it. It's been looked at by all the combatant commanders. It's gone through the National Security Council process."[4]

Meanwhile another plan, though categorically discarded by President Bush himself only shortly before, began showing signs of revival. As detailed previously, the neoconservatives had long schemed for Ahmed Chalabi to take power in Iraq. Yet on no less than two occasions, Bush had flatly ruled out the imposition of Chalabi as ruler. Chalabi had moved to northern Iraq, a guest of the Kurds. He had recruited his own militia of a thousand or so men, a motley group, described by journalist Charles Glass as "northerners and southerners, Kurds and Arabs, exiles and those who stayed, veterans of Saddam's army and veterans of no army."[5] Suddenly, as American forces closed in on Baghdad, Chalabi received a request from Centcom to send his men to help subdue the fedayeen guerrillas in the south. Wolfowitz and Feith made sure that Chalabi himself was allowed to travel with his little army, now christened the Free Iraq Forces. In early April, the entire group, some seven hundred men, was flown south on air force C-17s to a former Iraqi base outside the city of Nasiriyah.

"What was all that about?" a former senior White House official wondered aloud to me later. "George Bush had told them, 'No, Chalabi is not my man.' Then Chalabi is introduced almost covertly into Iraq [from Kurdistan]. What were Wolfowitz and company up to? Maybe they thought, 'Fuck the president. We're going to do it anyway.'"

The gambit didn't work. Once in southern Iraq, Chalabi and his men were effectively stranded and isolated by the U.S. military, left with little or no supplies, not even water, in the searing heat of the Iraqi desert.[6] Evidently, someone powerful had given the signal that the ambitious exile was not to be given too much encouragement. In media coverage of his move, the press described Chalabi as "a Pentagon favorite"[7] and "enjoying the support of Pentagon hawks such as Mr. Rumsfeld."[8] But that was misleading. Rumsfeld himself, encouraged by Cambone, disliked and distrusted the man, even despite his links with Perle.

Though few paid attention at the time or since, Rumsfeld made his feelings clear in a press briefing on April 7, the day after the famous exile landed in southern Iraq. Asked whether he was supporting Ahmed Chalabi, or endorsing him for any role in a postwar Iraq, Rumsfeld replied, "Of course not. I just said that the Iraqi people are going to make these decisions. Clearly, the United States is not going to impose a government on Iraq." He was, of course, echoing the words and sentiments of George Bush, a fact unknown to the journalists, but certainly familiar to Wolfowitz and Feith.

The shipment of Chalabi and his cohort to southern Iraq came not only as a surprise to the outside world, it was also news to the rest of the administration, including the CIA (who had long had their private feud with him), but it was by no means the only Pentagon action kept secret from other parts of the government. More than most men of power, Rumsfeld treated information as a weapon, to be hoarded as much as possible and shared only when necessary. At National Security Council meetings, when he was not ejecting lower-ranking staff from the room while he conferred with the president, he would often forbid the taking of notes, on security grounds, by such people as Frank Miller, who for decades had overseen the darkest secrets of American nuclear targeting policy. This passion for secrecy extended to even the most customary interactions between the Pentagon and other agencies, including the White House itself. The details of the Iraq invasion plan, for example, were a process closely held even within the Pentagon, and absolutely withheld even from the military staff at the NSC, let alone the State Department.

Such behavior clearly came easily to a secretary who refused to tell his deputy what had happened at White House meetings. But there was a deeper and more crafty logic behind Rumsfeld's policy of secrecy. He was determined at all costs to protect and maintain the chain of command that made Rumsfeld, and only Rumsfeld, the link between the Pentagon and George Bush. Hence his petty theatrics over the fighter escort for *Air Force One* three days after 9/11. In the months of apparent crisis after 9/11, he instituted the practice of going to see the president every single day. Most of the time there would be high-level White House aides sitting in on the meetings, National Security Adviser Rice, or Chief of Staff Andrew Card. But he also managed to garner the holy grail of Washington's imperial court: regular meetings alone with the president. These private conferences, usually once a week, were themselves deeply secret. Rumsfeld, I was told, "would literally sneak over to the White House," making every effort to be unobserved. According to one former high-ranking official, it was a full year before Powell found out they were happening.

However, skillful operators on the other side were loath to tolerate the defense secretary's control of information. Miller, for example, the former nuclear targeteer who carried the title of senior director for defense policy on the NSC staff, had spent almost three decades in the Pentagon before coming to the White House, and not only knew how the building worked but also enjoyed a huge range of contacts within the military high command. In addition, he had a number of capable military officers assigned to his own staff, and he deployed them to winkle out the defense secretary's secrets. To carry out their mission they not only turned to friends and associates working on the inside who could be persuaded to hand over an envelope containing the latest version of the war plan, they also resorted to cyberwar.

Alongside the Internet we all use, there exists a secret Internet known as Siprnet, available only to those with special clearances and equipment. Siprnet, which stands for Secret Internet Protocol Router Network, is the Pentagon's Internet, and is always kept carefully physically separated from its civilian counterpart. Access to it is severely restricted to special well-guarded terminals. Users must have a password, and all transmissions are highly encrypted. Furthermore, the system is internally compartmentalized, so access to one part does not automatically permit the user to get into a joint staff website, for example, still less Rumsfeld's videoconferences with his combatant commanders, which were transmitted over Siprnet. The officers on Miller's staff had clearance to access the Siprnet; their special skill was in knowing where to look, which secret Pentagon websites to scrutinize, thereby monitoring Rumsfeld's moves in real time. This operation enabled Miller to inform not only Rice, his direct superior, of the latest developments, but also Rumsfeld's detested rivals, Powell and Armitage, at the State Department. Amazingly, this was the only way these high-ranking officers were able to discover, for example, which reserve units the secretary had decided to mobilize, and when. Even more strangely, the bizarre system continued once the war had started, with the president's staff, as well as his senior diplomats, forced to spy on their colleague to find out how America's forces were faring.

Just as Rumsfeld strove for what Torie Clarke called information dominance over the rest of the government, he was at the center of efforts to control the picture that the American public was getting of the war. Part of his contribution came in the form of frequent public appearances, either at Pentagon press conferences or in TV studios, in which he displayed the bluff, confident style he had been perfecting since 9/11. (Wolfowitz was also very much in the public eye, thanks in part to the persistent efforts of his own public affairs staff, which he insisted should remain independent of Clarke.)

There were no subtleties in Rumsfeld's depiction of the war. "War is the last choice," he declared on the opening night. "The American people can take comfort in knowing that their country has done everything humanly possible to avoid war and to secure Iraq's peaceful disarmament." However, he had a less direct but possibly even more effective way of delivering the official message. The proliferation of cable news channels had created a sellers' market for former military officers, preferably high-ranking, who could comment with at least the appearance of expertise on the unfolding drama. For regulars who could deliver pearls of inside information not yet generally available, the rewards could be attractive in the form of lucrative exclusive contracts. Months before the war, therefore, Clarke's team had begun seeking out not only military retirees who were already regular TV guests, but also those who might serve as suitable candidates in the future and offered them an attractive proposition. "We would have them in for regular briefings from the secretary or the chairman," one of Clarke's former staff explained to me. "There was no requirement that they be absolutely uncritical of what we [the U.S. military] were doing; in fact, we welcomed mild criticism. But if they really crossed the line, attacked us strongly, then they were out." For a retired colonel or general who was getting used to regular TV exposure, admission to these briefings was a significant bonus, not to be given up lightly.

At the time of the invasion, the public affairs office on the second floor of the Pentagon had a row of TV monitors constantly tuned to all the news shows. At one point in the early days, one official looked up and saw "every single one had a retired officer on the screen discussing the campaign. Every single one of them was our guy."

Some were more reliable conduits of Rumsfeld's message than others. Retired army colonel Robert Maginnis, for example, was forthright in passing on the secretary's confident assertions regarding Saddam's alleged nuclear, chemical, and biological facilities, and remained a trusted member of the analysts' group almost to the end.[9] Others, notably Barry McCaffrey, a former four-star general with sensitive political antennae, began expressing criticism of Rumsfeld's troop deployment record with the first reports that the invasion force had run into difficulties, and was notified forthwith that he was no longer welcome at the Pentagon background briefings.[10] "He wasn't very happy about it," one of the staff in the public affairs office recalled later, "and asked if he could come back, but we thought he had crossed the line."

But McCaffrey was not alone. "Shock, awe, overconfidence," wrote Colonel Ralph Peters, a retired military intelligence officer, in the *Washington Post* five days into the war. "Military planners have argued for months that more and heavier ground forces were needed. . . . In [Rumsfeld's] vision of the future, one shaped by technocrats and the defense industry, ground forces can be cut drastically. But those who want to wage antiseptic wars for political purposes should not start wars in the first place."[11]

The criticism was wounding, and Rumsfeld did not take it well. Asked in a press conference if he was deliberately withholding reports of U.S. casualties, he angrily pounded the podium with his fist.[12] But the barrage of protest died down as the generals in Iraq recovered their nerve and the advance on Baghdad resumed. Nevertheless, a pattern had been set. If things went seriously wrong in Iraq, the blame would eventually land on Rumsfeld. To make matters worse, at this moment his old ally Richard Perle had to resign as chairman of the defense policy advisory board in the face of questions about his business dealings, notably his recent negotiations with an infamous Saudi arms dealer and his $725,000 contract with a communications company looking for Pentagon clearance for its sale to a Hong Kong billionaire. Rumsfeld issued a statement praising Perle as having "a deep understanding of our national security process."[13]

The furor over the stalled advance and the supposed lack of troops obscured a more fundamental problem, one that could not be

explained away with carefully briefed retired officers or hopeful predictions: the total absence of weapons of mass destruction. No
nuclear facilities of any kind, no biological weapons stocks, not even
a few stray chemical artillery rounds that could have been exhibited
as proof that the accusations had been true. All the intelligence
deployed before the war to indicate the contrary had either been
wishful thinking, or straightforward lies. Hussein Kamel had been
telling the truth.

Rumsfeld took the news badly. As the U.S. forces rolled northward, a dedicated unit searched for evidence of the weapons, and
found none. At his morning briefings on the progress of the war the
secretary grew increasingly angry when one site after another that
had previously been confidently predicted as a weapons site turned
out to be a "dry hole." One officer attending these daily meetings
later reported Rumsfeld as exclaiming, "They must be there." On
another occasion he picked up the paper briefing charts and threw
them at the briefers.[14] Reality was beginning to intrude, and there
was nothing he could do about it, except to move as expeditiously as
possible to devolve responsibility for the WMD hunt onto the CIA.

Ahmed Chalabi, who had done so much to popularize the concept of Saddam's WMD arsenal, later blithely conceded that he had
been totally wrong, but felt there was nothing of which he need be
ashamed. "We are heroes in error," he told Britain's *Daily Telegraph*.
"As far as we're concerned we've been entirely successful. That
tyrant Saddam is gone and the Americans are in Baghdad. What was
said before is not important."[15] Had Saddam's undeniably vicious
regime been succeeded by something clearly and immediately better,
Rumsfeld and his colleagues might have been able to take the same
tack. Unfortunately for the hundreds of thousands of people who
were going to die over the next few years, that was not to be.

Iraqi society had been fraying at the edges for years before the
invasion. I recall the astonished horror of Baghdadis in 1991 as a
crime wave swept across the Iraq capital, spurred by the U.N. sanctions strangling the economy. Along with the spreading plague of
violent robberies, previously incorruptible bureaucrats whose
salaries were being vaporized by inflation began accepting and
then demanding bribes for any and all services. More ominously,

during the bloody uprising and far bloodier suppression of the Shia uprising that followed the 1991 war, all museums across the south were looted. By the time the American invasion army reached Baghdad twelve years later, the Iraqi state had itself withered to a degree that could surprise only those who knew little and cared less about the society they had just conquered.

Looting broke out in Baghdad on April 9 at almost the moment that the last vestiges of the old regime's presence disappeared from the capital. People stormed out of the poorer areas of east Baghdad intent on stripping anything and everything of value from public buildings. The same thing happened in cities across Iraq. Notoriously, the National Museum in the heart of Baghdad was stormed and looted of artifacts dating back to the dawn of civilization. The tears of deputy museum director Nabhal Amin as she gazed in shock at the destruction became a symbol of the overall disaster that had suddenly descended on Iraq.[16]

Rumsfeld reacted to the compelling images of chaos and destruction beamed from Baghdad with both irritation and denial. In an April 11 press conference, where his remarks were interspersed with slides of cheerful GIs in company with happy Iraqis, he infamously exclaimed, "Stuff happens," citing the American urban riots of the 1960s as precedent. The main fault, he made clear, lay with the media. "In terms of what's going on in that country, it is a fundamental misunderstanding to see those images over, and over, and over again of some boy walking out with a vase and say, 'Oh, my goodness, you didn't have a plan.' That's nonsense. They [the U.S. military on the ground] know what they're doing, and they're doing a terrific job."

It was far from the truth. There was no plan for dealing with the situation. (However, Rumsfeld's complaints about misleading reporting would have their effect, as Baghdad news bureaus came under pressure from their headquarters to emphasize more of the good news in their reporting.) Rumsfeld had seized responsibility for postwar Iraq away from the State Department, and had seemingly then lost interest. One former official, who worked closely with Rumsfeld at the Pentagon at this time, suggested that having proved his point that a slimmed-down force moving quickly could defeat

Saddam, Rumsfeld would have been happy to wash his hands of the country and leave its problems for someone else to deal with. "That was clearly his style," he laughed.

A former White House official who had ample opportunity to monitor Rumsfeld during his years of power preferred to explain Rumsfeld's actions in terms of idle vanity: "The man had to be *acknowledged* to be in control. Once people gave him that acknowledgment, he didn't seem to care. They could more or less do what they wanted."

Mostly what the military appeared to want to do was nothing. No one had told the ground commanders what they should do once organized enemy resistance came to an end. These commanders themselves neglected to plan for "Phase IV," as the postconflict era was officially termed. General Mike Hagee, for example, commander of the First Marine Expeditionary Force, later described how he repeatedly asked his superiors to whom he should hand over the towns he captured. The answer was always "someone" whose identity was "undetermined," he said.[17] Accordingly, without orders, nothing was done to impede the looting. No one had the initiative to move an M-1 Abrams tank, already parked just a few yards away, in front of the museum—a move that might have stopped the looting. Even more damning, when looting first broke out on April 9, there were indeed tanks stationed on the bridges over the river Tigris, which divides east and west Baghdad. As a result, potential looters were confined to the eastern side for that day, and the next. West Baghdad remained relatively peaceful and secure. On April 11, however, someone ordered the tanks moved from the bridges. Unconstrained, the mob streamed across the river and west Baghdad was soon in the same state of anarchic mayhem as the rest of the city.[18] General David McKiernan, a cautious commander to say the least, refused to intervene in any way to stop the looting. "This is not my job," he reportedly snapped when urged to do something to arrest the destruction of Baghdad.[19]

Rumsfeld's flippant reaction to the total breakdown of law and order suggested that his knowledge of the people he now ruled was superficial at best. But this degree of ignorance was widespread among the occupiers. I myself had a small insight into this condition when I learned that I possessed the only copy available in Washington of *The Revolt in Mesopotamia*, a lucid account by Lieutenant General Sir Aylmer Haldane, the commander of British forces in Iraq in 1920, of the widespread and bloody popular uprising by the recently conquered Iraqis. I was asked to lend my copy for Xeroxing, to be distributed to some of the U.S. generals who were following in Haldane's footsteps. Subsequent events indicated little sign that any of them read it.

Jay Garner, a retired army general who had been designated as the civilian overseer for occupied Iraq, did not secure permission from Franks to move to Baghdad until ten days after the fall of the old regime. Long before that, Rumsfeld was already planning to replace him with someone with a higher profile, a special presidential envoy who would head up a colonial administration, the Coalition Provisional Authority, or CPA, under his overall supervision. Steve Herbits, charged with reviewing possible candidates to rule Iraq, opted for Paul Wolfowitz. Wolfowitz was very happy with this idea. Chalabi must have been equally thrilled, assuming he knew about it. The proposal was taken seriously at high levels, allegedly endorsed by Cheney.[20]

Sending a passionate Israel supporter to rule a large Arab country would certainly have had the merit of novelty. However, it has not previously been reported that there might have been not one but two of them, for that was what Herbits, later secretary general of the World Jewish Congress, had in mind. Well aware of Wolfowitz's managerial deficiencies, he included in his endorsement of the deputy secretary for the position a proposal that he *himself* go along as well, a de facto prime minister to Wolfowitz the viceroy. "Steve would have been the manager," chuckled one of the few individuals aware of this plan within the plan. "He knew perfectly well that Paul couldn't run the place." Wolfowitz is reported as suspecting that he was ruled out for the job because he was Jewish, but his relationship with Chalabi, who had already received specific nonendorsements from Bush and, by implication, Rumsfeld, may have been enough to put him out of the running.

Herbits's next recommendation appeared less contentious: L. Paul "Jerry" Bremer, a former diplomat and State Department official with no Middle East experience whatsoever. Acceptable to Rumsfeld, endorsed by Wolfowitz, and liked by Bush, Bremer seemed the perfect choice. After two weeks of preparation and briefings he arrived in Baghdad on May 13, primed with an agenda that probably did more than anything to ensure the ultimate doom of the American adventure in Iraq.

On May 14, Bremer unveiled a draft "De-Baathification of Iraqi Society" decree to U.S. officials in Baghdad that mandated the immediate dismissal of all full members of the Baath Party, which had ruled Iraq since 1968. It had been handed to him by Feith before he left Washington. Since party membership was mandatory for all government officials with any degree of responsibility under the old regime, this move deprived up to fifty thousand people of their livelihood and was guaranteed to cripple whatever remained of the administration of Iraq.

On May 15, Bremer showed his staff a draft of a second order. This one abolished the Iraqi army, thereby ensuring that some 400,000 men, all of them with military training and most having access to weapons and explosives, were suddenly on the street with nothing to lose and a very strong grudge against the occupation. Not surprisingly, the origins of this edict are somewhat murky. In his memoir of his year in Iraq, Bremer wrote that this decree had also been under discussion by Feith and others before he left Washington.[21]

The assertion is strange, because just ten days before the war, on March 10, there had been a full dress briefing for President Bush at the White House to discuss the plan for postwar Iraq. Most of the presentation was prepared and delivered by Frank Miller, the senior NSC defense aide. But when it came to the section dealing with the future of the Iraqi military, Rumsfeld had insisted beforehand that such matters were the prerogative of the Defense Department and should therefore be briefed by someone from the Pentagon. Accordingly, Feith took the slides already prepared by Miller, had them stamped with the Pentagon logo, and read them to the president at the briefing. They laid out in precise detail how the Iraqi army would be kept intact and be used to provide security after the war.

"So what happened?" wondered an official who had been present at that meeting. "Everything in that briefing had been reviewed and approved at the different agencies by the deputies and principals. It was absolutely clear that we intended to keep the army. Then two months later, Bremer arrives and abolishes it. The strange thing is that if [the neocons] were going to put Chalabi in power, they needed stability—there had to be some sort of government functioning for him to take over—but abolishing the army guaranteed that there would be no stability. Maybe by that point they had given up. Chalabi had been Plan A, but there was no Plan B." (On the other hand, Chalabi had a vested interest in the dissolution of the army, since it was thought to be a stronghold of support for the rival exile politician, Iyad Allawi.)

Anthony Zinni, the former commanding general of Centcom, has suggested that there was indeed a neocon Plan B, which was to let Iraq sink into chaos. Well before the first American soldier crossed the border, he concluded, "the neocons didn't really give a shit what happened in Iraq and the aftermath." He believed that though they may have hoped Chalabi would take power, an alternative scenario in which Iraq fell apart in chaos was entirely acceptable and they would welcome a "messy" outcome that diverted attention from the Israel-Palestine peace process, whatever the degree of bloodshed in Iraq itself.[22] Zinni based this depressing conclusion, as he told me, on his "observations of the neocons in action" rather than any direct evidence.

However, a month before the invasion, an important Shi'ite cleric, Majid al-Khoei, flew to Washington from London, where he had lived since fleeing Iraq in 1991. Al-Khoei was the son of Grand Ayatollah Mohammed al-Khoei, the most revered and influential cleric in the Shi'ite world until his death in 1992. The younger al-Khoei was himself a respected figure among Iraqi Shi'ites both outside and inside Iraq, and therefore of interest to officials and others involved in invasion planning. On his return to London he told friends that he had spoken with some "American Jews," which was how he might have described neocons, who had informed him that "preserving the unity of Iraq" was no longer a priority of American policy, and therefore the emergence of a separate Shi'ite state in southern Iraq would be entirely acceptable. This meant, as al-Khoei observed, that "there would be a Shia state in the south with lots of oil, a Kurdish state in the north with lots of oil, and a Sunni state in the middle with no oil at all!"[23]

Early in April 2006, the CIA flew al-Khoei to Iraq and escorted him to his native city of Najaf. A few days after his arrival, he was hacked to death by a mob with the apparent complicity or even encouragement of a younger and then relatively unknown cleric, Moqtada al-Sadr.

This evidence, though circumstantial, at least supplies some explanation for the curious decisions emanating from Washington at that time, including the abrupt abandonment of the prewar commitment to preserve the Iraqi army. Apologists for the abolition, including Bremer, argued later that the decree was purely pro forma, as the army had in any case dispersed and gone home at the end of the war, effectively abolishing itself. This was entirely untrue. American officers had been talking to army representatives, who were eager to cooperate. When the decision was announced, large numbers of former soldiers demonstrated angrily. Three days after the announcement the first U.S. soldier to die in an IED (improvised explosive device) attack was killed on the road to the Baghdad airport. American military intelligence officers assumed as a matter of course that it had been planted by newly unemployed and angry soldiers.

Meanwhile, documents similar to the directive passed on to the Pentagon by Indian intelligence weeks earlier were starting to turn up in Baghdad. Dated from before the war, they commanded members of Saddam's secret service, the Mukhabarat, to promote chaos by burning public buildings and records and discouraging collaboration.[24] Over the following months, further evidence emerged that there was a brain at work behind at least part, but only part, of the resistance to the occupation. Someone had apparently been studying the Western military occupation of Bosnia and Kosovo, noting the importance of helpful regional allies, NGOs (nongovernment organizations), and the United Nations to the comparative success of those undertakings. On August 7, a huge bomb tore apart the Baghdad embassy of Jordan, whose government then became rather less helpful to the United States. On August 17, an ever bigger blast ripped the U.N. office, killing the senior U.N. official in Iraq, Sergio Vieira de Mello. The United Nations sharply reduced its presence in Iraq. In October, another bomb exploded outside the Red Cross compound in Baghdad, with predictable effects on the enthusiasm of

NGOs for working in the country. If the United States was going to reconstruct Iraq, it would be doing so almost on its own. Contrary to the initial reaction to the Indian intelligence gift at the time of the invasion, it seemed that Iraqis were perfectly capable of "putting something like this together."

Rumsfeld did not see it that way, at least not for a very long time. On April 30, 2003, as the smoke of burning buildings clouded the sky above Baghdad, the secretary of defense told those Iraqis fortunate enough to have electricity to power their TVs: "Coalition forces are working in close partnership with Iraqi citizens to restore order and basic services. Each day that goes by, conditions in Iraq are improving."[25]

In the streets outside, U.S. troops on patrol were not only taking fire, they were also being stoned by gangs of youths emulating familiar scenes of Palestinians throwing stones at their Israeli occupiers.[26] The previous day, in Fallujah, a quiet city on the main highway to Jordan, hundreds of mourners chanted, "We will sacrifice our souls and our blood to you martyrs," as they followed coffins of some of the thirteen townspeople killed when soldiers of the 82nd Airborne Division, based in a schoolhouse, opened fire on a crowd outside. The crowd had been demonstrating to get their school back.[27]

The following day, May 1, Centcom announced that major combat operations were officially over, and President Bush dressed up in a flight suit to land on the aircraft carrier *Abraham Lincoln*. The White House had arranged for the ship to sport a banner with the words "Mission Accomplished" over the flight deck. Rumsfeld later asserted that he had been opposed to claiming that the mission was accomplished.

In the following six weeks, about fifty American soldiers died in Iraq due to attacks and accidents. Rumsfeld sought to put these casualties in perspective. "If Washington, D.C., were the size of Baghdad," he told a Pentagon press briefing, "we would be having something like 215 murders a month." In any event, resistance was coming merely from "small elements" of ten to twenty people, "dead-enders."[28]

A month later, the number of American dead since May 1 had risen to eighty-one, still mostly from accidents, but plans for a major withdrawal of troops—nine thousand men from the army's 3rd Division—were put on hold for an indefinite time. At the Pentagon, Rumsfeld defended as "imperfect but good" the intelligence the Bush administration had used to build its case for a war to disarm Saddam of weapons of mass destruction.

"I think the intelligence was correct in general," he said. "And you will always find out precisely what it was once you get on the ground and have a chance to talk to people and explore it." On the day the 3rd Division got the bad news, someone threw a grenade at the American occupation headquarters, Saddam's former Republican Palace. Jay Garner had selected the site to set up shop, apparently oblivious to the implications for ordinary Iraqis of the new rulers simply moving into the same quarters as the old.

This was one decision by the departed Garner left unchanged by Bremer, who was attempting to rule Iraq with the help of a drove of eager young Republicans, many recruited through the website of the right-wing Heritage Foundation. Senior Pentagon officials bridled at derisive criticism of these youths, some of whom were as ignorant as they were arrogant, claiming that due to a malign lack of cooperation from the diplomats, they had no other source of recruits. "When Rumsfeld got control of postwar Iraq," one former Pentagon official grumbled to me, "Powell said, 'Screw them, let the fuckers stew.' At that point the State Department began a determined rearguard action against us, discouraging their staff from working for the CPA."

By July, no one was pretending that Baghdad was a safe environment for the occupation authority staff. The entire sprawling city of 5.5 million people was designated as a "Red Zone" by the American military, the only exception being the increasingly fortified enclave around the Republican Palace, the "Green Zone." Inside the Green Zone, members of Iraq's new ruling class were assured of constant electric power, air-conditioning, clean water, and a lively social life. One visitor from Washington in July, invited to the Green Zone for a poolside buffet dinner, was surprised to find the Iraqi staff decked out in period costumes from the era of 1001 Nights.

Out in the Red Zone, resentment of the occupiers was increasing day by day. The Kurds in their northern mountains remained comparatively friendly toward Americans, not only because the invasion had destroyed the genocidal regime of Saddam Hussein, but also because they were not under foreign occupation. The Shi'ites, though also happy that the United States had rescued them from the Baathist yoke, had no affection for the foreigners, and within a year they would be fighting them. But in Baghdad, even by June, the killing of American soldiers was already sparking local celebrations in places where it occurred. In July, Richard Wild, a young British freelance journalist, was murdered in the street, almost certainly because his dress and close-cropped hair caused him to resemble someone from the CPA.[29]

Back on the E Ring of the Pentagon, "We were still high-fiving each other" in July 2003, one member of the inner circle told me. That month, Rumsfeld invited in the graying "formers"—former secretaries of defense. Henry Kissinger came as well. As was his custom, he stood while they sat down for lunch. "A little show of dominance," said one of his staff. The formers were treated to a briefing on progress in Iraq, but the skeptical old gentlemen persisted in quizzing Rumsfeld on what lay ahead. "What's your plan?" they pressed. Rumsfeld fudged. "I'm not in a position to show you what we're doing," he told them. "Everything's fluid."

Despite the ongoing upbeat mood along the wide Pentagon corridors, the small but steady trickle of casualties was an awkward reminder that Iraq was far from being at peace. This was a touchy subject. Though "dead-ender" was acceptable in Rumsfeld's company as a description for those mounting attacks on the occupation forces, his preferred term was "Former Saddam Loyalist," which quickly and inevitably became the acronym FSL. Other words that were beginning to come into use in the world outside, such as "insurgent" or "resistance," were completely out of bounds. Even Cambone thought this rule was silly, but Rumsfeld was adamant that the United States was not facing "anything like a guerrilla war, or an organized resistance." He took particular exception to a reporter's use of the word "quagmire," an unwelcome reminder of Vietnam. "It's a different time," he said. "It's a different era. It's a different place."[30]

On the other hand, the U.S. military in Iraq was definitely evoking memories of a different time that summer, launching massive

Vietnam-style "sweeps" with pretentious code names—Ivy Lightning, Desert Scorpion, Peninsula—aimed at rounding up the FSLs who were giving Operation Iraqi Freedom a bad name. As they crashed through the countryside, these operations tended to have one significant effect, which was to increase the level of hostility between both sides. That summer I heard the GI's refrain "They hate us and we hate them" for the first time. To the soldiers, all Iraqis were now "hajis," as all Vietnamese a generation before had been "gooks."

There is no reason to believe that the several hundred thousand troops trimmed by Rumsfeld from the invasion force would have had any different attitudes. Their presence was therefore as likely to have hastened the insurgency as prevented it.

The Geneva conventions, tossed aside almost casually in Afghanistan, were supposedly fully in effect in Iraq. But in reality, they were equally unwelcome and unobserved. Civilians picked up in the sweeps as suspected FSLs were "persons under confinement," or PUCs. A statement given by "Sergeant A" of the 82nd Airborne to Human Rights Watch in 2005 provides a chilling illustration of the consequences of this officially sanctioned policy at the farther end of the chain of command. From August 2003, the sergeant was stationed at Camp Mercury, a "forward operating base" close to the town of Fallujah, due west of Baghdad. As he explained, "To 'fuck a PUC' meant to beat him up. We would give them blows to the head, chest, legs, and stomach, pull them down, kick dirt on them. This happened every day. To 'smoke' someone is to put them in stress positions until they get muscle fatigue and pass out. That happened every day. . . . On their day off, people would show up all the time. Everyone in camp knew if you wanted to work out your frustration you show up at the PUC tent. In a way it was sport. The cooks were all U.S. soldiers. One day a sergeant shows up and tells a PUC to grab a pole. He told him to bend over and broke the guy's leg with a mini Louisville Slugger that was a metal bat. He was the fucking cook. He shouldn't be in with no PUCs. . . . People would just volunteer just to get their frustrations out. We had guys from all over the base just come to guard PUCs so they could fuck them up. Broken bones didn't happen too often, maybe every other week."[31]

Following this experience, PUCs and prisoners collected by other units were sent on to Abu Ghraib, the sinister prison just outside Baghdad where Saddam had held the bulk of his prisoners. His successors in the Republican Palace had deemed it too useful to discard. No one in the Green Zone, or in Washington, appears to have reflected on the symbolism of this decision.

Quite apart from the violence routinely meted out to "hajis," Iraqis had other reasons to feel disillusioned with the occupation. Traveling around the country a few months after the invasion, I was struck by the fact that every Iraqi I met, in Sunni and Shi'ite areas, was utterly convinced that the occupation was intrinsically corrupt. Many had concrete examples to back up their accusations. Businessmen complained that bribes were solicited in exchange for reconstruction work; ordinary citizens insisted that they were routinely robbed by military patrols searching their houses or cars at checkpoints. Thanks to a well-founded distrust of the banking system under Saddam, ordinary people often kept their entire life savings at home, often in the form of dollars, troves that occupation search parties all too often confiscated on the grounds that the money signified some connection to the dead-enders. "I keep hearing rumors about our attached infantry company. Apparently they are under investigation for a few 'incidents,' " a young infantry captain based in Baiji, a grim city in the northern Sunni Triangle, wrote home to his family that first August. "It seems that whenever they get the chance, they steal money from the locals. I'm not talking about small amounts of cash, I'm talking about a nice, fat bankroll. They take the money during raids, while searching cars, while detaining locals."

The immorality, as well as the practical consequences, of such behavior toward the local population was clearly apparent to many officers and men. "I really don't care for the Iraqi people, I don't care about helping them get back on their feet," the captain continued in his letter, which was later forwarded to me by his father, a decorated Vietnam veteran distraught at his son's involvement in this repetition of history. "However, I don't condone stealing from them, hurting them unnecessarily or threatening them with violence if it is not needed. We will never win hearts and minds here, but what these guys are doing is wrong. I am positive that this isn't happening in my company, and that's all I can really affect." Such determination to maintain the honor and standards of his profession was, unfortunately, all too rare.

Far away in Washington, oblivious to the ground truths of life under occupation, not to mention the everyday barbarism of the PUC tents, Rumsfeld was growing increasingly frustrated at the constant talk of "guerrilla war" and "resistance," which was infecting even the higher echelons of Centcom and the army staff. In August, for example, he arranged for a briefing for senior civilian and military staff that had been prepared by an officer at JFCOM (Paul Van Riper's bête noire) on "lessons learned" in the invasion of Iraq. Rumsfeld highly approved of the presentation, which had some very positive things to say about the "transformational" aspects of the campaign. But his mood was spoiled by some unexpectedly frank comments from General Jack Keane, the acting chief of staff of the army. (Shinseki had finally left in April; neither Rumsfeld nor Wolfowitz had been invited to his leaving ceremony.) "You never told us we'd be facing this insurgency," one attendee recalls Keane saying to Rumsfeld. "You never told us there would be resistance." Neither Rumsfeld nor Wolfowitz, who was also present, reacted to this outburst. "They both just sat there."

Sometime in mid-August, however, Rumsfeld took action to deal with the question of "insurgency" once and for all. During an intelligence briefing in his office he reportedly expressed outrage at the quality of intelligence he was receiving from Iraq, which he loudly and angrily referred to as "shit," banging the table with his fist "so hard we thought he might break it," according to one report. His principal complaint was that the reports were failing to confirm what he knew to be true—that hostile acts against U.S. forces in Iraq were entirely the work of FSLs and dead-enders. Scathingly, he compared the quality of the Iraqi information with the excellent intelligence that was now, in his view, being extracted from prisoners being held at Guantánamo, or "Gitmo," as the military termed it, under the able supervision of prison commander Major General Geoffrey Miller.[32] Rumsfeld concluded his diatribe with a forthright instruction to Cambone that Miller be ordered immediately to the Abu Ghraib prison and "Gitmoize it." Cambone, in turn, dispatched the deputy undersecretary of defense for intelligence, Lieutenant General William

Boykin, a fervent Christian fundamentalist given to deriding the Muslims' Allah as "an idol," to Cuba to brief Miller on his mission.[33]

Boykin must have given Miller careful instructions, for he arrived in Iraq fully prepared, bringing with him experts such as a female interrogator practiced in the art of sexually taunting prisoners, as well as useful tips on the use of dogs as a means of intimidating interviewees. First on his list of appointments was Lieutenant General Ricardo Sanchez, who had succeeded McKiernan as the commander of all U.S. forces in Iraq. It must have been an instructive conversation. Within thirty-six hours Sanchez issued instructions on detainee interrogation that mirrored those authorized by Rumsfeld for use at Guantánamo in December the previous year, which gave cover to techniques including hooding, nudity, stress positions, "fear of dogs," and "mild" physical contact with prisoners. There were, however, some innovations in Sanchez's instructions, such as sleep and dietary manipulation. Brigadier General Janis Karpinski, the overall commander of the U.S. military prison system in Iraq at that time, later insisted that she did not know what was being done to the prisoners at Abu Ghraib, though she did recall Miller remarking that "at Guantánamo Bay we learned that the prisoners have to earn every single thing that they have" and "if you allow them to believe at any point that they are more than a dog then you've lost control of them."

The techniques were apparently fully absorbed by the Abu Ghraib interrogators and attendant military police, as became apparent when photographs snapped by the MPs finally began to surface, initially on CBS News's *60 Minutes* in late April 2004. When Rumsfeld first learned that there were pictures extant of naked, humiliated, and terrified prisoners being abused by cheerful Americans, he said, according to an official who was present, "I didn't know you were allowed to bring cameras into a prison!"

It is not clear when Rumsfeld first saw the actual photographs. He himself testified under oath to Congress that he first saw them in expurgated form when they were published in the press, and only got to look at the originals nine days later after his office had been "trying to get one of the disks for days and days."[34]

The army's criminal investigation division began a probe on January 16, 2004, after Joseph Darby, a soldier not involved in the abuse, slipped them a CD containing some of the photos. As the CID investigation set to work, Karpinski, according to her later testimony, asked a sergeant at the prison "What's this about photographs?" The sergeant replied, "Ma'am, we've heard something about photographs, but I have no idea. Nobody has any details, and ma'am, if anybody knows, nobody is talking." When she asked to see the logbooks kept by the military intelligence personnel, she was told that the CID had cleared everything up. However, when she went to look for herself, she found they had missed a piece of paper stuck on a pole outside a little office used by the interrogators. "It was a memorandum signed by Secretary of Defense Rumsfeld, authorizing a short list, maybe six or eight techniques: use of dogs; stress positions; loud music; deprivation of food; keeping the lights on—those kinds of things," Karpinski said. Over to the side of the paper was a line of handwriting, which to her appeared to be in the same hand and with the same ink as the secretary's signature. The line read: "Make sure this happens!!"

Further indications of Rumsfeld's close interest in ongoing events at Abu Ghraib emerged in subsequent court proceedings. In May 2006, Sergeant Santos Cardona, an army dog handler, was court-martialed at Fort Meade, Maryland. In stipulated testimony, Major Michael Thompson, who had been assigned to the 325th Military Intelligence Battalion in the relevant period and reported to Colonel Tom Pappas, the battalion commander, stated that he was frequently told by Pappas's executive assistant that "Mr. Donald Rumsfeld and Mr. Paul Wolfowitz" had called and were "waiting for reports." The defense also read aloud stipulated testimony from Steve Pescatore, a civilian interrogator employed by CACI, a corporation contracted to assist in interrogations, who recalled being told by military intelligence personnel that Secretary Rumsfeld and Wolfowitz received "nightly briefings."

Needless to say, the numerous investigations of itself by the military high command concluded that no officer or official above the rank of colonel bore any responsibility for Abu Ghraib. Colonel Pappas was granted immunity in return for his testimony against a dog handler. One of the investigations, conducted by former defense secretary James Schlesinger (who had become a friend of Rumsfeld's since the distant days of the Ford administration), concluded that the whole affair had been simply "animal house on the night shift," the acts of the untrained national guard military police unit from Cumberland, Maryland, assigned to Abu Ghraib.

This strategy of deflecting responsibility downward appears to have been crafted in the three desperate weeks that followed the initial call for comment on the photographs from *60 Minutes* producer Mary Mapes. While General Myers bought time with appeals to the broadcasters' patriotism, Rumsfeld's public affairs specialists went into crisis mode under the urgent direction of Larry Di Rita, who had taken on Torie Clarke's responsibilities following her departure in April 2003. To help in developing tactics to deal with the storm they knew would break once *60 Minutes* went ahead with its story, Di Rita's staff summoned an "echo chamber" of public relations professionals, "all Republicans, of course," as one official assured me, from big Washington firms to advise them. Naturally, the well-oiled system for delivering the official line through the medium of TV military analysts was brought into play. Retired army general David Grange, one of the stars of this system, got the tone exactly right on CNN. Responding to a question from Lou Dobbs that though there were six soldiers facing charges, "their superiors had to know what was going on here," Grange responded quickly, "Or they didn't know at all because they lacked the supervision of those soldiers or [were not] inspecting part of their command." In other words, the higher command's fault lay not in their encouraging the torture at Abu Ghraib but simply in their failure to notice what the guards were up to. "These soldiers," continued Grange indignantly, "these few soldiers let down the rest of the force in Iraq and the United States, to include veterans like myself. It is unexcusable."[35]

Meanwhile, Rumsfeld accepted full responsibility without taking any blame, a standard response for high officials implicated in scandal. He said he'd had no idea what was going on in his Iraqi prisons until Specialist Darby, whom he commended, alerted investigators in January, though he also claimed that a vague press release on the investigation issued in Baghdad at that time had in fact "broken the story" and alerted "the whole world." (His very specific identification of Darby rendered the previously anonymous whistleblower liable to lethal sanctions from his fellow soldiers.) He said he had written not one but two letters of resignation to President Bush, which were rejected. General Myers testified under oath that he never informed Rumsfeld that he was trying to persuade CBS to suppress their report.[36] After a leaked internal report by General Antonio Taguba, detailing how "numerous incidents of sadistic, blatant, and wanton criminal abuses were inflicted on several detainees" at Abu Ghraib, had been published in the press and even on Fox TV a few days after the original CBS broadcast, Feith sent an urgent memo around the Pentagon warning officials not to read it, or even discuss it with family members.[37] What Rumsfeld did not mention in all his public protestations of regret over Abu Ghraib was that in the same month of May 2004, he had on his desk a report prepared by the navy inspector general's office detailing the interrogation methods, refined in their cruelty, being practiced on José Padilla and other inmates in the South Carolina naval brig.

By the time the Abu Ghraib photographs had ensured, as Senator Jack Reed (D-R.I.) put it, that "for the next fifty years in the Islamic world and many other parts of the world, the image of the United States will be that of an American soldier dragging a prostrate, naked Iraqi across the floor on a leash," it had become impossible even for Rumsfeld to blame the FSLs for the problems of Iraq. Casualties had been edging up steadily since the previous fall. In late October an imaginatively planned rocket attack on the Rashid Hotel in Baghdad had almost killed Wolfowitz. Apparently undismayed, he continued his tour of inspection, at one point landing his helicopter in a field near Tikrit to address a group of Iraqi farmers on the subject of De Tocqueville and democracy. A few days later, a shoulder-fired rocket brought down a Chinook helicopter, killing sixteen American servicemen. "In a long, hard war," said Rumsfeld, "we're going to have tragic days, as this is. But they are necessary." Gingrich, who was still in close contact with the secretary, told a friend that "we're going to use the Shia and the Kurds to go after the Sunni." Recruitment for the new Iraqi army was stepped up, most of the recruits coming from the Shi'ite and Kurdish communities. Whatever the intent, this had the inevitable effect of exacerbating sectarian tensions. The rebellious Sunni now perceived the Shi'ites as traitors, collaborators with the occupying enemy, and felt free to launch bloody attacks on them, which of course elicited equally bloody reprisals.

By April 2004, while Myers and others in Rumsfeld's entourage strove to keep Abu Ghraib off the air, all of Iraq was in flames. A team of private security consultants from the Blackwater Corporation were ambushed and killed in Fallujah, the city west of Baghdad that had been a center of resistance ever since U.S. troops had opened fire on a crowd of demonstrators shortly after the invasion. The Blackwater ambush occurred close by the spot where local day laborers customarily waited for employers, and it was these people who dragged the dead Americans from their vehicle and dismembered the bodies.

Contrary to the advice of local marine commanders, orders from Washington directed that "heads roll" in Fallujah, and the marines therefore launched a full-scale attack on the town. Simultaneously, the radical Shi'ite cleric Moqtada al-Sadr rose in revolt, seizing control of Najaf, the holiest site in the Shi'ite religion. After heavy fighting, the marines were forced to withdraw from Fallujah while al-Sadr remained in control of Najaf. So critical was the military situation at that point, a year after the triumphant entry into Baghdad, that the sybaritic Green Zone briefly ran short of food. The U.S. military was so caught off guard and oblivious to realities on the ground that they continued to send fuel convoys on roads controlled by insurgents, which were then promptly attacked and destroyed. Scrambling for reinforcements, army commanders were reduced to flying in individual tanks from Germany, at vast expense.

The war had settled into a pattern. U.S. successes, when they occurred, were temporary, or masked a setback elsewhere. In November 2004, for example, the marines launched a renewed assault on the town of Fallujah, reducing much of the city to ruins in the process of occupying it. But meanwhile, unnoticed by most of the outside world, the insurgents captured the far bigger and more important city of Mosul. A renewed effort to "kill or capture" al-Sadr with a heavy attack on his Najaf lair once again ended in a stalemate. In Washington, officials, including Rumsfeld, emphasized and reemphasized that the U.S. strategy was to train a new Iraqi army and police force to take responsibility for security. But despite a flood of statistics to demonstrate progress in this effort, the grimmer statistic of U.S. casualties in Iraq was what attracted the attention of Americans back home. Month by month, the toll of the dead and wounded mounted.

Rumsfeld showed every sign of being engrossed in the day-to-day details of the war. His daily schedule revealed hours blocked off for videoconferences with his commanders in Iraq. Yet it was hard to see any practical effects of this hands-on management. For example, though building the new Iraqi army was the highest priority, it emerged in 2005 that corrupt officials in the Iraqi government had stolen all—not a portion, *all*—of the fledgling force's budget for new weapons, some $1.3 billion. This enormous robbery had apparently proceeded unnoticed by any of the U.S. command in Baghdad, including General David Petraeus, the media favorite with specific responsibility for training the new army. Nor had Rumsfeld, it seemed, cared to ask after the equipping of the new force supposedly so important to administration plans for Iraq.

The lack of planning could be seen not only in broad terms but also in the most minute detail. While Iraqi soldiers were forced to ride to combat in battered pickup trucks because the money for proper armored vehicles had been stolen, U.S. forces were not that much better off. Although the Iraq war had already cost over $130 billion, $77 billion in 2004 alone,[38] families of American soldiers were spending their own money, in some cases going heavily into debt, in order to buy vital equipment such as body armor for their sons, brothers, or husbands in Iraq. In October 2004, *60 Minutes* reported that soldiers in Iraq were resorting to making their own makeshift protection for unarmored Humvees, using sandbags and plywood. In addition, they were scouring scrapheaps for discarded armor that they could use for a little extra protection. Asked by the program for comment, an army spokesman complacently replied, "As long as the army has a single vehicle without armor, we expect that our soldiers will continue to find ways to increase their level of protection."[39]

Pictures of American soldiers improvising wooden armor were more than just a reflection of the uncaring and incompetent civilian and military high command that sent them. In a literal sense they illustrated the defeat of an idea. Manifestos inspired by the revolution in military affairs, such as the neoconservatives' Rebuilding America's Defenses, had given little or no consideration to guerrilla insurgencies, and the techniques they might adopt to counter U.S. military technology. No one seemed to want to reflect on the Vietnam experience, which might have served as a reminder of the devastating effect of home-made mines.

So it was that the appearance of the improvised explosive device (IED) in Iraq came as a nasty surprise. The phenomenon can probably be dated from May 26, 2003, when Private First Class Jeremiah D. Smith of Odessa, Missouri, was killed when a bomb in a canvas bag exploded under his Humvee on the Baghdad airport highway. At the time, the Defense Department said he had been killed by "unexploded ordnance." By July, however, the military were officially listing IED as a cause of death, of which there were four cases that month. The number soon began to climb, as this was a weapon ideally suited to local conditions. Iraq was blessed with an extensive and well-built road system, limitless stocks of freely accessible explosives, many capable engineers, and a huge pool of trained military personnel who had been rendered recently and abruptly unemployed.

Equally necessary for IED utility, from the very beginning the commanders of the occupying army placed a premium on "presence," a concept that found practical expression in convoys of (lightly) armored vehicles traveling up and down the roads, often in predictable patterns. As a Defense Department analyst who carried out an in-depth study of the IED phenomenon remarked to me, "We have a contract with the insurgents; they bring the bomb, and we bring the target."

The military were ill equipped to deal with the problem. A combat engineer in a unit assigned to search for IEDs explained that he found an out-of-print Vietnam-era manual useful, and thought it had not been reissued because no one at the top wanted to encourage comparisons between Iraq and Vietnam. Combat engineers were trained to clear Soviet minefields with metal detectors, but they were of little use here, as Iraqi roadsides where IEDs were planted customarily doubled as garbage dumps, and were littered with cans and other metal junk.

Fairly speedily, according to the Pentagon specialist on the subject, the manufacture and distribution of IEDs were making a significant contribution to the Iraqi economy, employing upwards of twenty thousand people. The forty or fifty separate resistance groups, though of widely differing ideological persuasions, all tended to be organized in similar fashion. Under a senior commanding figure, four or five organizers would each supply roughly five bomb makers with the necessary finance. Each of the bomb makers would in turn supply bombs to five or so "placers," who selected the sites for the bomb and put them in place. Finally, the "triggermen" would wait for a suitable target to pass within lethal range of the bomb and detonate it. On average, intelligence collected over the years indicated, one week would elapse between production of a bomb and its detonation. Despite differing political agendas among the groups, technical and tactical information on innovations in bomb-making techniques, and developments in U.S. counter-IED tactics, appeared to flow rapidly from group to group.

The success of the weapon was summed up in the a DoD study in one devastating statistical ratio: seven to one. "We lose seven people for every one bomb planter we kill or capture. Given that thousands of people are engaged in the activity, this means that the risk for an individual in planting a bomb, for which he gets paid $100, is essentially zero."

Early in 2006, the IED problem, already responsible for roughly half of all U.S. casualties, took on a new urgency. Almost since the beginning of the occupation, units had occasionally been hit by an IED variant known as EFPs, which stood for "explosively formed projectiles," against which even up-to-date armor, let alone plywood and sandbags, was no defense at all. These were "shaped charge" bombs: high explosives packed around a metal cone, easily manufactured in any machine shop. When detonated, the explosives compress the cone, squeezing it forward, so that it becomes a high-speed jet of molten metal capable of piercing the armor even of an M-1 tank "like butter." This had far-reaching implications for any occupation force. "EFPs are the reason the Israelis left Lebanon [in 2000]. There comes a point where you simply cannot afford to travel by road," one specialist told me.

By the spring of 2006, EFP detonations were at one hundred a month and climbing. In April, Rumsfeld came to Baghdad and asked officers he encountered to tell him their biggest concerns. EFPs, he was told, every time. He was in fact already aware of the problem, throwing his weight behind the preferred military solution: money. At Fort Belvoir, Virginia, a few miles south of Washington, a new organization had sprung up endowed with limitless funds and hundreds of engineers. Its one task was summed up in its name: Joint IED Defeat. In 2006, this rapidly expanding enterprise spent $3.32 billion, without practical result. Since the other side often relied on cell phones or car-door openers to detonate their explosives, the engineers did develop a device to jam the signal. It cost $100,000 apiece, the same as the Humvees on which it was mounted, although when it was discovered that one jammer did not cover the full spectrum that could be used by the other side, IED Defeat recommended the use of a second $100,000 jammer on all vehicles. IED makers quickly responded by shifting to nonradio means of detonating their weapons, such as infrared beams, pressure plates, and other mechanisms. "What did that $3.32 billion really buy us?" a former high-ranking Pentagon official said to me. "Zero."

In December 2004, before the spread of EFPs began to nullify even the thickest armor, Rumsfeld was passing through Kuwait and scheduled one of his "town meetings," at which he was accustomed to exhort the troops and answer a few deferential questions. Specialist Thomas Wilson of the Tennessee National Guard drew cheers from his comrades when he asked why, after three years of fighting, "do we soldiers have to dig through local landfills for pieces of scrap metal and compromised ballistic glass to up-armor our vehicles, and why don't we have those resources readily available to us?"

Rumsfeld replied that matters were improving but "as you know, you go to war with the army that you have . . . not the army you might want or wish to have at a later time." He might have added that in his mind the entire invasion of Iraq had been intended as a showcase for the army he wished to have, which was now being defeated. But he didn't bring up transformation that day in Kuwait. The battle-weary troops might not have understood.

CHAPTER TEN

Downfall

As the wars in Iraq and Afghanistan got bloodier, the Pentagon began staging parades that ran around the innermost A Ring of the building, which overlooked the central courtyard. One morning in March 2006 I went along to watch what was billed as the "Parade of Heroes." All offices in the building had been notified by e-mail the day before. "As a side note," the message read, "the visit this Friday will be all amputees, and will be our first visit with military members from all four services." The Pentagon loves milestones. A few minutes before the scheduled start time—noon—the hallways were lined with office workers, many of them in the combat fatigues that had become fashionable for day-to-day wear at the Pentagon since 9/11. As the first two men in wheelchairs rolled into view, everyone began applauding. They were both double amputees. The older of the two, in his late twenties, bore a look of resignation. The other, a young man barely out of his teens, seemed more upbeat, cheerfully acknowledging handclasps thrust out from the spectators lining the walls.

After a pause, the soldiers, marines, and sailors in wheelchairs and on gurneys began coming in clusters. All were young, all men except for one pretty dark-haired girl missing both legs, one above the knee. Some were walking wounded, either because they had already learned to use their new legs or because they had lost only hands or arms to the bombs. Some had only hospital staff to walk with them, others had brought family. The mood in these little groups appeared to vary. A girl wearing a sky blue Rolling Stones T-shirt chatted cheerfully with her brother as she pushed him along. A more somber family followed them, a mother and father flanking their son, a double amputee. The constant patter of applause waxed and waned as the clusters passed, until dozens had gone by and disappeared out of sight around the corner. Given suitable support and medical care, these young people, and the thousands of others they represented, could expect to survive as living components of the Rumsfeld legacy for at least half a century.

Those Americans who do not come into direct contact with wounded veterans may feel the impact in other ways. At the beginning of 2006, Nobel Prize–winning economist Joseph Stiglitz had estimated the total war cost at up to $2 trillion, thanks in part to the cost of long-term health care for those wounded both in body and mind—one in five returning veterans was reported to be suffering from post-traumatic stress disorder.[1]

Meanwhile, around the country, inanimate mementos of the war were accumulating in ever-greater quantities. At Anniston Army Depot, for example, over a thousand ripped and battered weapons and vehicles littered fifteen thousand acres of Alabama countryside. Among them were field upon field of M-1 tanks, a legacy of Rumsfeld's first incarnation as defense secretary. The blades of the turbine tank engines he was so proud of imposing on the army corroded especially fast in the Iraqi desert sand, eventually snapping off with disastrous results for the engines. Anniston rebuilt eight hundred M-1 engines in 2006, and another twelve hundred the following year. The depressing scene was repeated at the Red River Army Depot in Texas, where hundreds of Bradley Fighting vehicles awaited major repair, as did the thousand Humvees at the depot in Letterkenny, Pennsylvania. Altogether, $17 billion worth of military equipment was being destroyed or worn out annually on the distant battlefields. After three years of war, the army and marines were literally breaking down as fighting forces.[2]

Maimed veterans and fields of broken armor were visible, dramatic examples of the human and material impact of this war and those who had fostered it. Even more dramatically, the entire country of Iraq lay shattered. One hard-line Iraqi opponent of the occupation gave eloquent expression to the feelings of many of his countrymen when he declared that the occupation had "destroyed Iraq—state, people, institutions, and resources. Since the first day of the occupation, it has been taking Iraq from bad to worse."

Future generations will almost certainly point to Iraq as Rumsfeld's most visible legacy. But they will also contemplate other fruits of his years in power. Shortly after viewing the procession of war-wounded, I sought out an official who has spent his career in the arcane world of high-technology weapons systems, many of them "black"—that is, secret from taxpayers lacking the requisite level of security clearance. "Things are about as fouled up as Iraq," he announced laconically, "it's just that it's going to take longer for the consequences to become obvious." Rattling off a slew of acronyms—"TSAT, TCA, SBIRS"— interspersed with uninhibited comments on the merits of the systems they represented—"a concept of truly astounding badness"—his summation of the situation was straightforward and bleak. "When all these new things they set in motion don't field [that is, become operational] we are going to be in a world of hurt."

Such systems were at the core of the revolution in military affairs. For example, TSAT, or Transformational Satellite, was a program born in 2004 and billed as an "Internet in the sky" that would allow all parts of the military to communicate with all other parts simultaneously and instantly. The system would reduce the processing time for the image from a radar reconnaissance drone on the other side of the world from twelve minutes to one second. Furthermore, the recipient could be on the move anywhere in the world with a portable receiver. Similar conveniences would be provided for a host of other military activities. "We had two comparatively more simple systems under development to do much of the same job," my friend explained, "but we were having problems with the easy programs, so did we take a step back? No, no, no-o-o, we went straight to the hard part, and started in on TSAT, which is already years late, technically sick [meaning it doesn't work], and half a billion dollars overbudget, which is an underestimate. It's exactly the same pattern as Iraq, Rumsfeld never learned from failure." There would come an awkward moment sometime around 2014, my friend added with gloomy relish, when Milstar II, the satellite system that TSAT was designed to replace, starts to wear out, at which time the new system would be in no condition to replace it.

Spewing technical data at an accelerating rate, the official predicted similarly disastrous fates for other lofty symbols of Rumsfeld's transformation, including the Space Radar, designed as a means of universal global surveillance from an orbit four hundred miles above the earth, transcending any and all obstacles of darkness, weather, or location. This very expensive dream was fervently promoted by Cambone and Wolfowitz, although another and more senior official with whom I discussed the radar made derisive comments about Wolfowitz's ability to understand the technology involved and claimed that "Cambone and Aldridge [formerly in charge of acquisition at the Pentagon] put the whole thing together in Aldridge's conference room one night." With such a low orbit, the required "constellation" of these satellites to cover the globe on a continual basis would have to number at least twenty-four, at $700 million per satellite, or $16 billion in total. The individual satellites would last no more than ten years, so replacement costs would probably be on the order of $1 billion a year after the first few years, but for what purpose? "This would be the only way to track a moving truck with a terrorist bomb on board in the middle of China," my informant explained. "Anywhere else, there are other less ambitious systems that do the job without having to be in space. But in any event, how would you know this was a terrorist truck? Suppose you see an individual who might be Osama bin Laden? Someone has to figure it out for sure, and do it near real time. You couldn't do that with a million analysts. It's just another very stupid, very expensive idea that we will be paying for, for a long time." At a recent high-level meeting on missile defense, he added for light relief, he had heard the commanding general of the Missile Defense Agency declare that the function of missile defense was now to guard against "an emerging offensive missile threat from Venezuela."

Although Rumsfeld and Bush routinely invoked the "global war on terror" when unveiling their annual budget demands, most of the money requested was for programs conceived before the 9/11 attacks. Up until 9/11, the Pentagon's publicly announced future budget plans showed no increase in spending at all up through 2006. This was politically vital, since it helped President Bush justify his drastic tax cuts.

Internally, however, Rumsfeld's budget planners were keeping a very different set of books, a fact unearthed by C. Franklin Spinney, an analyst in the Pentagon's office of plans, analysis, and evaluation. Spinney, who has since retired, took the trouble to look up the spending projections in the Future Years Defense Plans stored in the department computers and not intended for outside eyes. He found that during the summer of 2001 the planners were assuming that spending, so far from remaining flat at just over $300 billion, would in fact be climbing rapidly to about $400 billion by 2008. "When 9/11 came along, they simply tacked on a little bit extra to what they had already planned and justified the whole increase by the war on terror," Spinney explained to me later. Furthermore, as he testified to Congress in 2002, the projected 2003 defense budget was higher, even after accounting for inflation, than the average of the cold war, "when America faced the threat of a nuclear-tipped Soviet superpower instead of a criminal network of terrorists funded by a fanatical anti-American Saudi millionaire."[3]

By 2006, the annual Pentagon budget had reached $412.3 billion—more than the secret 2001 plan. Yet that did not include the wars, which accounted for at least an extra $125.8 billion, and the nuclear weapons programs in the Department of Energy budget—$18.1 billion; along with other defense items, such as the skyrocketing costs for homeland security and veterans affairs, the overall bill presented to the taxpayer for defending the United States was now running at just under $700 billion.[4] Growth in weapons spending had been particularly explosive. In September 2001 the Pentagon was financing seventy-one major programs. By December 2005 that had increased to eighty, an increase of 13 percent. Most of the programs were the same. But their total "lifetime" costs—that is, what it would cost to build and maintain them—had gone from $790 billion to $1,585 trillion, an increase of 100 percent.[5] In other words, the military was now paying roughly twice as much for the same items, most of which had been designed to face an enemy—the cold war Soviets—that didn't exist anymore. Long after Rumsfeld and Wolfowitz and the rest of the cast of characters who presided over this process had gone to their rewards, the bills for this spending frenzy would still be coming due. Spinney calculated for me that as of late 2006 it would take a generation to pay for the weapons *already on order,* assuming absolutely no "cost growth" in these programs. Such stability is unlikely; the price of Future Combat Systems, the army's most important project, had shot up by 80 percent in the previous two years. "If all the wars stopped tomorrow," Spinney explained to me, "we will be spending at Bush budget levels for at least the next seventeen years and probably longer."

In the midst of this financial tsunami, Rumsfeld himself tried to claim that he had been too busy to pay attention. "If you think back at the time period you are talking about here," he told investigators probing a scandal-ridden program in April 2005, "we had the attack on 9/11; we had the war on Afghanistan and continuing difficulties with the Taliban and Al Qaeda, the global war on terror; we had the war in Iraq. . . . My time basically in the Department was focused on these things and certainly not on acquisitions or—or what have you."

The issue under discussion in that interview is worth examining in further detail, since the circumstances may help explain just how defense spending may have got so far out of control. The scandal involved senior officials of the Boeing Corporation, the U.S. Air Force, the Office of the Secretary of Defense, and the White House. The affair began in late September 2001 when Boeing executives met with Darlene Druyun, then deputy assistant secretary of the air force for acquisition. Boeing was facing severe financial difficulties in the wake of the airline slump that followed 9/11 and was looking for a bailout. It was therefore agreed at this and subsequent meetings that the air force would acquire one hundred aerial refueling tankers from Boeing, but instead of buying them in the normal fashion, the planes would be leased, a much more profitable deal for Boeing. Structured in this fashion, the $26 billion deal cost the taxpayers as much as an extra $10 billion, for planes the air force did not actually need. Soon afterward, air force secretary James Roche gave his enthusiastic support to the deal. "Privately, between us," he e-mailed a friend, "Go Boeing!" While negotiating with Boeing on behalf of the government, Druyun was simultaneously negotiating with Boeing for a $250,000-a-year postretirement job for herself. Others who involved themselves in the affair also forgot to declare conflicts of interest. Richard Perle, for example, coauthored an article in the *Wall Street Journal* touting the proposed deal as vital to defense transformation, but failed to mention that Boeing had invested $20 million in Trireme Partners, a venture capital firm Perle had launched in November 2001 to capitalize on investment opportunities arising out of the war on terror.[6]

Ultimately, following an unrelenting effort by Senator John McCain to uncover the truth and a series of reports by the Defense Department's inspector general, Druyun and a Boeing executive went to jail. Roche had been slated to succeed the obstreperous army secretary Thomas White, who had finally been fired in April 2003. Instead, he quietly resigned. Rumsfeld's acquisitions chief, Edward C. "Pete" Aldridge, who had ordered an air force official to exempt the Boeing contract from normal Pentagon safeguards and oversight, also resigned and joined the board of defense giant Lockheed Martin. Asked by Senator John Warner (R-Va.) whether, in thirty-three years of government service, he had "ever seen a deal as dirty as this one," the chief auditor of the Pentagon's Inspector General's Office replied, "No sir, I have not."[7] Boeing ultimately paid a $615 million fine.

Those portions of the inspector general's 256-page final report that touched on the role of Rumsfeld, the White House, and members of Congress in the affair were blacked out before release. Nevertheless, Rumsfeld's name does occasionally appear, as in a July 2003 note by Roche, at a time when Congress was beginning to turn up the heat, reporting that Rumsfeld had just called him in Newport, Rhode Island, to say "he did not want me to budge on the tanker lease proposal."[8]

The investigators who finally managed to interview Rumsfeld on the subject of the tanker deal may have expected to get clear answers from the chief executive of the Department of Defense. If so, they were disappointed. Not only did Rumsfeld indicate an inability to remember any role he might have played in the affair, he exhibited a curious ignorance of other significant events and dates. For example, asked whether he remembered giving Aldridge his approval for the leasing scheme—the largest lease in the history of the United States—in May 2003, he cited his preoccupation with the Iraq invasion, though he was apparently uncertain of when the war had happened:

Rumsfeld: "We had the war in Iraq that began in—what, March—"

Investigator: "March."

Rumsfeld: "February, March, April."

Investigator: "March of 2003."

Rumsfeld: "Two"

Investigator: "Three."

Rumsfeld: "Three."

When he got around to answering the question, Rumsfeld was carefully noncommittal. Aldridge "clearly had the authority to make that decision. And he may very well have told me he was going to make it that way. And I may very well have said fine. But in terms of involvement it was modest. And I don't . . . I don't remember approving it. But I certainly don't remember not approving it, if you will." Asked about memos linking him to specific decisions, Rumsfeld insisted that department officials were in the habit of quoting him even when he had not been involved. Queried about other major acquisition programs he had approved, he cited the ancient precedent of his decision on the M-1 tank gun twenty-nine years earlier.

Overall, Rumsfeld presented a picture of a defense chief who didn't bother to read half the memos that crossed his desk and generally handed off responsibility to others: "Day in and day out I rely on the senior officials of the department to fulfill their statutory responsibilities." He spent most of his time "functioning as the link between the President, Commander in Chief, and the combatant commanders conducting the wars." As for defense contractors, he didn't meet with them "unless I ran into them at a party some place."[9]

The picture of a secretary so disengaged from an important part of his responsibilities was hardly complimentary, but convincing enough to dispel any idea that he might have been connected to the grubby machinations described above. Yet someone intimately familiar with the intersecting worlds of Rumsfeld, government contracting, and the political economy of Chicago suggested that Rumsfeld at least had to have been aware that the deal was happening. "Don't believe it," he said of Rumsfeld's protestation of ignorance. "Denny Hastert [then Speaker of the House of Representatives] has a Chicago district. Boeing headquarters are in Chicago. Rumsfeld is from Chicago."

Whether or not they encountered the secretary personally, contractors and the business community at large certainly appreciated what was happening on his watch. Heidi Wood, star aerospace and defense stock analyst at Morgan Stanley, had greeted news of the tanker lease deal with enthusiasm, calling the deal a "serious plus" in view of the $2.3 billion profit she expected the company to reap. Although such hopes were ultimately dashed when the deal was canceled, good times continued for others. In the five years following 9/11, the principal defense stock index climbed 103 percent, more than five and a half times the corresponding rise in the broad S&P 500 market index. "The U.S. may not be preparing for battles with legions of tanks, but the battle against a shadowy, stateless enemy is no cheaper," wrote one bullish analyst in September 2006. "The U.S. is . . . plowing ahead with new weapons systems, more accurate 'smart bombs,' and cutting edge anti-terror technology."[10]

The trouble was that as of December 9, 2004, people outside of Wall Street were becoming less interested in cutting-edge weapons technology and a lot more concerned about the fact that American soldiers in Iraq were picking through garbage dumps, looking for pieces of scrap metal to use as makeshift armor against the enemy bombs and rockets. Rumsfeld's insensitive rejoinder to Army Specialist Thomas Wilson in Kuwait—"You go to war with the army you have . . ."—helped crystallize public resentment at the apparently pointless and bloody war. From that time on, the percentage of people who thought he was doing a "poor" job never fell below 50 percent. Nor were matters improved when it emerged in that same month of December that the secretary's letters of condolence to the families of soldiers killed on active service were in fact signed by an autopen machine. Rumsfeld apologized, stating that although he did not personally sign individual letters, "I wrote and approved the now more than 1000 letters sent to family members. . . . I have directed that in the future I sign each letter."[11]

Just as the public perception of the secretary began to harden, so, too, did the attitudes of powerful political antagonists. Senator John

McCain told the Associated Press in December 2004 that he had "no confidence" in Rumsfeld's leadership.[12] Rumsfeld himself worried that his political problems could be terminal, telling old friends that he thought Bush might get rid of him for the second term. White House chief of staff Andrew Card was indeed recommending that very idea to Bush, but the day had not yet come when someone like Card could displace a Rumsfeld. Instead, it was Colin Powell, whose approval rating had never dropped below 50 percent all the time he was in office,[13] who was shown the door in January 2005.

Though Rumsfeld survived, he would from now on be on his own. Wolfowitz had cherished ambitions to move on and up in the second Bush term, becoming either secretary of state or national security adviser. He had even hoped that Rumsfeld would support him in this endeavor, but whether or not the secretary was disposed to do this, the White House political operation had already concluded they could never get Wolfowitz confirmed by the Senate. Condoleezza Rice had long earmarked the State Department for herself and didn't much care for Wolfowitz anyway. So the deputy secretary took himself off to the World Bank. From then on, criticism for the fatal miscalculations that had led to ruin in Iraq—the decision to invade with a light force, the lack of planning for the occupation, the incompetent and deeply corrupt occupation regime, the official endorsement of torture, and many others—all were laid solely at the door of Donald Rumsfeld while the former deputy who had done so much to shape events was off delivering stern lectures to third-world countries on corruption and human rights.

Wolfowitz was not the only participant in the Iraqi adventure to devolve his share of responsibility onto Rumsfeld. The generals, who had accepted his original vision of invasion without demur, ensured the failure of the occupation through lapses both moral, tolerating routine abuse of prisoners, and tactical, such as running pointless "presence" patrols that chiefly served as effective IED magnets. Faced with the consequences of their actions, however, the military could always point to the defense secretary's original withholding of troops as an excuse for everything that had subsequently gone wrong.

Carping by the "uniforms" mattered little so long as Rumsfeld retained the unquestioning support of George W. Bush. So while public opinion was turning steadily against him from early 2005 onward, his power appeared undiminished, as illustrated by the atmosphere of fear that surrounded him in the Pentagon or on his travels. On any given day in his outer office, military staff waiting to brief him would be nervously pacing, rehearsing their lines, foreheads damp with perspiration.

Yet there was a strange aspect to Rumsfeld's reign of terror over the officer corps: very few of them actually lost their jobs. Though I heard senior military personnel seriously compare him to Stalin, who executed officers by the thousand, Rumsfeld's victims are hard to find, and amount to perhaps two generals who were actually dismissed, as well as General Gregory Newbold, who made his own principled decision to retire. Former chief of staff Eric Shinseki, repeatedly invoked as a martyr by disgruntled army officers, served out his full term. "Timidity," one former high-ranking general with experience of the Rumsfeld Pentagon said to me vehemently one day early in 2006. "If you're looking for an explanation for the cut in troop levels in 2003, for Abu Ghraib, and many other disasters, you'll find it in a timid military."

As years went by, increasing numbers of generals owed their promotions and postings to Rumsfeld and his aging consigliere on such matters, retired admiral Staser Holcomb, still poring over lists of suitable candidates at his home in Washington state. Joint Chiefs chairman Peter Pace was the most prominent example of Rumsfeld's heavy hand on the promotion process. At a November 2005 Pentagon press briefing, Pace surprised everyone by contradicting his patron, who was standing by his side. Asked about the recent discovery by American troops of torture victims in an Iraqi-run Baghdad jail, he said it was "absolutely the responsibility of every U.S. service member, if they see inhumane treatment being applied, to intervene to stop it."

Rumsfeld did not think much of this idea. "But I don't think you mean they have an obligation to physically stop it," he intervened, "it's to report it."

Pace refused to be quashed. "If they are physically present when inhumane treatment is taking place, sir, they have an obligation to stop it," he said. "I'm not trainable today!" he joked a few minutes later, after again contradicting his boss.[14] Despite this commendable message from the top of the uniformed chain of command, signals to the troops at lower levels were more confused. Ten days before Pace spoke out, fellow marines based in Haditha, Iraq, had responded to an IED attack by entering nearby houses and killing twenty-four men, women, and children, a massacre that was then covered up by their superior officers.[15] In any event, Pace was soon back in training, dutifully endorsing a call by Rumsfeld for "clarification" of the rules on what a soldier should do when confronted with torture.[16]

It was not until the following spring that the American public finally got proper insight into the true state of high-ranking military opinion toward Rumsfeld. On March 19, 2006, under a graphic display summarizing deteriorating conditions in Iraq, the *New York Times* carried an op-ed by Paul Eaton, a retired army two-star, that forthrightly declared, "Donald Rumsfeld is not competent to lead our armed forces." Laced with vivid phrases—"incompetent strategically, operationally and tactically," "bullying," "intimidated," "groupthink"—Eaton's diagnosis of a military in crisis was tart and pithy: "Donald Rumsfeld demands more than loyalty. He wants fealty. And he has hired men who give it."

For Eaton, as he explained to me soon afterward while fielding "a flood" of supportive e-mails and letters from the army fraternity, the breaking point had been Rumsfeld's recently unveiled second Quadrennial Defense Review. This report was supposed to depict Rumsfeld's transformation come to maturity, his true and enduring legacy. Rhetoric aside ("the department has . . . executed urgently needed transformation. As a result of recent combat experience, U.S. armed forces today are more battle-hardened and combat ready than in decades"), the review revealed no indication of real change. Cold war programs such as the air force's F-22 and the navy's DDX destroyer remained untouched. Acknowledgments of "the Long War," as the "War on Terror" had lately been officially renamed, were limited to tokens such as a fifteen-hundred-man increase in army Special Forces.

The lack of any plan to increase the size of the regular army most enraged Eaton. "No one is fighting for the forty-thousand-man increase we need," he told me. This enforced limitation, he believed, was merely the latest stage in a malign longtime effort by Rumsfeld—"he came in to reduce the army from ten to six divisions"—

abetted by renegades in the ranks who had accepted high-level posts in return for acquiescence in limiting army numbers.

Soon after Eaton's broadside came an eloquent cri de coeur in *Time* magazine from Greg Newbold, the one high-ranking officer to have quit rather than go along with what he now witheringly denounced as a "fundamentally flawed plan executed for an invented war," to which American forces had been committed with "a casualness and swagger that are the special province of those who have never had to execute these missions, or bury the results." Significantly, he made sure to mention that he was writing "with the encouragement of some in positions of military leadership." Rumsfeld, he made clear, had to go.

Unlike Eaton's motivating indignation over army force size, Newbold had been moved to action by a more urgent concern. Rumors and leaks swirling out of the Pentagon had convinced him that those who had invented the Iraq war were getting ready to do it again, this time with Iran as the target. Hence the criticism in his essay of "leaders in uniform who chose inaction" thanks to intimidation or a belief that it was not their place to speak out. This time, he concluded, "we won't be fooled again."[17]

Before long the "revolt of the generals" had spread to include as many as eight retirees from the army and marines. Among them were two former divisional commanders from Iraq.[18] Charles Swannack, who had led the 82nd Airborne when the division was occupying Fallujah and Camp Mercury (home of the PUC tent), complained that Rumsfeld had "micromanaged the generals" and also bore "culpability associated with the Abu Ghraib prison scandal." The other, John Batiste, had been one of the army's golden boys, a former military assistant to Paul Wolfowitz who had more recently been offered promotion to lieutenant general and commander of U.S. forces in Iraq, only to turn it down. "The trouble with Don Rumsfeld," he repeated in interviews with myself and others, "is that he's contemptuous, he's dismissive, he's arrogant, and he doesn't listen." Unwilling to remain part of the system, Batiste said, he had turned down the offer of a third star and retired.

Those speaking out unanimously denied that their efforts were coordinated, though I was interested to note that Batiste received help in placing an op-ed in the *Washington Post* from an assistant to retired general Barry McCaffrey, the early and influential Rumsfeld critic, who nevertheless within weeks returned from a trip to Iraq, describing ongoing operations as "simply a brilliant success story"[19] and was soon afterward summoned to the White House to brief the president.

Rumsfeld reacted to these attacks with carefully directed counter-fire. I got a taste of the strategy over lunch with a Rumsfeld intimate. This individual made pointed reference to the section of the Uniform Code of Military Justice that prohibits "speaking contemptuously" about the secretary of defense, while passing additional remarks about the morals of one of the complainants. Turning to the subject of Batiste, he said the former general had turned down V Corps, the Iraq command, merely because of a dispute over the staff he would be allowed to bring with him. Elsewhere, Steve Herbits dove into print with a broad-based attack on the army, which for years had "not produced the needed talent . . . Mr. Rumsfeld's changes corrected that problem." At least one of the attackers, Herbits mentioned in passing, "was passed over for promotion because of personal behavior which did not clear a routine morals examination."[20] Meanwhile, following a Pentagon briefing, the team of military commentators were deployed into the TV studios. General David Grange duly informed the CNN audience that the attacks on Rumsfeld were "inappropriate" and came from a "small group." General Thomas McInerney, a retired air force three-star, said the criticism came mostly from two-stars.

At the Pentagon, Rumsfeld's heaviest weapon was Pace, who told a joint press conference that he had "zero questions" about Rumsfeld's leadership. At the same briefing the secretary himself once again told the story of his triumphant imposition of the M-1 tank gun on a recalcitrant army thirty years before. The following day, April 18, 2006, George W. Bush settled the matter by expressing full confidence in Rumsfeld. "I'm the decider, and I decide what is best. And what's best is for Don Rumsfeld to remain as the secretary of defense."

He had survived, but like a Wall Street takeover target, Rumsfeld was now "in play." In the background, Rumsfeld's old antagonist, George H. W. Bush, even began quietly scouting a possible replacement for Rumsfeld.[21] That effort came to nothing, but as the November 2006 midterm congressional elections loomed ever larger on the horizon, it was becoming increasingly clear that Rumsfeld had become the personification of the Iraq war. Far more than his role in barbarities such as Abu Ghraib, it was Rumsfeld's insistence on curtailing troop numbers that earned him the fiercest condemnation. If only the original Centcom scheme for a four-hundred-thousand-man invasion force had been allowed to stand, so the argument went, all would have been well with the occupation. Few in the internal American debate seemed to understand that it was the occupation itself that had ignited Iraqi resistance, and that a larger force of foreign occupiers might well have hastened the insurgency. By inference, therefore, it seemed plausible to argue that the dispatch of more troops would help solve the problem, a dangerous misconception.

By the fall, a call for Rumsfeld's resignation was becoming mandatory for embattled candidates such as Connecticut senator Joseph Lieberman, a former Democratic vice presidential candidate whose obsequious support for George W. Bush's policies had cost him the support of Connecticut democrats.

Lieberman remained among the most ardent proponents of the war itself, but the war was becoming harder to defend as the mounting toll of Iraqi civilian dead indicated how little was being accomplished by the occupation. Earlier in the year, Rumsfeld had said that the U.S. military would not intervene in a civil war, leaving that to Iraqi forces. "May God damn you, sir," responded the radical Shi'ite cleric Moqtada al-Sadr. "You said in the past that civil war would break out if you were to withdraw, and now you say that in case of civil war you won't interfere." It seemed a justifiable complaint.

Though the public saw an apparently unruffled Rumsfeld, as confident as ever, at least one person in closer contact noticed that every so often, Rumsfeld appeared to forget where he was for a brief moment, before collecting himself and focusing on the conversation once more. But even when undeniably in control of his faculties, Rumsfeld was still more distanced from realities, especially unpleasant ones, than in former times. "Torie Clarke used to make it a habit once every week or so to bring in a bundle of magazines—*Time, Newsweek*, a wide assortment—so that Rumsfeld would have an idea of what people are reading about out there," a former official in his office told me. No one was doing that now. It was not that Rumsfeld was cut off from information. On the contrary, he was spending just as many hours every day in videoconferences with his commanders in Iraq and Afghanistan, endlessly questioning on obscure details, still intimidating, still putting people off-balance, but he was talking in an echo chamber, with no one daring to contradict him.

Renaming the regional commanders, once known as commanders in chief, had been a symbol of his assertion of civilian dominance over the military. But ever since the creation of the Defense Department, the real key to civilian control of the military services had been control of the purse strings. Extraordinarily, in September 2006, Rumsfeld ceded this vital instrument back to the military, following what amounted to a mutiny by the army high command.

Every August, each service is required to submit a budget plan, known as the Program Objective Memorandum, or POM, to the secretary's office, outlining how much money it needs to meet its obligations in the upcoming fiscal year. The defense secretary and his staff then renew and rework the figures until a final budget is ready for presentation to the White House and Congress. But in August 2006, the army simply refused to submit a POM, claiming that it could not possibly meet its obligations in Iraq and elsewhere with the money it had been told would be available. Instead, the army was demanding $138.8 billion, $25 billion more than Rumsfeld had offered, and forty-one percent above the previous year's budget. Rumsfeld's response was to surrender, telling the army chief of staff, General Peter Schoomaker, to try and raise the money on his own from the White House and Congress. Rumsfeld, who had come into office pledging to reassert civilian control, was now giving up the very function his office had been designed to perform.[22]

Meanwhile, former national security adviser Brent Scowcroft and former secretary of state James Baker, respected and even revered in some quarters as eminent exponents of "realism" as opposed to the eccentric messianism flourishing in the administration of George W. Bush, spent a summer's day in Scowcroft's 17th Street office in downtown Washington composing a comprehensive paper listing what they considered to be the most serious faults in the

administration's foreign policy. According to a former official familiar with this episode, the two elder statesmen put forward some suggestions, "almost certainly" including a change in leadership at
the defense department. Scowcroft put his name on it and sent it to
George H. W. Bush in hopes he could pass it to the president.

According to later reports circulating among those aware of the
Baker-Scowcroft initiative, the elder Bush waited until the First
Family arrived at the Bush seaside house in Kennebunkport, Maine,
in late August before calling his son aside and presenting him with
the paper. The president glanced at it disdainfully for a few seconds
before tossing it aside, reportedly with the words "I'm sick and tired
of getting papers from Brent Scowcroft telling me what to do, and
I never want to see another one again." With that, he exited, slam-
ming the door behind him.

Notwithstanding this episode, Bush 43 still sometimes drew on
his father's wide knowledge of the world. Though he refused to
read newspapers, he was aware of criticism that his administration had been excessively beholden to a particular clique, and
wanted to know more about them. One day during that holiday,
according to friends of the family, 43 asked his father, "What's a
neocon?"

"Do you want names, or a description?" answered 41.

"Description."

"Well," said the former president of the United States, "I'll give
it to you in one word: Israel."

Whether or not the neocons agreed with this description, they
could see that their successful campaign for an attack on Iraq had led
to total disaster, and that they might suffer for it unless they could
deflect blame elsewhere. The neocon flagship *Weekly Standard* had
already been criticizing Rumsfeld as the architect of defeat since early
2005. As Iraq spiraled to disaster, many of the original promoters of
the war began cataloging mistakes that had deprived the United
States of victory. John Podhoretz, for example, son of Rumsfeld
biographer Midge Decter, suggested that the problem might stem
from an excess of humanitarian morality. "What if the tactical mistake we made in Iraq was that we didn't kill enough Sunnis?" he
wrote in the *New York Post*. "Wasn't the survival of Sunni men

between the age of 15 and 35 the reason there was an insurgency and the basic cause of the sectarian violence now?"[23]

It was only in October 2006, however, just weeks before the election, that bigger guns of the movement weighed in to make it clear that nothing of what had happened was their fault. Kenneth Adelman, for example, who had worked with Rumsfeld in the distant days of the Office of Economic Opportunity and had proclaimed early in 2002 that attacking Iraq would be a "cakewalk," now told *Vanity Fair* magazine that "I'm very, very fond of [Rumsfeld], but I'm crushed by his performance."

Richard Perle was equally forthright: "Huge mistakes were made, and I want to be very clear on this: They were not made by neoconservatives, who had almost no voice in what happened, and certainly almost no voice in what happened after the downfall of the regime in Baghdad. I'm getting damn tired of being described as an architect of the war. I was in favor of bringing down Saddam. Nobody said, 'Go design the campaign to do that.' I had no responsibility for that."[24]

This crude buck-passing ignited outrage in many quarters, including those who had been in a position to observe the neoconservative contribution to war planning. "Interesting that they are not going after their puppet," one former senior official e-mailed me, in reference to the absence of Wolfowitz not only in the neocon complaints but in other finger-pointing books that were being published at the time. "This kind of stuff really pisses me off. I sat there and watched Perle and Wolfowitz craft the strategy. . . . Rumsfeld may never have stood a chance."

Over at the White House, said one senior official just weeks before the November congressional elections, "Every day there's a discussion about whether to fire Rumsfeld, and every day the conclusion is no."

Two weeks before the election, a former colleague called Rumsfeld to see how he was bearing up under the hail of criticism. "I serve at the pleasure of the president," said Rumsfeld portentously.

"Sounds to me like you serve at the pleasure of [White House political director] Karl Rove," replied the former colleague jocularly.

Rumsfeld was outraged at such flippancy. "I serve at the will of the American people," he angrily replied. His defensive state of mind was clear to all at an October 26 press conference in the Pentagon briefing room, scene of so many triumphs in the past. "Just back off," he said to critics of the war policy, "take a look at it, relax, understand that it's complicated, it's difficult." Rumsfeld had long brooded on supposed enemy mastery of the press, a malign enterprise he often ascribed to al Qaeda "media committees." Now his staff instituted a novel feature on the Pentagon website "For the Record," to answer back. An October 27, 2006, posting illustrates the tone: "Several news outlets . . . reported or headlined incorrectly that Secretary Rumsfeld told 'critics' to 'back off' during yesterday's press briefing. In fact, the Secretary was referring specifically to journalists who were seeking to create a perception of major divisions between the positions of the U.S. and Iraqi governments. He was not referring to critics of the administration's Iraq policy."

A week before the election, Bush appeared to settle the issue, telling journalists on November 1 that he wanted Rumsfeld and Vice President Cheney to remain with him until the end of his presidency. "Both those men are doing fantastic jobs," said the president, "and I strongly support them."[25]

It was a straightforward lie, as Bush himself candidly admitted on November 8 when he announced Rumsfeld's "resignation" and replacement by former CIA director Robert Gates. The day before, voters had given their verdict on the administration and its war by turning control of the Congress back to the Democrats after years of Republican control. Rumsfeld was duly offered up as a sacrifice. Just who had finally maneuvered the dismissal of a man who had exercised such an overpowering influence on the president was not clear, and Rumsfeld himself was unaware that a plot to remove him was so close to success until the president told him he was going, probably on Sunday, November 5, the day Gates was summoned for a meeting with Bush. "He didn't expect it," said Ray Dubois, who had served under Rumsfeld as a special assistant during his two Pentagon terms and stayed in close touch with the secretary. "You always know it can happen, but when it happens to you, it comes as a shock. He didn't expect it."

Dubois told me he got news of what had happened soon after

Rumsfeld's senior aides were informed. Almost exactly thirty-one years before, he himself had been an aide in the office of defense secretary James Schlesinger and got a similar call on the day Schlesinger returned from the White House having just been fired by President Ford, an event in which, as we know, Donald Rumsfeld had played a significant role.

Schlesinger had rapidly removed himself from the stage, at least temporarily, following his dismissal. Rumsfeld seemed determined to go out with more of a bang. Within weeks of his dismissal *New York Times* correspondent Michael Gordon received two leaks that were clearly designed to embarrass the president. One was a highly disobliging report by National Security Adviser Stephen Hadley (which was circulated to the defense secretary) on Iraqi prime minister Nouri Kamel al-Maliki, whom Bush was about to meet. The memo, composed after a recent Hadley trip to Baghdad, cast grave doubt on the Iraqi prime minister's abilities. Publication prompted al-Maliki to cancel a meeting with the president. The second document was a classified paper presented by Rumsfeld himself to Bush the day before the election. In total contradiction to years of protestations by the defense secretary that Iraq policy was yielding satisfactory progress, the memo called for a "major adjustment" because "what U.S. forces are currently doing in Iraq is not working well enough or fast enough." There followed a slew of haphazard suggestions, many of them echoing ideas recently advanced by Democrats opposed to the administration's war policy. "Recast the U.S. military mission and the U.S. goals (how we talk about them)—go minimalist" ran one suggestion. Some of the suggestions (helpfully labeled as "less attractive") were for options that Bush, and until recently Rumsfeld himself, had repeatedly rejected, such as "Set a firm withdrawal date to leave." For a president determined to "stay the course" this was a cruel blow, as the leaker must have known.[26]

Rumsfeld, as we have seen, was well practiced in the art of the damaging leak, a fact that Bush may well have known and pondered in the difficult weeks that followed. Cynics, including several of Rumsfeld's former subordinates, assumed as a matter of course, though without proof, that he had either leaked it personally—"he probably faxed it himself," laughed one former official—or made sure that it made its way into print.

The exiting secretary meanwhile had embarked on a ritual of departure mapped out at a conference at his seaside retreat in St. Michaels, Maryland, the weekend after he was fired. The Pentagon website sported a new item, "Six Years of Accomplishment with Secretary of Defense Donald H. Rumsfeld," hailing triumphs ranging from the liberation of "50 million people in Afghanistan and Iraq" to "New technologies and tactics to counter IED threat" to the largest round of base closures in history, "saving taxpayers $5.5 million per year." There was even a defiant reference to his grim record on torture: "Suspected terrorists held at Guantanamo Bay, Cuba, have revealed information that has helped thwart attacks against our troops, the American people and our allies."[27] There was no mention of the largest defense budgets in history, a lost war, a ground force at breaking point, a politicized general officer corps, a vastly expanded and empowered defense intelligence sector, unprecedented military involvement in domestic intelligence and security, or many other significant Rumsfeld bequests, including 22,000 wounded and 2,900 dead. This was his legacy, one that would not be reversed but rather expanded in the hands of his successors.

There followed a final "Pentagon Town Meeting" at which he reiterated many of his accomplishments. It was a performance of bantering superficiality, reminiscent of the thousands of briefings and appearances he had made over his years at the Pentagon. Sniffles from a slight head cold caused some commentators to speculate that he might have actually been emotional enough to cry. He said he remembered being "stunned" by the news of the abuse at Abu Ghraib but was cheered by "watching so many determined people spend so many months trying to figure out exactly how in the world something like that could have happened," a presumed reference to the numerous official inquiries that had for the most part obscured his own direct involvement in the "abuse." He told the story of a "young fellow with multiple wounds" he had met recently at Walter Reed Army Hospital in Washington, "he was on his back and he had a tube in his nose," who had looked at Rumsfeld and said, "If only the American people will give us the time, we can do this. We're getting it done." Rumsfeld did not mention his recently published memo that stated that what U.S. forces were doing in Iraq was "not working well enough" and suggested the possibility of major troop reductions as an option. Nor did he mention the lawsuits filed by two prestigious human rights groups, the American Civil Liberties Union and the Center for Constitutional Rights, holding him personally responsible for documented cases of torture and abuse. On the day of this last Pentagon meeting, the morning papers were reporting efforts by government attorneys to have one of the suits dismissed.[28]

Within days, Rumsfeld was off to Iraq for one last visit to the country he had changed in so many ways. Ray Dubois sincerely thought it an opportunity not only for Rumsfeld to thank the troops, but for "the troops to thank him." Flying into bases at Al Asad, Balad, where all the water and fuel was now being flown in because of enemy attacks on ground convoys, and Mosul, he communed one more time with the troops. In Mosul, a soldier asked him why he didn't "have more patience in looking for WMDs before going to war?"

"Interesting," replied Rumsfeld. "You're talking to the wrong person. That decision was made by the president. It was made by the Congress." As usual, it was someone else's fault, not part of his legacy at all.

There remained only a final extravaganza at the Pentagon, billed as a "Farewell Parade" for Rumsfeld. President Bush made playful allusions to the age of the honoree, whom he had just fired, and cited his role in helping "the Iraqi people establish a constitutional democracy in the heart of the Middle East, a watershed event in the story of freedom." Vice President Cheney unblushingly hailed Rumsfeld as "the finest secretary of defense this nation has ever had." Rumsfeld himself said he wanted to talk of the future, and how America's message was being "whispered in the coffeehouses and the streets of Damascus and Tehran and Pyongyang."

The whole event—complete with bands, a nineteen gun salute, honor guards in Revolutionary War costumes, and overwhelming security—cost, according to sources, millions of dollars. Asked what he would do next, Rumsfeld hinted he might write a book. It would show what a success everything had been.

NOTES

CHAPTER ONE: MAKING HISTORY

1. 9/11 Commission Report, p. 37.
2. Victoria Clarke, *Lipstick on a Pig* (New York: The Free Press, 2006) pp. 221–23.
3. 9/11 Commission Report, p. 43.
4. Day One, Transcript, 9/11 Commission Hearing, March 23, 2004.
5. CBS News, September 4, 2002.
6. Joint Investigation into September 11: First Public Hearing 18 September 2002—Joint House/Senate Intelligence Committee Hearing Joint Inquiry Staff Statement, Part I, Eleanor Hill, Staff Director.
7. "Rumsfeld, Ashcroft received warning of al Qaida attack before 9/11," McClatchy Newspaper, October 2, 2006.
8. CBS News, July 26, 2001, http://www.cbsnews.com/stories/2001/07/26/national/main303601.shtml; *Village Voice*, April 13, 2004, http://www.villagevoice.com/news/0415,mondo1,52614,6.html.
9. CBS News, September 4, 2002.

CHAPTER TWO: A RUTHLESS LITTLE BASTARD

1. *Washington Post,* February 22, 1970, p. 5.
2. Even in 2006, with her husband increasingly attacked and reviled by liberals, Joyce would step out every morning for a walk around her Washington neighborhood with four or five close women friends, all passionately liberal Democrats.
3. Carol Felsenthal, *Chicago Magazine,* June 2001.
4. Transcript of interview with Rowan Scarborough, *Washington Times,* on October 18, 2003, http://www.defenselink.mil/Transcripts/Transcript.aspx?TranscriptID=3577.
5. *Chicago Tribune,* March 30, 1962, p. C9.
6. *Chicago Tribune,* January 26, 1986, p. 6.
7. *Chicago Tribune,* December 5, 1989, p. 14.
8. James Carroll, *House of War* (New York: Houghton Mifflin, 2006).
9. *Chicago Tribune,* July 28, 1963, p. A8.
10. Ibid.
11. *New York Times,* May 1, 1969.
12. Jason West, *American Prospect,* February 26, 2001.

13. Robert Hartmann, *Palace Politics* (New York: McGraw Hill, 1980), p. 283.
14. Interview with Larry King, May 25, 2006.
15. *Chicago Tribune Sunday Magazine,* January 26, 1986, p. 6.
16. *New York Times,* November 21, 1970.
17. *New York Times,* November 24, 1970.
18. *The Haldeman Diaries* (New York: Putnam, 1994), p. 169.
19. http://www.whitehousetapes.org/clips/rmn_rumsfeld.html.
20. http://www.whitehousetapes.org/clips/1971_0722_nixon_rumsfeld.html.
21. James Mann, *Rise of the Vulcans* (New York: Penguin, 2004), p. 3.
22. *New York Times,* October 31, 1973, p. 1.
23. Robert Hartmann, *Palace Politics,* p. 272.
24. *Daily Telegraph,* February 2, 2003.
25. Robert Hartmann, *Palace Politics,* p. 274.
26. *Time,* May 26, 1975.
27. *New York Times,* November 11, 1975, p. 18.
28. Ford-Kissinger conversations, confidential source.
29. Rowland Evans and Robert Novak, *Washington Post,* September 27, 1975.

CHAPTER THREE: SECRETARY RUMSFELD: THE PREQUEL

1. Rumsfeld speech at Lone Sailor Award Ceremony, May 3, 2002.
2. http://www.cnn.com/SPECIALS/cold.war/episodes/12/interviews/mcnamara/. (He made the same mea culpa a number of times over the years.)
3. Frances FitzGerald, *Way Out There in the Blue* (New York: Simon & Schuster, 2001) p. 83.
4. *New York Times,* November 12, 1975, p. 29.
5. *Aviation Week,* January 12, 1976, p. 7.
6. *New York Times,* January 27, 1976.
7. *Washington Post,* January 28, 1976, p. A8.
8. Ibid.
9. Quoted by William Lanouette, *National Journal,* September 9, 1978.
10. "Rumsfeld Calls for More Funds, Citing Increased Soviet Power," *New York Times,* January 28, 1976.
11. Roper Center at University of Connecticut, Public Opinion Online, 1999.
12. Quotations from Anne Hessing Cahn, "Team B: the Trillion Dollar Experiment," *Bulletin of the Atomic Scientists,* April 1993.
13. *Washington Post,* November 5, 1975, p. A1.
14. *Larry King Live,* November 28, 2000.
15. "A Soviet–East Europe 'Organic Union,' " *Washington Post,* March 22, 1976, p. A19.
16. October 6, 1976; http://www.presidency.ucsb.edu/showdebate.php?debateid=7.
17. *Washington Post,* January 2, 1977, p. 1.
18. Nick Kotz, *Wild Blue Yonder* (New York: Random House, 1988), p. 135.
19. *New York Times,* June 9, 1976, p. 9.
20. *Newsweek,* May 3, 1976, p. 26.
21. *PBS Newshour,* February 14, 2001, http://www.defenselink.mil/transcripts/2001/t02152001_t0214pbs.html.

22. Pentagon Press Briefing, April 17, 2006.
23. I produced a TV program on these events in 1979 for ABC News. However, I have relied here on the comprehensive account by Richard Mendel in *Washington Monthly*, February 1987.
24. Robert Hartmann, *Palace Politics* p. 370.
25. *Washington Post*, January 18, 1977, p. A11.
26. *Aviation Week*, December 6, 1976, p. 12.
27. *Aviation Week*, January 24, 1977, p. 12.

CHAPTER FOUR: HOW $WEET IT IS

1. *Newsweek*, June 6, 1977, p. 68.
2. *Chicago Tribune*, April 17, 1978, p. E9.
3. In the biographical information supplied by Rumsfeld for his nomination as defense secretary in 2000, Rumsfeld stated that he had become a consultant to Searle in January 1977.
4. *Fortune*, April 21, 1980, p. 62.
5. *Chicago Tribune*, July 19, 1985.
6. *Fortune*, April 21, 1980.
7. Bressler report available at http://www.dorway.com/bressler.txt.
8. Greg Gordon, "Did Searle Ignore Early Warning Signs?" UPI, October 13, 1987.
9. E-mail from Jere Goyan to author, September 20, 2006.
10. *Washington Post*, June 26, 1983, p. A4. The piece attributes most of its information, including the quote from Hayes, to an earlier article in *Newsday*.
11. *Chicago Tribune*, November 10, 1981, p. C1.
12. *Fortune*, July 26, 1982, p. 28.
13. *Chemical Week*, July 6, 1983, p. 15.
14. *Wall Street Journal*, July 19, 1985.
15. *Chicago Tribune*, January 26, 1986.
16. *Fortune*, November 1, 1990.
17. Christopher Meyer, *D.C. Confidential* (London: Phoenix, 2006), p. 212.
18. *New York Times*, February 2006.

CHAPTER FIVE: POLITICS AND OTHER GAMES

1. *Chicago Tribune*, January 13, 1985.
2. *Fortune*, September 10, 1979.
3. For the declassified cables on Rumsfeld's meetings in Iraq, see http://www.gwu.edu/~nsarchiv/NSAEBB/NSAEBB82/.
4. Ibid.
5. Ibid., affidavit by Howard Teicher in "United States of America, Plaintiff, v. Carlos Cardoen [et al.]," January 31, 1995.
6. *Chicago Tribune Sunday Magazine*, January 26, 1986, p. 6.
7. UPI, January 21, 1986.
8. *New York Times*, March 28, 1987.
9. James Mann, *Rise of the Vulcans* (New York: Penguin, 2004), p. 167.

10. *Business Wire,* August 11, 1993,
11. *Crain's Chicago Business,* November 11, 1991.
12. *Electronic Media,* May 25, 1992.
13. Interview with John McWethy, *ABC Primetime,* March 25, 2004.
14. http://www.guardian.co.uk/korea/article/0,2763,952289,00.html
    http://www.swissinfo.org/eng/swissinfo.html?siteSect=105&sid=1648385.
    After he became secretary of defense in 2001, Rumsfeld liked to hand visitors to his office copies of a nighttime satellite picture of the Korean peninsula that is prominently displayed in his office. The photograph reveals prosperous South Korea as a blaze of light, while all is dark in the north, an illustration, he would explain, of the triumph of freedom versus totalitarianism. There is no record of his bringing up his own efforts to illuminate the north with nuclear power.
15. Compiled from separate entries recorded in FEC records, but more easily accessible through http://www.newsmeat.com/washington_political_donations/Donald_Rumsfeld.php.

CHAPTER SIX: FROM NOTION TO BUMPER STICKER

1. Coats's near miss is described in James Mann, *Rise of the Vulcans* (New York: Penguin, 2004), p. 266–67, but without some of the further details of the interview revealed here.
2. *Washington Post,* July 28, 1999, p. A1.
3. http://www.citadel.edu/pao/addresses/pres_bush.html.
4. Robert Coram, *Boyd: The Fighter Pilot who Changed the Art of War* (New York: Little Brown, 2002), pp. 268–69. Also interviews by author with the late Colonel John Boyd, who was dispatched to Thailand to terminate the project.
5. Operation Desert Storm; Evaluation of the Air Campaign. General Accounting Office, GAO/NSIAD-97–134. June 1997.
6. *Newsweek,* May 15, 2000, p. 23, as well as interviews at the time with serving DoD officials.
7. http://www.iasps.org/strat1.htm.
8. See Report of Investigation by the Special Committee of the board of directors of Hollinger International Inc. http://www.sec.gov/Archives/edgar/data/868512/000095012304010413/y01437exv99w2.htm, pp. 482–89.
9. *The Nation,* August 23, 2002.
10. Bob Woodward, *Bush at War* (New York, Simon & Schuster, 2004), p. 281.
11. http://www.commondreams.org/views01/0224–02.htm.
12. Office of the Inspector General, Department of Defense, Audit Report, Department Level Accounting Entries for FY 1999, August 18, 2000.
13. Confidential sources at meeting, see also Thomas P. Barnett, *Esquire,* July 1, 2005.
14. *Inside the Pentagon,* July 19, 2001, p. 1.
15. http://www.robertbryce.com/092104aascheneyandv-22.htm.
16. Rumsfeld press conference, August 17, 2001.
17. Richard Clarke, *Against All Enemies* (New York: Free Press, 2004), p. 23.
18. http://www.defenselink.mil/Speeches/Speech.aspx?SpeechID=430.

CHAPTER SEVEN: WARLORD

1. *New York Times,* January 22, 2002.
2. Rowan Scarborough, *Rumsfeld's War* (Washington, Regnery, 2004).
3. Tommy Franks, *American Soldier* (New York: Regan Books, 2004).
4. *Los Angeles Times,* June 9, 2004; navy medic testimony: *United States of America v. John Philip Walker Lindh,* U.S. District Court, E.D. Va., Crim. No. 02-37-A, Proffer of facts in Support of Defendant's Motion to Suppress, June 13, 2002, http://www.lindhdefense.info/20020613_FactsSuppSuppress.pdf.
5. Most of these details, including Ali's deal to let people escape Tora Bora, are taken from Philip Smucker, "How Bin Laden Got Away," *Christian Science Monitor,* March 4, 2002.
6. *Messages to the World, The Statements of Osama bin Laden* (London: Verso, 2006), p. 183.
7. Pentagon briefing, April 17, 2002, http://www.defenselink.mil/Transcripts/Transcript.aspx?TranscriptID=3405.
8. Sean Naylor, *Not a Good Day to Die* (Berkley Hardcover, 2005).
9. *Washington Post,* December 16, 2006, p. A1.
10. Documents most easily accessible online through the National Security Archive, http://www.gwu.edu/~nsarchiv/NSAEBB/NSAEBB127/. See also Karen J. Greenberg and Joshua Bratel, eds., *The Torture Papers: The Road to Abu Ghraib* (Cambridge University Press, 2005), pp. 223–37.
11. The statement was obtained under the Freedom of Information Act by Michael Scherer and Mark Benjamin of *Salon* magazine (the point about verbal approval is stated on page 18 of the report), http://www.salon.com/news/feature/2006/04/14/rummy/index.html; http://images.salon.com/ent/col/fix/2006/04/14/fri/Schmidt.pdf.
12. Ibid., p. 14.
13. Ibid., p. 25.

CHAPTER EIGHT: A GAME OF WAR

1. News of Kamel's interview was broken by John Barry in *Newsweek,* issue dated March 3, 2003. Full text can be found at http://www.globalsecurity.org/wmd/library/news/iraq/un/unscom-iaea_kamel-brief.htm.
2. Hearing of the Senate Armed Forces Committee on U.S. policy toward Iraq, September 22, 1998.
3. Address by President George W. Bush, October 7, 2002.
4. August 26, 2002. These and other misrepresentations of Kamel's debrief collected by Glen Rangwala of Cambridge University; http://www.iraqwatch.org/perspectives/rangwala-kamel-022703.htm.
5. John Dizard, "How Ahmed Chalabi Conned the Neocons," Salon.com, May 4, 2004.
6. Jane Mayer, *New Yorker,* June 7, 2004.
7. Department of State, Office of Inspector General, Review of Awards to Iraqi National Congress Support Foundation. Report 01-FMA-R-092, September 2001; http://oig.state.gov/documents/organization/7508.pdf.

8. Michael Gordon and Bernard Trainor, *Cobra II* (New York: Pantheon, 2006), p. 18.
9. Senate Armed Forces Committee, hearing on U.S. policy toward Iraq, September 28, 1998.
10. www.defenselink.mil/transcripts/2002/t02052002_t0109wp.html.
11. *New York Times,* November 21, 2001.
12. William Arkin, *Los Angeles Times,* November 10, 2002.
13. American Forces Press Service, March 16, 2001.
14. Project for the New American Century, *Rebuilding America's Defenses,* p. v.
15. Stephen Herbits, letter in *Washington Times,* April 20, 2006, p. A21.
16. *Washington Post,* May 8, 2002, p. A2.
17. Press briefing by Secretary of Defense Rumsfeld, Pentagon, May 8, 2002; http://www.defenselink.mil/transcripts/2002/t05082002_t0508sd.html.
18. GovernmentExecutive.com, April 15, 2005; http://www.govexec.com/features/0405-15/0405-15s3.htm.
19. Military.com, July 20, 2006; http://www.military.com/features/0,15240,106071,00.html.
20. William Arkin, *Bulletin of the Atomic Scientists,* May/June 2000.
21. See JFCOM glossary at http://www.jfcom.mil/about/glossary.htm-D.
22. Gordon and Trainor, *Cobra II,* p. 35.
23. http://www.jfcom.mil/newslink/storyarchive/2002/pa072902.htm.
24. "Gen. William F. Kernan and Maj. Gen. Dean W. Cash Discuss Millennium Challenge's Lessons Learned," September 22, 2002; http://www.jfcom.mil/newslink/storyarchive/2002/no091702a.htm.
25. Gordon and Trainor, *Cobra II,* p. 311.
26. Tom Ricks, *Fiasco* (New York: Penguin Press, 2006), p. 84.
27. *Washington Post,* December 18, 2002, p. A1.
28. Ricks, *Fiasco,* pp. 66–67.
29. Press conference with Donald Rumsfeld and President Hamid Karzai, February 27, 2003; Fox News Network, *Hannity & Colmes,* February 28, 2003, *Los Angeles Times,* February 26, 2003, p. 1.
30. *The Independent,* London, February 17, 2002, p. 2.

CHAPTER NINE: REALITY INTRUDES

1. Patrick Cockburn, *The Occupation* (London: Verso, 2006), p. 2.
2. *Washington Post,* April 13, 2003, p. A1.
3. Michael Gordon and Bernard Trainor, *Cobra II* (New York: Pantheon, 2006), pp. 304, 309. Douglas Macgregor, "Fire the Generals," http://www.cdi.org/program/issue/document.cfm?DocumentID=3486&IssueID=227&StartRow=11&ListRows=10&appendURL=&Orderby=DateLastUpdated&ProgramID=37&issueID=227.
4. ABC News, *This Week with George Stephanopoulos,* March 30, 2003; http://www.defenselink.mil/transcripts/2003/t03302003_t0330sdabcsteph.html.
5. Charles Glass, *The Northern Front* (London: Saqi Books, 2006), p. 232.
6. Ibid., pp. 236–56.
7. *New York Times,* April 26, 2003, p. 1.
8. *Financial Times,* April 8, 2003, p. 7.

9. For example, his op-ed for UPI, January 15, 2003.
10. For example, *CNBC News with Brian Williams,* March 27, 2003.
11. *Washington Post,* March 25, 2003.
12. Pentagon press briefing, March 28, 2003; http://www.defenselink.mil/Transcripts/Transcript.aspx?TranscriptID=2180.
13. *New York Times,* March 28, 2003.
14. Rowan Scarborough, *Rumsfeld's War* (Washington, D.C.: Regnery, 2004), p. 48.
15. *Daily Telegraph,* February 19, 2004.
16. *Daily Telegraph,* April 13, 2003; http://www.telegraph.co.uk/news/main.jhtml?xml=%2Fnews%2F2003%2F04%2F13%2Fwirq13.xml.
17. *CBS News,* November 13, 2006; http://www.cbsnews.com/stories/2006/11/13/national/main2177031.shtml.
18. Jon Lee Anderson, *The Fall of Baghdad* (New York, Penguin, 2005), p. 257.
19. Bob Woodward, *State of Denial* (New York: Simon & Schuster, 2006), p. 179.
20. Ibid., pp. 167–69.
21. L. Paul Bremer, *My Year in Iraq* (New York: Simon & Schuster, 2006), p. 39.
22. Thomas E. Ricks, *Fiasco* (New York: Penguin Press, 2006), p. 87.
23. Personal recollection by Patrick Cockburn of interview with Majid al-Khoei, London, February 2003.
24. Woodward, *State of Denial,* p. 184; Bremer, *My Year in Iraq,* pp. 126–27; *USNews & World Report,* December 20, 2004; *Boston Globe,* October 11, 2004.
25. Town hall meeting Baghdad, April 30, 2003; http://www.defenselink.mil/Transcripts/Transcript.aspx?TranscriptID=2543.
26. *Independent* (London), April 27, 2003, p. 16.
27. Reuters, April 29, 2003.
28. Media availability with Secretary Rumsfeld and Jay Garner, June 18, 2003, http://www.defenselink.mil/transcripts/2003/tr20030618-secdef0282.html.
29. Patrick Cockburn, *The Occupation* (London: Verso, 2006), p. 77.
30. Pentagon press briefing, June 30, 2003.
31. Human Rights Watch; http://hrw.org/reports/2005/us0905/2.htm_Toc115161401.
32. Expert report of Scott Horton to the German prosecutor lawsuit against Donald Rumsfeld, January 28, 2005; http://www.ccr-ny.org/v2/legal/september_11th/docs/ScottHortonGermany013105.pdf, p. 5.
33. John Barry, Michael Hirsh, Michael Isikoff, *Newsweek,* May 24, 2004. See also Horton, ibid.
34. http://news.bbc.co.uk/1/hi/world/americas/3806713.stm. Major General Miller denies that he ever made the remarks.
35. Rumsfeld testimony to Senate Armed Services Committee, May 7, 2003.
36. CNN, *Lou Dobbs Tonight,* April 30, 2004.
37. Testimony of Rumsfeld and Myers to Senate Armed Services Committee, May 7, 2004.
38. *Newsweek,* May 7, 2004.
39. "The Cost of Iraq, Afghanistan, and Other Global War on Terrorism Operations since 9/11." CRS Report for Congress RL33110, p. CRS-4.
40. CBS, *60 Minutes,* October 31, 2004. The story was produced by Leslie Cockburn, wife of the author.

CHAPTER TEN: DOWNFALL

1. "Meeting the Mental Health Needs of Veterans of the Wars in Iraq and Afghanistan: An Expert Interview with Colonel Elspeth Cameron Ritchie, MD, MPH"; http://www.medscape.com/viewarticle/515397.
2. *Washington Post,* December 5, 2006.
3. Statement by Franklin C. Spinney before Subcommittee on National Security Veterans Affairs and International Relations, Government Reform Committee, U.S. House of Representatives, June 4, 2002; http://www.d-n-i.net/fcs/spinney_testimony_060402.htm.
4. Winslow Wheeler, Military Reform Project briefing, "Old Wine, Bigger Bottles," February 21, 2006.
5. Budget Bulletin, Republican Staff, Senate Budget Committee, July 28, 2006; http://www.cdi.org/PDFs/SBC on SARs.pdf.
6. *Wall Street Journal,* August 14, 2003.
7. Joe Galloway, Military.Com, June 9, 2005.
8. Jeffrey St. Clair, *Grand Theft Pentagon* (Monroe, Me.: Common Courage Press, 2005), p. 192.
9. Interview with Donald Rumsfeld, Department of Defense, Deputy Inspector General for Investigations, April 1, 2005. Obtained under Freedom of Information Act, 2006.
10. Martin Weiss's "Safe Money Report," September 2006.
11. *Stars and Stripes,* December 17, 2004.
12. Associated Press, December 13, 2004.
13. http://www.pollingreport.com/p-z.htm.
14. Pentagon press briefing, November 29, 2005; http://www.defenselink.mil/Transcripts/Transcript.aspx?TranscriptID=1492.
15. *Time,* June 12, 2006.
16. Voice of America News, December 8, 2005.
17. *Time,* April 9, 2006.
18. CNN.com, April 13, 2006.
19. http://fallbackbelmont.blogspot.com/2006/05/mccaffrey-trip-report.html; http://www.military.com/features/0,15240,96000,00.html.
20. *Washington Times,* op-ed, April 20, 2006.
21. Sidney Blumenthal, Salon.com, June 8, 2006.
22. *Los Angeles Times,* September 25, 2006.
23. John Podhoretz, NYPost.com, July 25, 2006.
24. http://www.vanityfair.com/politics/features/2006/12/neocons200612?printable=true&currentPage=all.
25. Associated Press, November 2, 2006.
26. *New York Times,* December 3, 2006.
27. http://www.defenselink.mil/.
28. http://www.defenselink.mil/Transcripts/Transcript.aspx?TranscriptID=3823.

ACKNOWLEDGMENTS

It has been my terrific good fortune to work on this book under the auspices of Colin Harrison of Scribner, a living refutation of the notion that editors don't give books and authors the maximum care and insightful attention anymore. Karen Thompson kept track of an extraordinarily complicated schedule with unflappable patience and good humor.

My agent, Anna Stein, did an extraordinary job, first in making me think through the shape of the project and second in representing me and finding the book a home. Almost all of those who assisted significantly in the research for this book must remain anonymous, for reasons that should be all too clear. I do, however, extend sincere thanks to Winslow Wheeler, director of the Straus Military Reform Project at the Center for Defense Information, who was ever ready with a fact, a figure, or an encouraging word.

INDEX

ANDREW COCKBURN is a writer and lecturer on defense and national affairs, and is also the author of five nonfiction books. He has written for *The New York Times, The New Yorker, Playboy, Vanity Fair,* and *National Geographic,* among other publications. He currently lives in Washington, D.C.